T0283414

Principles of
Computer Science

Principles of Computer Science

Penelope Maynard

Larsen & Keller
www.larsen-keller.com

Principles of Computer Science
Penelope Maynard
ISBN: 978-1-64172-637-5 (Hardback)

 **Larsen & Keller**

Published by Larsen and Keller Education,
5 Penn Plaza,
19th Floor,
New York, NY 10001, USA

Cataloging-in-Publication Data

Principles of computer science / Penelope Maynard.
    p. cm.
Includes bibliographical references and index.
ISBN 978-1-64172-637-5
1. Computer science. 2. Electronic digital computers. 3. Computer software.
4. Computer engineering. 5. Computers. I. Maynard, Penelope.
QA76 .P75 2022
004--dc23

For more information regarding Larsen and Keller Education and its products, please visit the publisher's website www.larsen-keller.com

Table of Contents

Preface

The discipline that is concerned with the study of the processes that interact with data and can be represented as data in various forms of programs is referred to as computer science. It enables the use of algorithms for storing, manipulating and communicating digital information. The academic field of computer science includes the study of theories of computation and the practice of designing software systems. It is classified into various theoretical and practical disciplines, which include computational complexity theory, computer graphics, programming language theory, computer programming, as well as human-computer interaction. This textbook presents the complex subject of computer science in the most comprehensible and easy to understand language. The various sub-fields of computer science along with technological progress that have future implications are glanced at in this textbook. For all those who are interested in this field, this book can prove to be an essential guide.

A detailed account of the significant topics covered in this book is provided below:

Chapter 1- A machine that can be instructed to carry out sequences of arithmetic and logical operations automatically through computer programming is termed as a computer. Computer science is the domain that deals with the study of processes that interact with data and in which data can be represented in the forms of programs. This is an introductory chapter which will introduce briefly all the significant aspects of computers and computer science.

Chapter 2- The numbers that are classified into sets are known as a number system. A logic gate is a physical device that implements a boolean function. It performs a logical operation on one or more than one binary input and produces a single binary output. Devices like arithmetic logic units, registers, unit's multiplexers, and computer memory fall under the umbrella of logic circuits. This chapter discusses in detail the theories and applications of number system, logic gates and logic circuits, with respect to computer science.

Chapter 3- An operating system is system software that provides common services for computer programs through the management of computer hardware and software resources. The set of rules and methods that describe the functionality, organization, and implementation of computer systems is termed as computer architecture. This chapter has been carefully written to provide an easy understanding of the varied facets of the operating systems and computer architecture.

Chapter 4- The recording of information in a storage medium is known as data storage. Computer data storage is a technology that comprises of recording media and computer components via which digital data are retained. Computer data storage includes primary, secondary, tertiary and off-line storage. The chapter closely examines the key concepts of data storage and manipulation to provide an extensive understanding of the subject.

Chapter 5- Algorithm is a set of instruction that is primarily used to solve a problem and to perform a computation. It includes algorithm design, algorithm implementation and algorithm analysis. A formal language that consists of a set of instructions to produce various kinds of outputs is known as a programming language. It is majorly used in computer programming in order to implement algorithms. The diverse applications of algorithms and programming language in the current scenario have been thoroughly discussed in this chapter.

Chapter 6- A data organization, management and storage format that facilitates efficient access and modification is known as a data structure. It provides a means to manage large amounts of data such as large databases and internet indexing services for various uses. An organized collection of data that is generally stored and accessed electronically from a computer system is termed as database. The topics elaborated in this chapter will help in gaining a better perspective about computer databases and data structures.

I would like to make a special mention of my publisher who considered me worthy of this opportunity and also supported me throughout the process. I would also like to thank the editing team at the back-end who extended their help whenever required.

Penelope Maynard

Introduction to Computers and Computer Science

A machine that can be instructed to carry out sequences of arithmetic and logical operations automatically through computer programming is termed as a computer. Computer science is the domain that deals with the study of processes that interact with data and in which data can be represented in the forms of programs. This is an introductory chapter which will introduce briefly all the significant aspects of computers and computer science.

A computer is a programmable device that can automatically perform a sequence of calculations or other operations on data once programmed for the task. It can store, retrieve, and process data according to internal instructions. A computer may be either digital, analog, or hybrid, although most in operation today are digital. Digital computers express variables as numbers, usually in the binary system. They are used for general purposes, whereas analog computers are built for specific tasks, typically scientific or technical. The term "computer" is usually synonymous with digital computer, and computers for business are exclusively digital.

Elements of the Computer System

The core, computing part of a computer is its central processing unit (CPU), or processor. It comprises an arithmetic-logic unit to carry out calculations, main memory to temporarily store data for processing, and a control unit to control the transfer of data between memory, input and output sources, and the arithmetic-logic unit. A computer is not fully functional without various peripheral devices, however. These are typically connected to a computer through cables, although some may be built into the same unit with the CPU. These include devices for the input of data, such as keyboards, mice, trackballs, scanners, light pens, modems, magnetic strip card readers, and microphones, as well as items for the output of data, such as monitors, printers, plotters, loudspeakers, earphones, and modems. In addition to these input/output devices, other types of peripherals include computer data storage devices for auxiliary memory storage, where data is saved even when the computer is turned off. These devices most often are magnetic tape drives, magnetic disk drives, or optical disk drives.

Finally, for a digital computer to function automatically, it requires programs, or sets of instructions written in computer-readable code. To be distinguished from the physical or hardware components of a computer, programs are collectively referred to as software.

A computer *system*, therefore, is a computer combined with peripheral equipment and software so that it can perform desired functions. Often the terms "computer" and "computer system" are used interchangeably, especially when peripheral devices are built into the same unit as the computer or when a system is sold and installed as a package. The term "computer system," however, may also refer to a configuration of hardware and software designed for a specific purpose, such as a manufacturing control system, a library automation system, or an accounting system. Or it may refer to a network of multiple computers linked together so that they can share software, data, and peripheral equipment.

Computers tend to be categorized by size and power, although advancements in computers' processing power have blurred the distinctions between traditional categories. Power and speed are influenced by the size of a computer's internal storage units, called words, which determine the amount of data it can process at once and is measured in bits (binary digits). Computer speed is also determined by its clock speed, which is measured in megahertz. Additionally, the amount of main memory a computer has, which is measured in bytes (or more precisely, kilobytes, megabytes, or gigabytes) of RAM (random access memory), plays a role in determining how much data it can process. The amount of memory that auxiliary storage devices can hold also determines the capabilities of a computer system.

The Microcomputer

The development of the microprocessor, a CPU on a single integrated-circuit chip, enabled the development of affordable single-user microcomputers for the first time. The slow processing power of the early microcomputers, however, made them attractive only to hobbyists and not to the business market. In 1977, however, the personal computer industry got under way with the introduction of off-the-shelf home computers from three manufacturers.

The term "personal computer" (PC) was coined by IBM with the launch of its PC in 1981. This model became an instant success and set the standard for the microcomputer industry. By the early 1990s personal computers had become the fastest-growing category of computers. This was largely due to the adoption of their use in businesses of all sizes. The availability of these small, inexpensive computers brought computer technology to even the smallest of enterprises.

The most recent category of microcomputer to enter the business world is the portable computer. These small and light—but increasingly powerful—computers are commonly known as laptop or notebook computers. Laptop computers have the same power as desktop personal computers, but are built more compactly and use flat screen monitors, usually using liquid crystal display, that fold down to form a slim unit that fits in a briefcase and usually weigh under 15 pounds. A notebook computer is one that weighs under 6 pounds and may or may not have a full-size keyboard. A pocket computer is a hand-held calculator-size computer. A personal digital assistant is a pocket computer that uses a pen and tablet for input, has a fax/modem card, and is combined with the capabilities of a cellular telephone for remote data communications. Portable computers are increasingly popular among businesspeople who travel, such as executives or sales representatives.

Open Systems

Today, most computer systems are "open"—compatible with computer hardware and software from different manufacturers. In the past, all components of a computer system originated from the same manufacturer. There were no industry-wide standards. As a result, printers, monitors, and other peripheral equipment from one manufacturer would not operate when matched with the computer of another manufacturer. More significantly, software could only run on the specific computer brand for which it was designed. Today, however, "open systems," wherein various equipment from different manufacturers can be matched together, is common. Open systems are especially popular among small business owners because they allow enterprises to upgrade or expand their computer systems more easily and cheaply. Open systems provide business owners with more buying options, enable them to minimize expenses of employee retraining on new systems, and give them greater freedom to share computer files with outside clients or vendors.

Networking

Computers on a network are physically linked by cables and use network software in conjunction with the operating system software. Depending on the hardware and software used, different types of computers may be put on the same network. This may involve computers of different sizes—such as mainframes, mid-ranges, and microcomputers—or computers and peripherals of different manufacturers, which the trend toward open systems has facilitated. Local area networks (LANs) link computers within a limited geographical area, while Wide area networks (WANs) connect computers in different geographic regions. Networks may have various architectures which determine whether computers on the network can act independently. A commonly used system architecture is client-server, whereby a server computer is designated as the one storing and processing data and is accessed by multiple users each at a client computer.

LANs have transformed how employees within an organization use computers. In organizations where employees formerly accessed midrange computers through "dumb" terminals, these employees now typically have more capabilities. These users have their own personal computers at their desks, but are still able to access needed data from a midrange or other server through the network. Whereas smaller businesses typically favor LANs, WANs are often used by companies with multiple facilities located over a wide geographic area. After all, under a WAN system, a company's databases can be accessed at headquarters in one city, at a manufacturing plant in other city, and at sales offices in other locations.

Characteristics of Computer

As you know computer can work very fast. It takes only few seconds for calculations that we take hours to complete. Suppose you are asked to calculate the average monthly income of one thousand persons in your neighborhood. For this you have to add income from all sources for all persons on a day to day basis and find out the average for each one of them. How long will it take for you to do this? One day, two days or one week? Do you know your small computer can finish this work in few seconds? The weather forecasting that you see every day on TV is the results of compilation and analysis of huge amount of data on temperature, humidity, pressure, etc. of various places on computers. It takes few minutes for the computer to process this huge amount of data and give the result.

You will be surprised to know that computer can perform millions (1,000,000) of instructions and even more per second. Therefore, we determine the speed of computer in terms of microsecond (10-6 part of a second) or nano-second (10-9 part of a second). From this you can imagine how fast your computer performs work.

Accuracy

Suppose some one calculates faster but commits a lot of errors in computing. Such result is useless. There is another aspect. Suppose you want to divide 15 by 7. You may work out up to 2 decimal places and say the dividend is 2.14. I may calculate up to 4 decimal places and say that the result is 2.1428. Some one else may go up to 9 decimal places and say the result is 2.142857143. Hence, in addition to speed, the computer should have accuracy or correctness in computing.

The degree of accuracy of computer is very high and every calculation is performed with the same accuracy. The accuracy level is determined on the basis of design of computer. The errors in computer are due to human and inaccurate data.

Diligence

A computer is free from tiredness, lack of concentration, fatigue, etc. It can work for hours without creating any error. If millions of calculations are to be performed, a computer will perform every calculation with the same accuracy. Due to this capability it overpowers human being in routine type of work.

Versatility

It means the capacity to perform completely different type of work. You may use your computer to prepare payroll slips. Next moment you may use it for inventory management or to prepare electric bills.

Power of Remembering

Computer has the power of storing any amount of information or data. Any information can be stored and recalled as long as you require it, for any numbers of years. It depends entirely upon you how much data you want to store in a computer and when to lose or retrieve these data.

No IQ

Computer is a dumb machine and it cannot do any work without instruction from the user. It performs the instructions at tremendous speed and with accuracy. It is you to decide what you want to do and in what sequence. So a computer cannot take its own decision as you can.

No Feeling

It does not have feelings or emotion, taste, knowledge and experience. Thus it does not get tired even after long hours of work. It does not distinguish between users.

Storage

The Computer has an in-built memory where it can store a large amount of data. You can also store data in secondary storage devices such as floppies, which can be kept outside your computer and can be carried to other computers.

Classification of Computers

Analog Computers

Analog computers are used to process continuous data. Analog computers represent variables by physical quantities. Thus any computer which solve problem by translating physical conditions such as flow, temperature, pressure, angular position or voltage into related mechanical or electrical related circuits as an analog for the physical phenomenon being investigated in general it is a computer which uses an analog quantity and produces analog values as output. Thus an analog computer measures continuously. Analog computers are very much speedy. They produce their results very fast. But their results are approximately correct. All the analog computers are special purpose computers.

Digital Computers

Digital computer represents physical quantities with the help of digits or numbers. These numbers are used to perform Arithmetic calculations and also make logical decision to reach a conclusion, depending on, the data they receive from the user.

Hybrid Computers

Various specifically designed computers are with both digital and analog characteristics combining the advantages of analog and digital computers when working as a system. Hybrid computers are being used extensively in process control system where it is necessary to have a close representation with the physical world. The hybrid system provides the good precision that can be attained with analog computers and the greater control that is possible with digital computers, plus the ability to accept the input data in either form.

Classification of Computers According to Size

Super Computers

Large scientific and research laboratories as well as the government organizations have extra ordinary demand for processing data which required tremendous processing speed, memory and other services which may not be provided with any other category to meet their needs. Therefore very large computers used are called Super Computers. These computers are extremely expensive and the speed is measured in billions of instructions per seconds.

Main Frame Computers

The most expensive, largest and the most quickest or speedy computer are called mainframe computers. These computers are used in large companies, factories, organizations etc. the mainframe computers are the most expensive computers, they cost more than 20 million rupees. In this computers 150 users are able to work on one C.P.U. The mainframes are able to process 1 to 8 bits at a time. They have several hundreds of megabytes of primary storage and operate at a speed measured in nano second.

Mini Computers

Mini computers are smaller than mainframes, both in size and other facilities such as speed, storage capacity and other services. They are versatile that they can be fitted where ever they are needed. Their speeds are rated between one and fifty million instructions per second (MIPS). They have primary storage in hundred to three hundred megabytes range with direct access storage device.

Micro Computers

These are the smallest range of computers. They were introduced in the early 70's having less storing space and processing speed. Micro computers of todays are equivalent to the mini computers of yesterday in terms of performing and processing. They are also called "computer of a chip" because its entire circuitry is contained in one tiny chip. The micro computers have a wide range of applications including uses as portable computer that can be plugged into any wall.

Laptop Computers

The smallest computer in size has been developed. This type of small computers look like an office brief case and called "LAPTOP" computer. The laptops are also termed as "PORTABLE COMPUTERS." Due to the small size and light weight, they become popular among the computer users. The businessmen found laptop very useful, during traveling and when they are far away frm their desktop computers. A typical laptop computer has all the facilities available in microcomputer. The smallest laptops are called "PALMTOP".

Physical Size

Computers range in size and capability. At one end of the scale are supercomputers, very large computers with thousands of linked microprocessors that perform extremely complex calculations. At the other end are tiny computers embedded in cars, TVs, stereo systems, calculators, and appliances. These computers are built to perform a limited number of tasks.

The personal computer, or PC, is designed to be used by one person at a time.

Desktop Computers

Desktop computers are designed for use at a desk or table. They are typically larger and more powerful than other types of personal computers. Desktop computers are made up of separate components. The main component, called the system unit, is usually a rectangular case that sits on or underneath a desk. Other components, such as the monitor, mouse, and keyboard, connect to the system unit.

Laptop Computers

Laptop computers are lightweight mobile PCs with a thin screen. They are often called notebook computers because of their small size. Laptops can operate on batteries, so you can take them anywhere. Unlike desktops, laptops combine the CPU, screen, and keyboard in a single case. The screen folds down onto the keyboard when not in use.

Handheld Computers

Handheld computers, also called personal digital assistants (PDAs), are battery-powered computers small enough to carry almost anywhere. Although not as powerful as desktops or laptops, handhelds are useful for scheduling appointments, storing addresses and phone numbers, and playing games. Some have more advanced capabilities, such as making telephone calls or accessing the Internet. Instead of keyboards, handhelds have touch screens that you use with your finger or a stylus (a pen-shaped pointing tool).

Tablet PCs

Tablet PCs are mobile PCs that combine features of laptops and handhelds. Like laptops, they're powerful and have a built-in screen. Like handhelds, they allow you to write notes or draw pictures on the screen, usually with a tablet pen instead of a stylus. They can also convert your handwriting into typed text. Some Tablet PCs are "convertibles" with a screen that swivels and unfolds to reveal a keyboard underneath

Importance of Computers

Computers are now a fact of life. Computers have created a very effective information system to help streamline the management of an organization. This makes it a much needed tool for every business, banking, government, entertainment, daily life, industry, education, and administration. It can be said of all large organizations, whether the department government or private, use a computer for a variety of their daily business and it is the fastest growing industries in the world today. Each organization usually has one or more large computer systems and a number of microcomputer. The system is a great computer for data processing tasks, while many small microcomputer to use as word processing. Computers have become part of our lives is essential. In general, the use of computers can be divided into several groups.

The first extensive data processing in order to avoid abuse of the workload while increasing the effectiveness of trade and industry. Both as a prediction for decision-makers on the planning, development, and growth based on past data. In addition, it also as a means of control and non-power electric system based on our needs, such as closing the air conditioner if the temperature is lower and save energy, connecting the parts and so on. It is also a link to link data around the world in a short time. For the fields of use mentioned above, the programs needed to be developed, tested, and implemented on a computer. The various programs should be written and linked to form a system for specific tasks. In general, the system means that the software and hardware. As the system -the system used to process the data or information, call our information systems.

Main Body

Role of Computer in Many Areas

It is known that the rapid growth of computer usage time. In all areas have been using computers to launch a business.

Role of Computer in Business

The use of computers among maximum practiced in the field of business. In fact, small businesses also use the computer as there are now very cheap microcomputers. Business organizations now have a number of facts and a lot of numbers to be processed. So many businesses have started using the computer, for example to calculate the salary, to identify the goods sold and are still in stock, to issue and send or receive business statements, letters, invoices and more.

The use of computers and office equipment to assist other managers, clerks, and the management of office automation mentioned. One of them is a word processing type of electronic method that enables us to produce and edit letters, reports, documents, and other than work in a few seconds to type manually. Many of the office to produce standard letters, such as payment of the balance, invitations and more. In addition, local business organizations to use computers to create, save, and send envoys to a particular place. The advantages of using computers in this area, clearly it is very important in a business organization.

Role of Computers in Banking and Financial

Processing data involving savings accounts, fixed deposits, loans, investments, profitability analysis, and so on are among the organizations operating budget. The measures used are standard and recurrent. And with that, the financial institution is the first user is aware of the importance of computers to save time. Use of financial institutions including electronic fund transfer activities for example a bank has a terminal in each branch in the country and also in supermarkets, petrol stations, schools, factories, homes, hotels, and so on.

The company will move employees' salary into the account by entering employee identification numbers then pay the money transferred into the account supermarkets, hotels, or gas station when making a purchase. Money transfer facility is referred to the electronic transfer of money is very effective use is safe and quick method for financial transactions. With the facility, known as ETC is also individual can issue, transfer, and include cash or checks to the current balance at any time. Clearly the main purpose of the use of computers in financial institutions can assist in arranging the affairs of clients and provide services better and more efficient, reduce fraud in financial transactions also eliminate cash transactions involving the community with the goal to create a cashless society.

Role of Computers in Industrial Areas

Industry is a lot of benefit from the use of computers and the development of a human machine that 'robot'. Industrial production, for example requires a lot of computers to process data collected from employees, customers, sales, product information, production schedules, and so on. The computer used to control the production process.

Especially the production of information processing inventory control to keep the latest information about the remaining inventory of raw materials and finished goods used to determine the value of inventory and stock status. This computer can alert the staff involved if he should order the raw materials and when to deliver the goods completed to the customer. Similarly, to store information about the structure of an item, but the material requirement planning processes also use computers to facilitate the work. Appear in the computer industry is very broad and also affect the development of industry in a country.

Role of Computers in Education

Now in this era of science and technology become more advanced, the computer may take over the role of books in the store and disseminate knowledge to the public. In other words, the computer will change the way we learn and the way we store knowledge. Hal-related matters such as student registration, class scheduling, processing of examination results, students 'and teachers' personal storage can be implemented by a computer with a fast and effective in helping the administration. Now exams results were processed by computer. The IPT also the duties of office automation, processing, scientific research results and also use the computer. In fact, cataloging books in libraries also apply to computer use. Last but not least is used for teaching and learning process is not only at institutions of higher learning in the schools, both for teaching and studying computer-assisted education on computer is very emphasized that in the field of education for helping in the administrative process, research is what is important is the ease and help students and teachers in the teaching and learning.

Role of Computers in the Medical

Hospitals and clinics use computers to store patient records, scheduling doctors, nurses and other personnel, inventory and purchase of medicines, medical research and medical diagnosis. Applications of computer-based equipment or use of information technology has help doctors to diagnose diseases. It is clear that the use of computers in the medical field to provide solutions to complex problems. Among the new computer technology that provides assistance to those who are disabled. Microprocessor-based voice systems assist people with disabilities speaking with a terminal that directs the computer to perform a verbal task. Similarly, the development of computers has helped the blind to see, the deaf to communicate, whether with the help of speech synthesizer or using the keyboard. This can be help them become more active and can do what they could not do before. Besides works of traditional data processing, such as issuing bills of patients, medical statistics and scheduling of staff and others have also streamlined and processed by computer.

Hospital Information System that is used can be stored in a centralized patient database. In fact, the use of information technology the computer is programmed to culture and analyze bacteria, viruses, and other infections agents to automatically detect and identify a disease thus enabling the hospitals and laboratories to begin treatment. For example, Computer Help Demography machine (Computer Aided Demography, CAT) used for the purpose. Similarly, computers are used for a patient oversee psychological variables such as blood pressure, body temperature, ECG (Electro-Cardiograph) and sounded a warning if something unusual happens. For this purpose the computer to read different variables and make comparison with standard values. If there is something extraordinary happens the computer will draw the attention of doctors and nurses to issue a warning. Clearly, it was found that the computer has a wide range of accommodation in the medical field.

Role of Computers in Legal

Computers have been used in the legislative process in recent years. The use of the most important is the preparation of documents using a word processor. The use of computer accounting legislation also includes processing to produce weekly and monthly reports, keep records of payments consulting, diary for the latest attorney information consumers about the various court procedures and also to keep records of users. As this area is very complicated, it is the need to retrieve the required information either on journal of law, an important case, scale, and statistics or important decisions for the purpose of making the decision to retain legal data bank. Thus the use of one computer will help lawyers and trainee lawyers and law students find relevant data without wasting time and get better service.

Role of Computers in Government

Government sector is one of the largest users of computer usage practices in implementing administrative matters. All the necessary data can be obtained in a short time such as information about people, services, economic planning, and land development projects and for planning and decision making. Through long-term weather forecasting computer can now be done. With tie loss of life can be because of better information and faster. "The success of Neil Am strong on July 23, 1969 landing on the moon is also made possible with the help of computers used to design spacecraft, space for clothes astronauts, and flight schedules". This shows the very important use of computers in the field of space transportation. Service tax and income tax collection was simplified by using the computer. Keeping records of taxpayers who do it manually, and bring many problems have been addressed with the use of computer and services can make the task more efficiently and quickly.

Similarly, in the military, use of computer store inventory held until the war simulation on the screen. Computers are also used to follow the movement of the enemy in the border areas. Traffic flow can be managed effectively by detecting the direction of traffic using the many tools of detection. In this way, if there are more vehicles from one direction, the computer will let the green light goes on for a suitable period of time. "In the field of transport, Cosmos- 11 introduced by Mass by providing facilities for passengers to know the status including those booking hotel reservations, from anywhere in the world". Similarly, business owners and vehicle registration can be performed with the use of computers. Many of the all administrative affairs are managed by using the computer. This not only saves time but can do all things more practical.

Role of Computers in Entertainment

Now the computer can be programmed to play music. Places of entertainment with music controlled by computer are cheaper and can be used at any time. Computers are also used to arrange the order of dance and music. Each game requires movement. Movement can best be obtained by detailed analysis of a physical system. Computers also can be programmed to depict images of high quality. Drawing using the computer speeds up the process of creating. The work of art can be done and made a review in a short time compared with traditional Kedah. Cartoon films produced by computers have grown so widely.

Role of Computers at Daily Life

Microcomputer use also home to control the safety and control of air conditioning and lighting. The use of computers in the home allows housewife get the latest information about fashion and can make orders to use supermarket with and video. In addition to budget planning and inventory at home. This is all to do with a microcomputer that is connected to the national data bank. Children can use computers to learn school subjects or educational games. But it is clear that computers have become machines of information in our society.

Computer and Marketing

Creating a product or service that fulfills a consumer need is necessary for a small business to achieve success, but a strong concept alone is not enough to ensure profitability. Small businesses have to convince consumers to try a new product and find ways to deliver those products to consumers to be successful. Computers can be a powerful tool for assisting small companies in many aspects of marketing new products and services.

Web-Based Promotion

The Internet provides businesses with an advertising channel that can potentially reach millions of customers all around the world. Web advertising can take many forms, including banner and in-text advertisements on popular websites, emails sent to past or potential customers and video advertisements played before or during online videos. Advertising on the web can be cheaper than traditional advertising through media such as TV, radio and print, which can make it attractive to new companies with small advertising budgets.

Market Research

Market research is the collection of data concerning the current state of a market, consumer preferences and competitors. Administering surveys to customers is one of the most common ways that businesses conduct market research. Computers offer a way for companies to give surveys without actually going out and meeting customers. Businesses can gather data by offering surveys on their own official websites, using third-party Internet surveying services or sending out email questionnaires.

Distribution

The methods that a company uses to distribute products and services to customers are a core component of its overall marketing strategy. Computers allow companies to distribute their products and services to remote users via the Internet, without the need for a physical office or retail storefront. Digital distribution can be advantageous to small companies that want to sell to consumers all across the country and keep start-up costs low.

Creating Advertisements for Other Media

While the Internet allows companies to use computers for promotion, research and distribution, computers are also used to help prepare advertisements for other media. For example, modern print magazines and newspapers often use computers to help design the layouts of pages. Graphic designers and media specialists use computers to edit photographs for print media ads, audio for the radio spots and video for TV commercials.

Computer Science

Computer science is the *study of computation*. Computer scientists look for answers to questions such as:

- What can (and can't) be computed?

- How can we devise general, reusable solutions to common classes of problems?

- How can we describe computations in a manner that can be understood by both computers and humans?

- How can we make computers more user-friendly?

1. Computational Thinking: More than anything, studying computer science is about developing a way of thinking, an approach to solving problems.

2. Software and Hardware: Typically, computer science is more focused on *software* than *hardware*. Our friends in computer engineering design and build the hardware. Computer scientists focus on what computers can do and how to create applications that make them do it.

3. Programming: Most people assume that computer science is all about programming writing code to tell a computer what to do. While all computer scientists need some understanding of programming, this is really just a skill or tool that enables us to express the result of our work in a manner that a computer can understand.

4. Mathematics: The early years of computing research were dominated by

mathematicians. This was natural and necessary since the first step in beginning to build and use computers required mathematical techniques for expressing processes and data in the binary language understood by computers. Unfortunately, this has resulted in a perception that computer science is a highly mathematical field. While some of the theoretical subfields of computer science remain highly mathematical, many other aspects of computer science do not require excessive mathematics.

5. Science and Engineering: As many of the fundamental questions about computing have been answered, the focus has shifted from "How can we do this thing that no one has ever done before? to "How can we reuse and improve on what has already been done?" and "How can we define processes for developing software systems efficiently and reliably?". This is reflected in a shift from a scientific approach to an engineering approach.

6. People and Processes: As computers have become faster, with large capacities, software systems have become larger and more complex. This is great, since it allows for greater functionality and more user-friendly interfaces. However, larger systems require more labor and larger teams of people to develop them. The consequence is that the skill set required to be a successful computing professional is increasingly built on "soft-skills" such as communication, management and teamwork. Working in larger teams also requires shared knowledge of common processes and methodologies for developing software.

7. Computing Domains: Looking Outward: One thing that makes computing particularly interesting is that it reaches into virtually all aspects of society and our personal lives. Specialized domains for software applications are everywhere: finance, health care, entertainment, government, science, education, virtually every possible domain has some need for specialized computing. The consequence is that most computing professionals actually need to understand two fields: computer science and the application area. Often, this second area of specialization comes through practice on the job, but aspiring computer scientists often select elective courses or minor programs aimed at particular application domains.

Visual Computing

Visual computing is a field of computing that deals with the acquisition, analysis and synthesis of visual data through the use of computer resources. It encompasses several fields of science (computer science, in particular), mathematics, physics and the cognitive sciences. Visual computing aims to let us control and interact with activities through the manipulation of visual images, either as direct objects or, simply, representations of nonvisual objects. The media involved can be images, 3D models, videos, block diagrams and even simple icons.

Visual computing is a rather large field with many subfields, but all are related to the visual aspect of computing. Visual computing deals with everything related to computer visuals - from hardware to mathematical equations behind each pixel of color. Its primary aim is to use visual entities for the manipulation of everything around us, tangible or intangible. Visual computing can be broken down into two main branches, as follows:

- Visual computer environment: The visual paradigm used in the human interaction with computers - the combination of multimedia and text, rather than simple text alone.

- Visual applications: These deal with massive amounts of image data, such as video and 3D sequences, along with the images, diagrams and any visible entity related to computers. Commonly, however, people understand and associate visual computing with video, animation and 3D modeling and design (CAD), which is only one of two main areas of the field.

Computer Engineering

Computer engineering refers to the study that integrates electronic engineering with computer sciences to design and develop computer systems and other technological devices. Computer engineering professionals have expertise in a variety of diverse areas such as software design, electronic engineering and integrating software and hardware.

Computer engineering allows professionals to engage in a number of areas such as analyzing and designing anything from simple microprocessors to highly featured circuits, software design, and operating system development. Computer engineering is not limited to operating computer systems but is aimed at creating a broad way to design more comprehensive technological solutions. Also known as computer system engineering.

The term computer engineering is often confused with computer science, but these two terms are different. Computer scientists are responsible for electrical and software manufacturing, while computer engineers are trained to design software and perform and integrate that software with hardware components. Computer engineering also includes the engineers who write firmware specifically for embedded microcontrollers, design and develop analog sensors, design very-large-scale integration chips, and create schemes for mixed- and single-circuit boards. The engineering field of computer sciences also contributes to robotic research that requires digital systems to monitor electrical components like motors and sensors.

References

- Computers-and-computer-systems: inc.com, Retrieved 5 January, 2019

- Characteristics-of-computer, it-support: vskills.in, Retrieved 12 April, 2019

- Classification-of-computers, it-support: vskills.in, Retrieved 28 February, 2019

- Importance-of-computers-in-society-information-technology, information-technology: ukes-says.com, Retrieved 30 July, 2019

- Computers-used-marketing: chron.com, Retrieved 15 June, 2019

- What-is-computer-science, computer-science: pacific.edu, Retrieved 2 March, 2019

- Visual-computing: techopedia.com, Retrieved 8 May, 2019

- Computer-engineering: techopedia.com, Retrieved 23 July, 2019

2

Numbers System, Logic Gates and Logic Circuits

The numbers that are classified into sets are known as a number system. A logic gate is a physical device that implements a boolean function. It performs a logical operation on one or more than one binary input and produces a single binary output. Devices like arithmetic logic units, registers, unit's multiplexers, and computer memory fall under the umbrella of logic circuits. This chapter discusses in detail the theories and applications of number system, logic gates and logic circuits, with respect to computer science.

Binary Number System

Computers don't understand words or numbers the way humans do. Modern software allows the end user to ignore this, but at the lowest levels of your computer, everything is represented by a binary electrical signal that registers in one of two states: on or off. To make sense of complicated data, your computer has to encode it in binary.

Binary is a base 2 number system. Base 2 means there are only two digits—1 and 0—which correspond to the on and off states your computer can understand. You're probably familiar with base 10—the decimal system. Decimal makes use of ten digits that range from 0 to 9, and then wraps around to form two-digit numbers, with each digit being worth ten times more than the last (1, 10, 100, etc.). Binary is similar, with each digit being worth two times more than the last.

Counting in Binary

```
                                    1
    0     1     0     1     1       1
   +0    +0    +1    +1    +1      +1
   ――    ――    ――    ――    ――     ――
   00    01    01    10    11     100
                      ↖     ↑    ↗
                       carried bit
```

In binary, the first digit is worth 1 in decimal. The second digit is worth 2, the third worth 4, the fourth worth 8, and so on—doubling each time. Adding these all up gives you the number in decimal. So,

$$1111 \text{ (in binary)} = 8 + 4 + 2 + 1 = 15 \text{ (in decimal)}$$

Accounting for 0, this gives us 16 possible values for four binary bits. Move to 8 bits, and you have 256 possible values. This takes up a lot more space to represent, as four digits in decimal give us 10,000 possible values. It may seem like we're going through all this trouble of reinventing our counting system just to make it clunkier, but computers understand binary much better than they understand decimal. Sure, binary takes up more space, but we're held back by the hardware. And for some things, like logic processing, binary is better than decimal.

There's another base system that's also used in programming: hexadecimal. Although computers don't run on hexadecimal, programmers use it to represent binary addresses in a human-readable format when writing code. This is because two digits of hexadecimal can represent a whole byte, eight digits in binary. Hexadecimal uses 0-9 like decimal, and also the letters A through F to represent the additional six digits.

Reasons for using Binary

Hardware and the laws of physics. Every number in your computer is an electrical signal, and in the early days of computing, electrical signals were much harder to measure and control very precisely. It made more sense to only distinguish between an "on" state—represented by negative charge—and an "off" state—represented by a positive charge. For those unsure of why the "off" is represented by a positive charge, it's because electrons have a negative charge—more electrons mean more current with a negative charge.

So, the early room-sized computers used binary to build their systems, and even though they used much older, bulkier hardware, we've kept the same fundamental principles. Modern computers use what's known as a transistor to perform calculations with binary. Here's a diagram of what a field-effect transistor (FET) looks like:

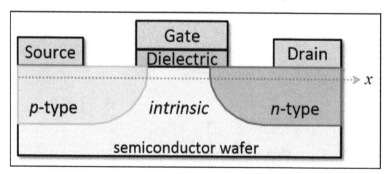

Essentially, it only allows current to flow from the source to the drain if there is a current in the gate. This forms a binary switch. Manufacturers can build these transistors incredibly small—all the way down to 5 nanometers, or about the size of two strands of DNA. This is how modern CPUs operate, and even they can suffer from problems differentiating between on and off states (though that's mostly due to their unreal molecular size, being subject to the weirdness of quantum mechanics).

Reason behind Base 2

So you may be thinking, "why only 0 and 1? Couldn't you just add another digit?" While some of it comes down to tradition in how computers are built, to add another digit would mean we'd have to distinguish between different levels of current—not just "off" and "on," but also states like "on a little bit" and "on a lot."

The problem here is if you wanted to use multiple levels of voltage, you'd need a way to easily perform calculations with them, and the hardware for that isn't viable as a replacement for binary computing. It indeed does exist; it's called a ternary computer, and it's been around since the 1950s, but that's pretty much where development on it stopped. Ternary logic is way more efficient than binary, but as of yet, nobody has an effective replacement for the binary transistor, or at the very least, no work's been done on developing them at the same tiny scales as binary.

The reason we can't use ternary logic comes down to the way transistors are stacked in a computer—something called "gates"—and how they're used to perform math. Gates take two inputs, perform an operation on them, and return one output.

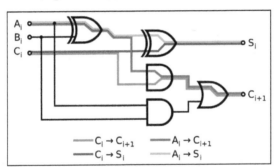

This brings us to the long answer: binary math is way easier for a computer than anything else. Boolean logic maps easily to binary systems, with True and False being represented by on and off. Gates in your computer operate on boolean logic: they take two inputs and perform an operation on them like AND, OR, XOR, and so on. Two inputs are easy to manage. If you were to graph the answers for each possible input, you would have what's known as a truth table:

A	B	A AND B	A OR B	NOT A
False	False	False	False	True
False	True	False	True	True
True	False	False	True	False
True	True	True	True	False

A binary truth table operating on boolean logic will have four possible outputs for each fundamental operation. But because ternary gates take three inputs, a ternary truth table would have 9 or more. While a binary system has 16 possible operators ($2\wedge2\wedge2$), a ternary system would have 19,683 ($3\wedge3\wedge3$). Scaling becomes an issue because while ternary is more efficient, it's also exponentially more complex.

Decimal Number System

Decimal number system is a base 10 number system having 10 digits from 0 to 9. This means that any numerical quantity can be represented using these 10 digits. Decimal number system is also a positional value system. This means that the value of digits will depend on its position. Let us take an example to understand this.

Say we have three numbers – 734, 971 and 207. The value of 7 in all three numbers is different–

- In 734, value of 7 is 7 hundreds or 700 or 7×100 or 7×10^2

- In 971, value of 7 is 7 tens or 70 or 7×10 or 7×10^1

- In 207, value of 7 is 7 units or 7 or 7×1 or 7×10^0

The weightage of each position can be represented as follows –

10^5	10^4	10^3	10^2	10^1	10^0

In digital systems, instructions are given through electric signals; variation is done by varying the voltage of the signal. Having 10 different voltages to implement decimal number system in digital equipment is difficult. So, many number systems that are easier to implement digitally have been developed.

Octal Number System

Octal Number System is one the type of Number Representation techniques, in which there value of base is 8. That means there are only 8 symbols or possible digit values, there are 0, 1, 2, 3, 4, 5, 6, 7. It requires only 3 bits to represent value of any digit. Octal numbers are indicated by the addition of either an 0o prefix or an 8 suffix.

Position of every digit has a weight which is a power of 8. Each position in the Octal system is 8 times more significant than the previous position, that means numeric value of an octal number is determined by multiplying each digit of the number by the value of the position in which the digit appears and then adding the products. So, it is also a positional (or weighted) number system.

Representation of Octal Number

Each Octal number can be represented using only 3 bits, with each group of bits having a distich values between 000 (for 0) and 111 (for 7 = 4+2+1). The equivalent binary number of Octal number are as given below –

Octal Digit Value	Binary Equivalent
0	000
1	001
2	010
3	011
4	100
5	101
6	110
7	111

Octal number system is similar to Hexadecimal number system. Octal number system provides convenient way of converting large binary numbers into more compact and smaller groups, however this octal number system is less popular.

Most Significant Bit (MSB)			Octal Point			Least Significant Bit (LSB)
8^2	8^1	8^0		8^{-1}	8^{-2}	8^{-3}
64	8	1		1/8	1/64	1/512

Since base value of Octal number system is 8, so there maximum value of digit is 7 and it can not be more than 7. In this number system, the successive positions to the left of the octal point having weights of 8^0, 8^1, 8^2, 8^3 and so on. Similarly, the successive positions to the right of the octal point having weights of 8^{-1}, 8^{-2}, 8^{-3} and so on. This is called base power of 8. The decimal value of any octal number can be determined using sum of product of each digit with its positional value.

Example– The number 111 is interpreted as:

$$111 = 1 \times 8^2 + 5 \times 8^1 + 7 \times 8^0 = 157$$

Here, right most bit 7 is the least significant bit (LSB) and left most bit 1 is the most significant bit (MSB).

Example– The number 65.125 is interpreted as:

$$65.125 = 1 \times 8^2 + 0 \times 8^1 + 1 \times 8^0 + 1 \times 8^{-1} = 101.10$$

Here, right most bit 0 is the least significant bit (LSB) and left most bit 1 is the most significant bit (MSB).

Example– A decimal number 21 to represent in Octal representation:

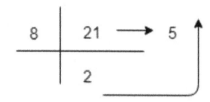

$(21)_{10} = 2 \times 8^1 + 5 \times 8^0 = (25)_8$

So, decimal value 21 is equivalent to 25 in Octal Number System.

Applications of Octal Number System

The octal numbers are not as common as they used to be. However, Octal is used when the number of bits in one word is a multiple of 3. It is also used as a shorthand for representing file permissions on UNIX systems and representation of UTF8 numbers, etc.

Advantages and Disadvantages

The main advantage of using Octal numbers is that it uses less digits than decimal and Hexadecimal number system. So, it has fewer computations and less computational errors. It uses only 3 bits to represent any digit in binary and easy to convert from octal to binary and vice-versa. It is easier to handle input and output in the octal form.

The major disadvantage of Octal number system is that computer does not understand octal number system directly, so we need octal to binary converter.

7's and 8's Complement of Octal (Base-8) Number

Simply, 7's complement of a octal number is the subtraction of it's each digits from 7. For example, 7's complement of octal number 127 is 777 - 127 = 650.

8's complement of octal number is 7's complement of given number plus 1 to the least significant bit (LSB). For example. 8's complement of octal number 320 is (777 - 320) + 1 = 457 + 1 = 460. Please note that maximum digit of octal number system is 7, so addition of 7+1 will be 0 with carry 1.

Hexadecimal Number System

The one main disadvantage of binary numbers is that the binary string equivalent of a large decimal base-10 number can be quite long.

When working with large digital systems, such as computers, it is common to find binary numbers consisting of 8, 16 and even 32 digits which makes it difficult to both read or write without producing errors especially when working with lots of 16 or 32-bit binary numbers.

One common way of overcoming this problem is to arrange the binary numbers into groups or sets of four bits (4-bits). These groups of 4-bits uses another type of numbering system also commonly used in computer and digital systems called Hexadecimal Numbers.

Hexadecimal Number String

The "Hexadecimal" or simply "Hex" numbering system uses the Base of 16 system and are a popular choice for representing long binary values because their format is quite compact and much easier to understand compared to the long binary strings of 1's and 0's.

Being a Base-16 system, the hexadecimal numbering system therefore uses 16 (sixteen) different digits with a combination of numbers from 0 through to 15. In other words, there are 16 possible digit symbols.

However, there is a potential problem with using this method of digit notation caused by the fact that the decimal numerals of 10, 11, 12, 13, 14 and 15 are normally written using two adjacent symbols. For example, if we write 10 in hexadecimal, do we mean the decimal number ten, or the binary number of two (1 + 0). To get around this tricky problem hexadecimal numbers that identify the values of ten, eleven, . . . , fifteen are replaced with capital letters of A, B, C, D, E and F respectively.

Then in the Hexadecimal Numbering System we use the numbers from 0 to 9 and the capital letters A to F to represent its Binary or Decimal number equivalent, starting with the least significant digit at the right hand side.

As we have just said, binary strings can be quite long and difficult to read, but we can make life easier by splitting these large binary numbers up into even groups to make them much easier to write down and understand. For example, the following group of binary digits 1101 0101 1100 1111$_2$ are much easier to read and understand than 1101010111001111$_2$ when they are all bunched up together.

In the everyday use of the decimal numbering system we use groups of three digits or 000's from the right hand side to make a very large number such as a million or trillion, easier for us to understand and the same is also true in digital systems.

Hexadecimal Numbers is a more complex system than using just binary or decimal and is mainly used when dealing with computers and memory address locations. By dividing a binary number up into groups of 4 bits, each group or set of 4 digits can now have a possible value of between "0000" (0) and "1111" (8+4+2+1 = 15) giving a total of 16 different number combinations from 0 to 15. Don't forget that "0" is also a valid digit.

Binary Numbers that a 4-bit group of digits is called a "nibble" and as 4-bits are also required to produce a hexadecimal number, a hex digit can also be thought of as a nibble, or half-a-byte. Then two hexadecimal numbers are required to produce one full byte ranging from 00 to FF.

Also, since 16 in the decimal system is the fourth power of 2 (or 2^4), there is a direct relationship between the numbers 2 and 16 so one hex digit has a value equal to four binary digits so now q is equal to "16".

Because of this relationship, four digits in a binary number can be represented with a single hexadecimal digit. This makes conversion between binary and hexadecimal numbers very easy, and hexadecimal can be used to write large binary numbers with much fewer digits.

The numbers 0 to 9 are still used as in the original decimal system, but the numbers from 10 to 15 are now represented by capital letters of the alphabet from A to F inclusive and the relationship between decimal, binary and hexadecimal is given below.

Hexadecimal Numbers

Decimal Number	4-bit Binary Number	Hexadecimal Number
0	0000	0
1	0001	1
2	0010	2
3	0011	3
4	0100	4
5	0101	5
6	0110	6
7	0111	7
8	1000	8
9	1001	9

10	1010	A
11	1011	B
12	1100	C
13	1101	D
14	1110	E
15	1111	F
16	0001 0000	10 (1+0)
17	0001 0001	11 (1+1)
Continuing upwards in groups of four		

Using the original binary number from above 1101 0101 1100 1111_2 this can now be converted into an equivalent hexadecimal number of D5CF which is much easier to read and understand than a long row of 1's and 0's that we had before.

So by using hexadecimal notation, digital numbers can be written using fewer digits and with a much less likelihood of an error occurring. Similarly, converting hexadecimal based numbers back into binary is simply the reverse operation.

Then the main characteristics of a Hexadecimal Numbering System is that there are 16 distinct counting digits from 0 to F with each digit having a weight or value of 16 starting from the least significant bit (LSB). In order to distinguish Hexadecimal numbers from Denary numbers, a prefix of either a "#", (Hash) or a "$" (Dollar sign) is used before the actual Hexadecimal Number value, #D5CF or $D5CF.

As the base of a hexadecimal system is 16, which also represents the number of individual symbols used in the system, the subscript 16 is used to identify a number expressed in hexadecimal. For example, the previous hexadecimal number is expressed as: $D5CF_{16}$.

Counting using Hexadecimal Numbers

So we now know how to convert 4 binary digits into a hexadecimal number. But what if we had more than 4 binary digits how would we count in hexadecimal beyond the final letter F. The simple answer is to start over again with another set of 4 bits as follows.

0...to...9, A,B,C,D,E,F, 10...to...19, 1A, 1B, 1C, 1D, 1E, 1F, 20, 21....etc

Do not get confused, 10 or 20 is NOT ten or twenty it is 1 + 0 and 2 + 0 in hexadecimal. In fact twenty does not even exist in hex. With two hexadecimal numbers we can count up to FF which is equal to decimal 255. Likewise, to count higher than FF we would add a third hexadecimal digit to the left so the first 3-bit hexadecimal number would be 100_{16} (256_{10}) and the last would be FFF_{16} (4095_{10}). The maximum 4-digit hexadecimal number is $FFFF_{16}$ which is equal to 65,535 in decimal and so on.

Representation of a Hexadecimal Number

MSB	Hexadecimal Number							LSB
16^8	16^7	16^6	16^5	16^4	16^3	16^2	16^1	16^0
4.3G	2.6G	16M	1M	65k	4k	256	16	1

This adding of additional hexadecimal digits to convert both decimal and binary numbers into an Hexadecimal Number is very easy if there are 4, 8, 12 or 16 binary digits to convert. But we can also add zero's to the left of the most significant bit, the MSB if the number of binary bits is not a multiple of four.

For example, 11001011011001_2 is a fourteen bit binary number that is to large for just three hexadecimal digits only, yet too small for a four hexadecimal number. The answer is to ADD additional zero's to the left most bit until we have a complete set of four bit binary number or multiples thereof.

Adding of Additional 0's to a Binary Number

Binary Number	0011	0010	1101	1001
Hexadecimal Number	3	2	D	9

The main advantage of a Hexadecimal Number is that it is very compact and by using a base of 16 means that the number of digits used to represent a given number is usually less than in binary or decimal. Also, it is quick and easy to convert between hexadecimal numbers and binary.

Hexadecimal Numbers

Example:

Convert the following Binary number $1110\ 1010_2$ into its Hexadecimal number equivalent.

11101010_2			
Group the bits into four's starting from the right hand side			
=	1110	1010	
Find the Decimal equivalent of each individual group			
=	14	10	(in decimal)
Convert to Hexadecimal using the table above			
=	E	A	(in Hex)
Then, the hexadecimal equivalent of the binary number $1110\ 1010_2$ is $\#EA_{16}$			

Hexadecimal Numbers

Example:

Convert the following Hexadecimal number $\#3FA7_{16}$ into its Binary equivalent, and also into its Decimal or Denary equivalent using subscripts to identify each numbering system.

$\#3FA7_{16}$

$\quad\quad = 0011\ 1111\ 1010\ 0111_{2}$

$\quad\quad = (8192 + 4096 + 2048 + 1024 + 512 + 256 + 128 + 32 + 4 + 2 + 1)$

$\quad\quad = 16,295_{10}$

Then, the Decimal number of 16,295 can be represented as:-

$\quad\quad \#3FA7_{16}$ in Hexadecimal

or

$\quad\quad 0011\ 1111\ 1010\ 0111_{2}$ in Binary.

Then to summarise. The Hexadecimal, or Hex, numbering system is commonly used in computer and digital systems to reduce large strings of binary numbers into a sets of four digits for us to easily understand. The word "Hexadecimal" means sixteen because this type of digital numbering system uses 16 different digits from 0-to-9, and A-to-F.

To convert binary numbers into *hexadecimal numbers* we must first divide the binary number up into a 4-bit binary word which can have any value from 0_{10} (0000_{2}) to 15_{10} (1111_{2}) representing the hexadecimal equivalent of 0 through to F.

Conversions in Number Systems

There are many methods or techniques which can be used to convert numbers from one base to another. We'll demonstrate here the following –

- Decimal to Other Base System
- Other Base System to Decimal
- Other Base System to Non-Decimal
- Shortcut method – Binary to Octal
- Shortcut method – Octal to Binary
- Shortcut method – Binary to Hexadecimal
- Shortcut method – Hexadecimal to Binary

Decimal to Other Base System

Steps

- Step 1 – Divide the decimal number to be converted by the value of the new base.

- Step 2 – Get the remainder from Step 1 as the rightmost digit (least significant digit) of new base number.

- Step 3 – Divide the quotient of the previous divide by the new base.

- Step 4 – Record the remainder from Step 3 as the next digit (to the left) of the new base number.

Repeat Steps 3 and 4, getting remainders from right to left, until the quotient becomes zero in Step 3.

The last remainder thus obtained will be the Most Significant Digit (MSD) of the new base number.

Example

Decimal Number: 29_{10}

Calculating Binary Equivalent –

Step	Operation	Result	Remainder
Step 1	29 / 2	14	1
Step 2	14 / 2	7	0
Step 3	7 / 2	3	1
Step 4	3 / 2	1	1
Step 5	1 / 2	0	1

As mentioned in Steps 2 and 4, the remainders have to be arranged in the reverse order so that the first remainder becomes the Least Significant Digit (LSD) and the last remainder becomes the Most Significant Digit (MSD).

Decimal Number – 29_{10} = Binary Number – 11101_2.

Other Base System to Decimal System

Steps

- Step 1 – Determine the column (positional) value of each digit (this depends on the position of the digit and the base of the number system).

- Step 2 – Multiply the obtained column values (in Step 1) by the digits in the corresponding columns.

- Step 3 – Sum the products calculated in Step 2. The total is the equivalent value in decimal.

Example

Binary Number – 11101_2

Calculating Decimal Equivalent –

Step	Binary Number	Decimal Number
Step 1	11101_2	$((1 \times 2^4) + (1 \times 2^3) + (1 \times 2^2) + (0 \times 2^1) + (1 \times 2^0))_{10}$
Step 2	11101_2	$(16 + 8 + 4 + 0 + 1)_{10}$
Step 3	11101_2	29_{10}

Binary Number – 11101_2 = Decimal Number – 29_{10}

Other Base System to Non-Decimal System

Steps

- Step 1 – Convert the original number to a decimal number (base 10).

- Step 2 – Convert the decimal number so obtained to the new base number.

Example

Octal Number – 25_8

Calculating Binary Equivalent –

- Step 1 – Convert to Decimal

Step	Octal Number	Decimal Number
Step 1	25_8	$((2 \times 8^1) + (5 \times 8^0))_{10}$
Step 2	25_8	$(16 + 5)_{10}$
Step 3	25_8	21_{10}

Octal Number – 25_8 = Decimal Number – 21_{10}

- Step 2 – Convert Decimal to Binary

Step	Operation	Result	Remainder
Step 1	21 / 2	10	1
Step 2	10 / 2	5	0
Step 3	5 / 2	2	1
Step 4	2 / 2	1	0
Step 5	1 / 2	0	1

Decimal Number – 21_{10} = Binary Number – 10101_2

Octal Number – 25_8 = Binary Number – 10101_2

Shortcut Method - Binary to Octal

Steps

- Step 1 – Divide the binary digits into groups of three (starting from the right).

- Step 2 – Convert each group of three binary digits to one octal digit.

Example

Binary Number – 10101_2

Calculating Octal Equivalent –

Step	Binary Number	Octal Number
Step 1	10101_2	010 101
Step 2	10101_2	$2_8\ 5_8$
Step 3	10101_2	25_8

Binary Number – 10101_2 = Octal Number – 25_8

Shortcut Method - Octal to Binary

Steps

- Step 1 – Convert each octal digit to a 3 digit binary number (the octal digits may be treated as decimal for this conversion).

- Step 2 – Combine all the resulting binary groups (of 3 digits each) into a single binary number.

Example

Octal Number – 25_8

Calculating Binary Equivalent –

Step	Octal Number	Binary Number
Step 1	25_8	$2_{10}\ 5_{10}$
Step 2	25_8	$010_2\ 101_2$
Step 3	25_8	010101_2

Octal Number – 25_8 = Binary Number – 10101_2

Shortcut Method - Binary to Hexadecimal

Steps

- Step 1 – Divide the binary digits into groups of four (starting from the right).

- Step 2 – Convert each group of four binary digits to one hexadecimal symbol.

Example

Binary Number – 10101_2

Calculating hexadecimal Equivalent –

Step	Binary Number	Hexadecimal Number
Step 1	10101_2	0001 0101
Step 2	10101_2	$1_{10}\ 5_{10}$
Step 3	10101_2	15_{16}

Binary Number – 10101_2 = Hexadecimal Number – 15_{16}

Shortcut Method - Hexadecimal to Binary

Steps

- Step 1 – Convert each hexadecimal digit to a 4 digit binary number (the hexadecimal digits may be treated as decimal for this conversion).

- Step 2 – Combine all the resulting binary groups (of 4 digits each) into a single binary number.

Example

Hexadecimal Number – 15_{16}

Calculating Binary Equivalent –

Step	Hexadecimal Number	Binary Number
Step 1	15_{16}	$1_{10}\ 5_{10}$
Step 2	15_{16}	$0001_2\ 0101_2$
Step 3	15_{16}	00010101_2

Hexadecimal Number – 15_{16} = Binary Number – 10101_2

Logic Gates

A logic gate is a building block of a digital circuit. Most logic gates have two inputs and one output and are based on Boolean algebra. At any given moment, every terminal is in one of the two binary conditions false (high) or true (low). False represents 0, and true represents 1. Depending on the type of logic gate being used and the combination of inputs, the binary output will differ. A logic gate can be thought of like a light switch, wherein one position the output is off—0, and in another, it is on—1. Logic gates are commonly used in integrated circuits (IC).

Basic Logic Gates

There are seven basic logic gates: AND, OR, XOR, NOT, NAND, NOR, and XNOR.

The *AND gate* is so named because, if 0 is called "false" and 1 is called "true," the gate acts in the same way as the logical "and" operator. The following illustration and table show the circuit symbol and logic combinations for an AND gate. (In the symbol, the input terminals are at left and the output terminal is at right.) The output is "true" when both inputs are "true." Otherwise, the output is "false." In other words, the output is 1 only when both inputs one AND two are 1.

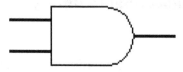

And Gate

Input 1	Input 2	Output
	1	
1		
1	1	1

The *OR gate* gets its name from the fact that it behaves after the fashion of the logical inclusive "or." The output is "true" if either or both of the inputs are "true." If both inputs are "false," then the output is "false." In other words, for the output to be 1, at least input one OR two must be 1.

OR gate

Input 1	Input 2	Output
	1	1
1		1
1	1	1

The *XOR* (*exclusive-OR*) *gate* acts in the same way as the logical "either/or." The output is "true" if either, but not both, of the inputs are "true." The output is "false" if both inputs are "false" or if both inputs are "true." Another way of looking at this circuit is to observe that the output is 1 if the inputs are different, but 0 if the inputs are the same.

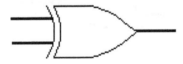

XOR Gate

Input 1	Input 2	Output
	1	1
1		1
1	1	

A logical *inverter*, sometimes called a *NOT gate* to differentiate it from other types of electronic inverter devices, has only one input. It reverses the logic state. If the input is 1, then the output is 0. If the input is 0, then the output is 1.

Inverter or not Gate

Input	Output
1	
	1

The *NAND gate* operates as an AND gate followed by a NOT gate. It acts in the manner of the logical operation "and" followed by negation. The output is "false" if both inputs are "true." Otherwise, the output is "true."

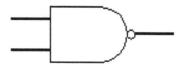

NAND Gate

Input 1	Input 2	Output
		1
	1	1
1		1
1	1	

The *NOR gate* is a combination OR gate followed by an inverter. Its output is "true" if both inputs are "false." Otherwise, the output is "false."

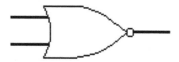

NOR Gate

Input 1	Input 2	Output
		1
	1	
1		
1	1	

The *XNOR (exclusive-NOR) gate* is a combination XOR gate followed by an inverter. Its output is "true" if the inputs are the same, and"false" if the inputs are different.

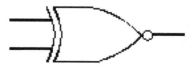

XNOR Gate

Input 1	Input 2	Output
		1
	1	
1		
1	1	1

Using combinations of logic gates, complex operations can be performed. In theory, there is no limit to the number of gates that can be arrayed together in a single device. But in practice, there is a limit to the number of gates that can be packed into a given physical space. Arrays of logic gates are found in digital ICs. As IC technology advances, the required physical volume for each individual logic gate decreases and digital devices of the same or smaller size become capable of performing ever-more-complicated operations at ever-increasing speeds.

Composition of Logic Gates

High or low binary conditions are represented by different voltage levels. The logic state of a terminal can, and generally does, change often as the circuit processes data. In most logic gates, the low state is approximately zero volts (0 V), while the high state is approximately five volts positive (+5 V).

Logic gates can be made of resistors and transistors, or diodes. A resistor can commonly be used as a pull-up or pull-down resistor. Pull-up or pull-down resistors are used when there are any unused logic gate inputs to connect to either a logic level 1 or 0 respectively. This prevents any false switching of the gate. Pull-up resistors are connected to Vcc (+5V), and pull-down resistors are connected to ground (0 V).

Commonly used logic gates are TTL and CMOS. TTL, or Transistor-Transistor Logic, ICs will use NPN and PNP type Bipolar Junction Transistors. CMOS, or Complementary Metal-Oxide-Silicon, ICs are constructed from MOSFET or JFET type Field Effect Transistors. TTL IC's may commonly be labeled as the 7400 series of chips, while CMOS ICs may often be marked as a 4000 series of chips.

Truth Table

As well as a standard Boolean Expression, the input and output information of any Logic Gate or circuit can be plotted into a standard table to give a visual representation of the switching function of the system.

The table used to represent the boolean expression of a logic gate function is commonly called a Truth Table. A logic gate truth table shows each possible input combination to the gate or circuit with the resultant output depending upon the combination of these input(s).

For example, consider a single 2-input logic circuit with input variables labelled as A and B. There are "four" possible input combinations or 2^2 of "OFF" and "ON" for the two inputs. However, when dealing with Boolean expressions and especially logic gate truth tables, we do not general use "ON" or "OFF" but instead give them bit values which represent a logic level "1" or a logic level "0" respectively.

Then the four possible combinations of A and B for a 2-input logic gate is given as:

Input Combination 1. – "OFF" – "OFF" or (0, 0)

Input Combination 2. – "OFF" – "ON" or (0, 1)

Input Combination 3. – "ON" – "OFF" or (1, 0)

Input Combination 4. – "ON" – "ON" or (1, 1)

Therefore, a 3-input logic circuit would have 8 possible input combinations or 2^3 and a 4-input logic circuit would have 16 or 2^4, and so on as the number of inputs increases. Then a logic circuit with "n" number of inputs would have 2^n possible input combinations of both "OFF" and "ON".

So in order to keep things simple to understand, in this we will only deal with standard 2-input type logic gates, but the principals are still the same for gates with more than two inputs.

Then the Truth tables for a 2-input AND Gate, a 2-input OR Gate and a single input NOTGate are given as:

2-input AND Gate

For a 2-input AND gate, the output Q is true if BOTH input A "AND" input B are both true, giving the Boolean Expression of: (Q = A and B).

Symbol		Truth Table		
		A	B	Q
A & Q		0	0	0
B		0	1	0
2-input AND Gate		1	0	0
		1	1	1
Boolean Expression Q = A.B		Read as A AND B gives Q		

Note that the Boolean Expression for a two input AND gate can be written as: A.B or just simply AB without the decimal point.

2-input or (Inclusive or) Gate

For a 2-input OR gate, the output Q is true if EITHER input A "OR" input B is true, giving the Boolean Expression of: (Q = A or B).

Symbol	Truth Table		
	A	B	Q
	0	0	0
	0	1	1
	1	0	1
	1	1	1
Boolean Expression Q = A+B	Read as A OR B gives Q		

NOT Gate (Inverter)

For a single input NOT gate, the output Q is ONLY true when the input is "NOT" true, the output is the inverse or complement of the input giving the Boolean Expression of: (Q = NOT A).

Symbol	Truth Table	
	A	Q
	0	1
	1	0
Boolean Expression Q = NOT A or $\bar{A}$	Read as inversion of A gives Q	

The NAND and the NOR Gates are a combination of the AND and OR Gates respectively with that of a NOT Gate (inverter).

2-input NAND (Not AND) Gate

For a 2-input NAND gate, the output Q is true if BOTH input A and input B are NOT true, giving the Boolean Expression of: (Q = not(A AND B)).

Symbol	Truth Table		
	A	B	Q
	0	0	1
	0	1	1
	1	0	1
	1	1	0
Boolean Expression Q = A .B	Read as A AND B gives NOT-Q		

2-input NOR (NOT OR) Gate

For a 2-input NOR gate, the output Q is true if BOTH input A and input B are NOT true, giving the Boolean Expression of: (Q = not(A OR B)).

Symbol	Truth Table		
	A	B	Q
A ≥ 1 B Q 2-input NOR Gate	0	0	1
	0	1	0
	1	0	0
	1	1	0
Boolean Expression Q = A+B	Read as A OR B gives NOT-Q		

As well as the standard logic gates there are also two special types of logic gate function called an Exclusive-OR Gate and an Exclusive-NOR Gate. The Boolean expression to indicate an Exclusive-OR or Exclusive-NOR function is to a symbol with a plus sign inside a circle, ($\oplus$).

The switching actions of both of these types of gates can be created using the above standard logic gates. However, as they are widely used functions they are now available in standard IC form and have been included here as reference.

2-input EX-OR (Exclusive OR) Gate

For a 2-input Ex-OR gate, the output Q is true if EITHER input A or if input B is true, but NOT both giving the Boolean Expression of: (Q = (A and NOT B) or (NOT A and B)).

Symbol	Truth Table		
	A	B	Q
A $=1$ B Q 2-input Ex-OR Gate	0	0	0
	0	1	1
	1	0	1
	1	1	0
Boolean Expression Q = A $\oplus$ B			

2-input EX-NOR (Exclusive NOR) Gate

For a 2-input Ex-NOR gate, the output Q is true if BOTH input A and input B are the same, either true or false, giving the Boolean Expression of: (Q = (A and B) or (NOT A and NOT B)).

Symbol	Truth Table		
	A	B	Q
A =1 B Q 2-input Ex-NOR Gate	0	0	1
	0	1	0
	1	0	0
	1	1	1
Boolean Expression Q = A ⊕ B			

2-input Logic Gates

The following Truth Table compares the logical functions of the 2-input logic gates above.

Inputs		Truth Table Outputs For Each Gate					
A	B	AND	NAND	OR	NOR	EX-OR	EX-NOR
0	0	0	1	0	1	0	1
0	1	0	1	1	0	1	0
1	0	0	1	1	0	1	0
1	1	1	0	1	0	0	1

The following table gives a list of the common logic functions and their equivalent Boolean notation.

Logic Function	Boolean Notation
AND	A.B
OR	A+B
NOT	$\bar{A}$
NAND	$\overline{A.B}$
NOR	$\overline{A+B}$
EX-OR	$(A.\bar{B}) + (\bar{A}.B)$ or A ⊕ B
EX-NOR	$(A.B) + (\overline{A.B})$ or $\overline{A ⊕ B}$

2-input logic gate truth tables are given here as examples of the operation of each logic function, but there are many more logic gates with 3, 4 even 8 individual inputs. The multiple input gates are no different to the simple 2-input gates above, So a 4-input AND gate would still require ALL 4-inputs to be present to produce the required output at Q and its larger truth table would reflect that.

Logic Circuit

A logic circuit is a circuit that executes a processing or controlling function in a computer. This circuit implements logical operations on information to process it.

Logic circuits utilize two values for a physical quantity, like voltage, to denote the Boolean values true and false or 1 and 0 respectively. Logic circuits have inputs and the outputs can be dependent on the inputs. In logic circuit diagrams, connection from one circuit's output to another circuit's input is displayed as an arrowhead at the input end.

When it comes to performance, logic circuits are similar to programming language functions. The inputs are similar to function parameters while the outputs are similar to function returned values. A logic circuit can accommodate multiple outputs.

Two Types of Logic Circuitry:

- Combinational circuitry – performs like a simple function. The output is based on the present values of the input.

Combinational circuitry is theoretically built from basic logic gates: AND gates, OR gates, XOR gates, and inverters. The outputs of gates in combinational circuitry are never sent back directly to earlier inputs.

- An AND gate can conceptually have any number of inputs. Its output is true when all of its inputs are true.

An AND gate is frequently used to control a signal – turn it on or off depending on the value of control signals.

- An OR gate can conceptually have any number of inputs. Its output is true when any one of its inputs is true.

- An XOR gate has two inputs. Its output is true when one of its inputs, but not both are true.

An XOR gate is sometimes used to control a signal – invert it or not depending on the value of a control signal.

Basic logic gates can be combined to form a variety of higher-level units:

- Routing

  ○ Multiplexers – have several data input signals and a control input. The output is identical to one of the inputs. The value of the control signal determines which one.

  ○ Demultiplexers – have one data input signal, a control input and several output signals. All of the output signals are 0 (false) except for the one selected by the control input. The selected output is identical to the data input.

- Computational

  ○ Full adders – perform a single column of a binary addition. They are the primary building block for multi-bit adders and subtracters.

  ○ Adders and Subtracters – add or subtract two binary or two complement numbers. A subtracter is just an adder with extra circuitry to do a two-complement operation on one of the inputs. Usually they are designed to do either addition or subtraction as directed by a control signal.

  ○ Comparators – compare two binary or two complement numbers.

- State circuitry – performs like an object method. The output is not only based on the input. It is also based on the historical inputs. This is made possible due to the memory embedded in the circuitry.This is similar to an object method with values depending on the object's state, or its instance variables.State circuitry contains anything that can recollect bits of information including memory, registers and program counter.

  The basic element of state circuitry is a flip-flop. A flip-flop stores one bit of data. Multiple flip-flops can be combined to form a multi-bit state element called a register. Multiple registers can be combined into a register bank.

These two types of logic circuitry work hand in hand to form a processor datapath.

Processor Datapath

A processor's datapath is conceptually organized into two parts:

- Combinational logic determines the state of the processor for the next clock cycle. The ALU is combinational logic.

- State elements hold information about the state of the processor during the current clock cycle. All registers are state elements.

Combinational Logic Circuits

Combinational Logic Circuits are memoryless digital logic circuits whose output at any instant in time depends only on the combination of its inputs.

Unlike Sequential Logic Circuits whose outputs are dependant on both their present inputs and their previous output state giving them some form of *Memory*. The outputs of Combinational Logic Circuits are only determined by the logical function of their current input state, logic "0" or logic "1", at any given instant in time.

The result is that combinational logic circuits have no feedback, and any changes to the signals being applied to their inputs will immediately have an effect at the output. In other words, in a Combinational Logic Circuit, the output is dependant at all times on the combination of its inputs. Thus a combinational circuit is *memoryless*.

So if one of its inputs condition changes state, from 0-1 or 1-0, so too will the resulting output as by default combinational logic circuits have "no memory", "timing" or "feedback loops" within their design.

Combinational Logic

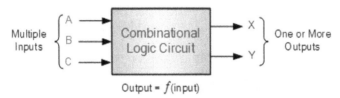

Combinational Logic Circuits are made up from basic logic NAND, NOR or NOT gates that are "combined" or connected together to produce more complicated switching circuits. These logic gates are the building blocks of combinational logic circuits. An example of a combinational circuit is a decoder, which converts the binary code data present at its input into a number of different output lines, one at a time producing an equivalent decimal code at its output.

Combinational logic circuits can be very simple or very complicated and any combinational circuit can be implemented with only NAND and NOR gates as these are classed as "universal" gates.

The three main ways of specifying the function of a combinational logic circuit are:

- Boolean Algebra – This forms the algebraic expression showing the operation of the logic circuit for each input variable either True or False that results in a logic "1" output.

- Truth Table – A truth table defines the function of a logic gate by providing a concise list that shows all the output states in tabular form for each possible combination of input variable that the gate could encounter.

- Logic Diagram – This is a graphical representation of a logic circuit that shows the wiring and connections of each individual logic gate, represented by a specific graphical symbol, that implements the logic circuit.

All three of these logic circuit representations are shown below.

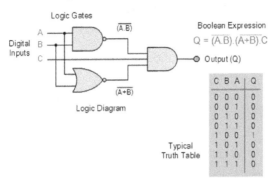

As combinational logic circuits are made up from individual logic gates only, they can also be considered as "decision making circuits" and combinational logic is about combining logic gates together to process two or more signals in order to produce at least one output signal according to the logical function of each logic gate. Common combinational circuits made up from individual logic gates that carry out a desired application include *Multiplexers, De-multiplexers, Encoders, Decoders, Full* and *Half Adders* etc.

Classification of Combinational Logic

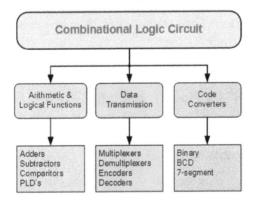

One of the most common uses of combinational logic is in Multiplexer and De-multiplexer type circuits. Here, multiple inputs or outputs are connected to a common signal line and logic gates are used to decode an address to select a single data input or output switch.

A multiplexer consists of two separate components, a logic decoder and some solid state switches.

Solid State Switches

Standard TTL logic devices made up from Transistors can only pass signal currents in one direction only making them "uni-directional" devices and poor imitations of conventional electro-mechanical switches or relays. However, some CMOS switching devices made up from FET's act as near perfect "bi-directional" switches making them ideal for use as solid state switches.

Solid state switches come in a variety of different types and ratings, and there are many different applications for using solid state switches. They can basically be sub-divided into 3 different main groups for switching applications and in this combinational logic section we will only look at the Analogue type of switch but the principal is the same for all types including digital.

Solid State Switch Applications

- Analogue Switches – Used in Data Switching and Communications, Video and Audio Signal Switching, Instrumentation and Process Control Circuits, etc.

- Digital Switches – High Speed Data Transmission, Switching and Signal Routing, Ethernet, LAN's, USB and Serial Transmissions, etc.

- Power Switches – Power Supplies and General "Standby Power" Switching Applications, Switching of Larger Voltages and Currents, etc.

Analogue Bilateral Switches

Analogue or "Analog" switches are those types that are used to switch data or signal currents when they are in their "ON" state and block them when they are in their "OFF" state. The rapid switching between the "ON" and the "OFF" state is usually controlled by a digital signal applied to the control gate of the switch. An ideal analogue switch has zero resistance when "ON" (or closed), and infinite resistance when "OFF" (or open) and switches with R_{ON} values of less than 1Ω are commonly available.

Solid State Analogue Switch

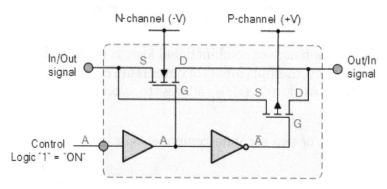

By connecting an N-channel MOSFET in parallel with a P-channel MOSFET allows signals to pass in either direction making it a "Bi-directional" switch and as to whether the N-channel or the P-channel device carries more signal current will depend upon the ratio between the input to the output voltage. The two MOSFET's are switched "ON" or "OFF" by two internal non-inverting and inverting amplifiers.

Contact Types

Just like mechanical switches, analogue switches come in a variety of forms or contact types, depending on the number of "poles" and "throws" they offer. Thus, terms such as "SPST" (single-pole single throw) and "SPDT" (single-pole double-throw) also apply to solid state analogue switches with "make-before-break" and "break-before-make" configurations available.

Analogue Switch Types

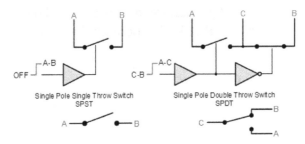

Individual analogue switches can be grouped together into standard IC packages to form devices with multiple switching configurations of SPST (single-pole single-throw) and SPDT (single-pole double-throw) as well as multi channel multiplexers.

The most common and simplest analogue switch in a single IC package is the 74HC4066 which has 4 independent bi-directional "ON/OFF" Switches within a single package but the most widely used variants of the CMOS analogue switch are those described as "Multi-way Bilateral Switches" otherwise known as the "Multiplexer" and "De-multiplexer" IC´s.

Then to summarise, Combinational Logic Circuits consist of inputs, two or more basic logic gates and outputs. The logic gates are combined in such a way that the output state depends entirely on the input states. Combinational logic circuits have "no memory", "timing" or "feedback loops", there operation is instantaneous. A combinational logic circuit performs an operation assigned logically by a Boolean expression or truth table.

Examples of common combinational logic circuits include: half adders, full adders, multiplexers, demultiplexers, encoders and decoders

Boolean Algebra

Boolean algebra is an algebra that deals with Boolean values((TRUE and FALSE). Everyday. we have to make logic decisions: "Should I carry the book or not?" , "Should I watch TV or not?" etc. Each question will have two answers yes or no, true or false. In Boolean Algebra we use 1 for true and 0 for false which are known as truth values.

Truth Table

A truth table is composed of one column for each input variable (for example, A and B), and one final column for all of the possible results of the logical operation that the table is meant to represent (for example, A XOR B). Each row of the truth table therefore contains one possible configuration of the input variables (for instance, A = true B = false), and the result of the operation for those values.

Logical Operators

In Algebraic function e use +,-,*,/ operator but in case of Logical Function or Compound statement we use AND, OR & NOT operator. Example: He prefers Computer Science NOT IP.

There are three Basic Logical Operator:

1. NOT

2. OR

3. AND

1. NOT Operator—Operates on single variable. It gives the complement value of variable.

X	$\bar{X}$
0	1
1	0

2. OR Operator -It is a binary operator and denotes logical Addition operation and is represented by "+" symbol

$0+0 =0$
$0+1 =1$
$1+0 =1$
$1+1 =1$

X	Y	X+Y
0	0	0
0	1	1
1	0	1
1	1	1

3. AND Operator – AND Operator performs logical multiplications and symbol is (.) dot.

    0.0 =0

    0.1 =0

    1.0 =1

    1.1 =1

Truth Table

X	Y	X.Y
0	0	0
0	1	0
1	0	0
1	1	1

Basic Logic Gates

A logic gate is an physical device implementing a Boolean function, that is, it performs a logical operation on one or more logic inputs and produces a single logic output. Gates also called logic circuits.

Or

A gate is simply an electronic circuit which operates on one or more signals to produce an output signal. NOT gate (inverter): The output Q is true when the input A is NOT true, the output is the inverse of the input:

Q = NOT A

A NOT gate can only have one input. A NOT gate is also called an inverter.

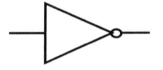

	Input A	Output Q
	0	1
	1	0

Traditional symbol   Truth Table

AND Gate

The output Q is true if input A AND input B are both true: Q = A AND B An AND gate can have two or more inputs, its output is true if all inputs are true.

Input A	Input B	Output Q
0	0	0
0	1	0
1	0	0
1	1	1

Traditional symbol   Truth Table

OR gate

The output Q is true if input A OR input B is true (or both of them are true): Q = A OR B An OR gate can have two or more inputs, its output is true if at least one input is true.

Input A	Input B	Output Q
0	0	0
0	1	1
1	0	1
1	1	1

Traditional symbol   Truth Table

Basic Postulates of Boolean Algebra

Boolean algebra consists of fundamental laws that are based on theorem of Boolean algebra. These fundamental laws are known as basic postulates of Boolean algebra. These postulates states basic relations in boolean algebra, that follow:

I If X != 0 then x=1 and If X!=1 then x=0

II OR relations(logical addition)

$$0+0 =0$$
$$0+1 =1$$
$$1+0 =1$$
$$1+1 =1$$

III AND relations (logical multiplication)

$$0.0 =0$$
$$0.1 =1$$
$$1.0 =1$$
$$1.1 =1$$

IV Complement Rules $\overline{0} = 1, \overline{1} = 0$

Principal of Duality

This principal states that we can derive a Boolean relation from another Boolean relation by performing simple steps. The steps are:-

1. Change each AND (.) with an OR (+) sign

2. Change each OR (+) with an AND (.) sign

3. Replace each 0 with 1 and each 1 with 0

e.g

0+0=0 then dual is 1.1=1

1+0=1 then dual is 0.1=0

Basic Theorem of Boolean Algebra

Basic postulates of Boolean algebra are used to define basic theorems of Boolean algebra that provides all the tools necessary for manipulating Boolean expression.

1. Properties of 0 and 1

$$(a) 0 + X = X$$
$$(b) 1 + X = 1$$
$$(c) 0.X = 0$$
$$(d) 1.X = X$$

2. Indempotence Law

$$(a) X + X = X$$
$$(b) X.X = X$$

3. Involution Law

$$(\overline{\overline{X}}) = X$$

4. Complementarity Law

$$(a) X + \overline{X} = 1$$
$$(b) X.\overline{X} = 0$$

5. Commutative Law

$$(a) X + Y = Y + X$$
$$(b) X.Y = Y.X$$

6. Associative Law

$(a) X+(Y+Z)=(X+Y)+Z$

$(b) X(YZ)=(XY)Z$

7. Distributive Law

$(a) X(Y+Z)=XY\_XZ$

$(b) X=YZ=(X+Y)(X+Z)$

8. Absorption Law

$(a) X+XY=X$

$(b) X+(X+Y)=X$

Some other rules of Boolean algebra

$X+\overline{XY}=X+Y$

Demorgan's First Theorem

It states that $\overline{X+Y}=\overline{X}\ \overline{Y}$

Demorgan's Second Theorem

This theorem states that : $\overline{X.Y}=\overline{X}+\overline{Y}$

Derivation of Boolean Expression

Minterm

Minterm is a product of all the literals within the logic System. Steps involved in minterm expansion of Expression

1. First convert the given expression in sum of product form.

2. In each term is any variable is missing(e.g. in the following example Y is missing in first term and X is missing in second term), multiply that term with (missing term +complement(missing term)) factor e.g. if Y is missing multiply with Y+Y").

3. Expand the expression.

4. Remove all duplicate terms and we will have minterm form of an expression.

Example: Convert X+Y

$$X+Y = X.1+Y.1$$
$$= X.(Y+Y")+Y(X+X")$$
$$= XY+XY"+XY+X"Y$$
$$= XY+XY"+XY$$

Other procedure for expansion could be:

1. Write down all the terms.

2. Put X"s where letters much be inserted to convert the term to a product term.

3. Use all combination of X"s in each term to generate minterms.

4. Drop out duplicate terms.

Shorthand Minterm Notation

Since all the letters must appear in every product, a shorthand notation has been developed that saves actually writing down the letters themselves. To form this notation, following steps are to be followed:

1. First of all, Copy original terms.

2. Substitute 0s for barred letters and 1s for nonbarred letters.

3. Express the decimal equivalent of binary word as a subscript of m.

Rule1: Find Binary equivalent of decimal subscript e.g.,for m6 subscript is 6, binary equivalent of 6 is 110.

Rule 2: For every 1s write the variable as it is and for 0s write variables complemented form i.e., for 110 t is XYZ. XYZ is the required minterm for m6.

Maxterm

A maxterm is a sum of all the literals (with or without the bar) within the logic system. Boolean Expression composed entirely either of Minterms or Maxterms is referred to as Canonical Expression.

Canonical Form

Canonical expression can be represented is derived from:

(i) Sum-of-Products(SOP) form

(ii) Product-of-sums(POS) form

Sum of Product (SOP)

1. Various possible input values

2. The desired output values for each of the input combinations

X	Y	R
0	0	X'Y'
0	1	X'Y
1	0	XY'
1	1	XY

Product of Sum (POS)

When a Boolean expression is represented purely as product of Maxterms, it is said to be in Canonical Product-of-Sum from of expression.

X	Y	Z	Maxterm
0	0	0	X+Y+Z
0	0	1	X+Y+Z'
0	1	0	X+Y'+Z
0	1	1	X+Y'+Z'
1	0	0	X'+Y+Z
1	0	1	X'+Y+Z'
1	1	0	X'+Y'+Z
1	1	1	X'+Y'+Z'

Minimization of Boolean Expressions

After obtaining SOP and POS expressions, the next step is to simplify the Boolean expression.

There are two methods of simplification of Boolean expressions.

1. Algebraic Method

2. Karnaugh Map

1. Algebraic Method: This method makes use of Boolean postulates, rules and theorems to simplify the expression.

Example: Reduce the expression

$$\text{Solution}, \overline{XY} + \overline{X} + XY$$

$$= \left(\overline{X} + \overline{Y}\right) + \overline{X} + XY \qquad \left(\text{using } DeMorgan'2^{nd} \text{ } theorem\, i.e, \overline{XY} = \overline{X} + \overline{Y}\right)$$

$$= \overline{X} + \overline{X} + \overline{Y} + XY$$

$$= \bar{X} + \bar{X} + \bar{Y} + XY$$

$$= \bar{X} + \bar{Y} + XY \qquad \left(\because \bar{X} + \bar{X} = \bar{X} \text{ as } X + X = X \right)$$

$$= \bar{X} + XY + \bar{Y}$$

$$= \left(\bar{X} + XY \right) + \bar{Y} = \left(\bar{X} + XY \right) + \bar{Y} \quad \left(\text{putting } X = \bar{X} \right)$$

$$= \bar{X} + Y + \bar{Y} \qquad \left(X + \bar{X}Y = X + Y \right)$$

$$= \bar{X} + 1 \qquad \left(\text{putting } Y + \bar{Y} = 1 \right)$$

$$= 1 \qquad \left(\text{putting } \bar{X} + 1 = 1 \text{ as } 1 + X = 1 \right)$$

$$\overline{XY} + \bar{X} + XY.$$

Example: Minimise $AB + \overline{AC} + A\bar{B}C(AB + C)$.

Solution: $AB + \overline{AC} + A\bar{B}C(AB + C)$

$$= AB + \overline{AC} + A\bar{B}CAB + A\bar{B}CC$$

$$= AB + \overline{AC} - AA\bar{B}BC + ABCC$$

$$= AB + \overline{AC} + 0 + ABCC \qquad \left(\text{putting } B\bar{B} - 0 \right)$$

$$= AB + \overline{AC} + A\bar{B}.C \qquad \left(\text{putting } C.C = C \right)$$

$$= AB + \bar{A} + \bar{C} + A\bar{B}C \qquad \left(\text{putting } \overline{AC} = \bar{A} + \bar{C} \text{ DeMorgan's } 2^{nd} \text{ theorem} \right)$$

$$= \bar{A} + AB + \bar{C} + A\bar{B}C \qquad (\text{rearranging the terms})$$

$$= \bar{A} + B + \bar{C} + A\bar{B}C \qquad \left(\text{putting } \bar{A} + AB = A + B \text{ because } X + XY = X + Y \right)$$

$$= \bar{A} + \bar{C} + B + A\bar{B}C = \bar{A} + \bar{C} + B + \bar{B}AC$$

$$= A + \bar{C} + B + AC \qquad \left(\text{putting } B + \bar{B} \ AC = B + AC \text{ because } X + \bar{X}Y - X + Y \right)$$

$$= \bar{A} + B + \bar{C} + CA$$

$$= \bar{A} + B + \bar{C} + A \qquad \left(\because \bar{C} + CA = \bar{C} + A \right)$$

$$= A + \bar{A} + B + \bar{C}$$

$$= 1 + B + C \qquad \left(\text{putting } A + \bar{A} = 1 \right)$$

$$= 1 \qquad (\text{as } 1 + X = 1 \text{ i.e., anything added to } 1 \text{ results in } 1)$$

2. **Karnaugh Maps:** Karnaugh map or K Map is a graphical display of the fundamental product in a truth table.

For example:

- Put a 1 in the box for any minterm that appears in the SOP expansion.

- Basic idea is to cover the largest adjacent blocks you can whose side length is some power of 2.

- Blocks can "wrap around" the edges.
- For example, the first K-map here represents $xy + x\bar{y} = x(y + \bar{y}) = x, (\text{since } y + y' = 1)$
- The second K-map, similarly, shows $xy + x\bar{y} = (x + \bar{x})y = y$

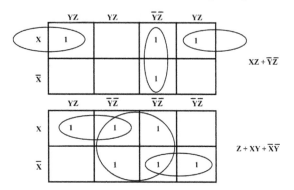

Remember, group together adjacent cells of 1s, to form largest possible rectangles of sizes that are powers of 2. Notice that you can overlap the blocks if necessary.

Sum of Products Reduction using K-Map

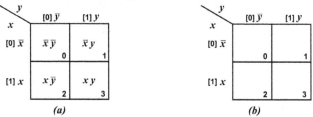

	[0] $\bar{y}$	[1] y
[0] $\bar{x}$	$\bar{x}\,\bar{y}$ 0	$\bar{x}\,y$ 1
[1] x	$x\,\bar{y}$ 2	$x\,y$ 3

(a)

	[0] $\bar{y}$	[1] y
[0] $\bar{x}$	 0	 1
[1] x	 2	 3

(b)

2-variable K-map representing mintorms.

	[00] $\bar{y}\bar{z}$	[01] $\bar{y}z$	[11] yz	[10] $y\bar{z}$
[0] $\bar{x}$	$\bar{x}\,\bar{y}\,\bar{z}$ 0	$\bar{x}\,\bar{y}\,z$ 1	$\bar{x}\,y\,z$ 2	$\bar{x}\,y\,\bar{z}$ 3
[1] x	$x\,\bar{y}\,\bar{z}$ 4	$x\,\bar{y}\,z$ 5	$x\,y\,z$ 6	$x\,y\,\bar{z}$ 7

(c)

	[00] $\bar{y}\bar{z}$	[01] $\bar{y}z$	[11] yz	[10] $y\bar{z}$
[0] $\bar{x}$	$\bar{x}\,\bar{y}\,\bar{z}$ 0	$\bar{x}\,\bar{y}\,z$ 1	$\bar{x}\,y\,z$ 2	$\bar{x}\,y\,z$ 3
[1] x	$x\,\bar{y}\,\bar{z}$ 4	$x\,\bar{y}\,\bar{z}$ 5	$x\,y\,z$ 6	$x\,y\,\bar{z}$ 7

(d)

3-variable K-map representing mintorms.

	[00] $\bar{y}\bar{z}$	[01] $\bar{y}z$	[11] yz	[10] $y\bar{z}$
[00] $\bar{w}\bar{x}$	$\bar{w}\,\bar{x}\,\bar{y}\,\bar{z}$	$\bar{w}\,\bar{x}\,\bar{y}\,z$	$\bar{w}\,\bar{x}\,y\,z$	$w\,x\,y\,z$
[01] wx	$\bar{w}\,x\,\bar{y}\,\bar{z}$	$w\,x\,y\,z$	$\bar{w}\,x\,y\,z$	$\bar{w}\,x\,y\,\bar{z}$
[11] wx	$w\,x\,\bar{y}\,\bar{z}$	$w\,x\,\bar{y}\,z$	$w\,x\,y\,z$	$w\,x\,y\,z$
[10] wx	$w\,\bar{x}\,\bar{y}\,\bar{z}$	$w\,x\,y\,z$	$w\,x\,y\,z$	$w\,\bar{x}\,y\,\bar{z}$

	[00] $\bar{y}\bar{z}$	[01] $\bar{y}z$	[11] yz	[10] $y\bar{z}$
[00] $\bar{w}\bar{x}$				
[01] wx				
[11] wx				
[10] wx				

4-variable K-map representing mintorms.

For reducing the expression first mark Octet, Quad, Pair then single.

- Pair: Two adjacent 1's makes a pair.

- Quad: Four adjacent 1's makes a quad.

- Octet: Eight adjacent 1's makes an Octet.

- Pair removes one variable.

- Quad removes two variables.

- Octet removes three variables.

Reduction of expression: When moving vertically or horizontally in pair or a quad or an boctet it can be observed that only one variable gets changed that can be eliminated directly in the expression.

In the above Example:

1. Step 1 : In K Map while moving from $m7$ to $m15$ the variable A is changing its state Hence it can be removed directly, the solution becomes $B.CD = BCD$. This can be continued for all the pairs, Quads, and Octets.

2. Step 2 : In K map while moving from $m0$ to $m8$ and $m2$ to $m10$ the variable A is changing its state. Hence B' can be taken similarly while moving from $m0$ to $m2$ and $m8$ to $m10$ the variable C is changing its state. Hence D' can be taken; the solution becomes B'.D' The solution for above expression using K map is BCD + B'D'.

Example: Reduce the following Boolean expression using K-Map:

$$F(P,Q,R,S)=\Sigma(0,3,5,6,7,11,12,15)$$

Soln:

This is 1 quad, 2pairs & 2 lock

Quad($m3+m7+m15+m11$) reduces to RS

Pair($m5+m7$) reduces to "PQS

Pair ($m7+m6$) reduces to P"QR

Block $m0$=P"Q"R"S"

$M12$=PQR"S"

Hence the final expressions is:

$$F=RS + P"QS + P"QR + PQR"S" + P"Q"R"S"$$

	R'S'	R'S	RS	RS'
P'Q'	1 0	 1	1 3	 2
P'Q	 4	1 5	1 7	1 6
PQ	1 12	 13	1 15	 14
PQ'	 8	 9	1 11	 10

Example: Reduce the following Boolean expression using K-Map:

$$F(A,B,C,D)=\Pi(0,1,3,5,6,7,10,14,15)$$

Soln:

Reduced expressions are as follows:

For pair 1, (A+B+C)

For pair 2, (A"+C"+D)

For Quad 1, (A+D")

For Quad 2, (B"+C")

Hence final POS expression will be:

$$Y(A,B,C,D)=(A+B+C)(A+\bar{C}+\bar{D})(A+\bar{D})(\bar{B}+\bar{C})$$

0	0	0	
	0	0	0
		0	0
			0

More about Gates:

NAND Gate (NAND = Not AND)

This is an AND gate with the output inverted, as shown by the 'o' on the output. The output is true if input A AND input B are NOT both true: Q = NOT (A AND B) A NAND gate can have two or more inputs, its output is true if NOT all inputs are true. NOR gate (NOR = Not OR)

This is an OR gate with the output inverted, as shown by the 'o' on the output. The output Q is true if NOT inputs A OR B are true: Q = NOT (A OR B) A NOR gate can have two or more inputs, its output is true if no inputs are true.

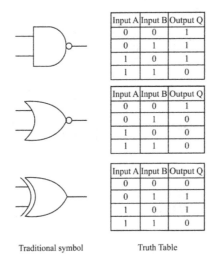

Input A	Input B	Output Q
0	0	1
0	1	1
1	0	1
1	1	0

Input A	Input B	Output Q
0	0	1
0	1	0
1	0	0
1	1	0

Input A	Input B	Output Q
0	0	0
0	1	1
1	0	1
1	1	0

Traditional symbol   Truth Table

EX-OR (EXclusive-OR) gate

The output Q is true if either input A is true OR input B is true, but not when both of them are true: Q = (A AND NOT B) OR (B AND NOT A) This is like an OR gate but excluding both inputs being true. The output is true if inputs A and B are DIFFERENT.

EX-OR gates can only have 2 inputs:

EX-NOR (EXclusive-NOR) gate

This is an EX-OR gate with the output inverted, as shown by the 'o' on the output. The output Q is true if inputs A and B are the SAME (both true or both false):

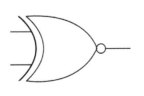

Input A	Input B	Output Q
0	0	1
0	1	0
1	0	0
1	1	1

Traditional symbol   Truth Table

Q = (A AND B) OR (NOT A AND NOT B) EX-NOR gates can only have 2 inputs.

Truth Tables

The summary truth tables below show the output states for all types of 2-input and 3-input gates.

summary for all 2-input gates							
Inputs		Output of each gate					
A	B	AND	NAND	OR	NOR	EX-OR	EX-NOR
0	0	0	1	0	1	0	1
0	1	0	1	1	0	1	0
1	0	0	1	1	0	1	0
1	1	1	0	1	0	0	1

Note that EX-OR and EX-NOR gates can only have 2 inputs.

summary for all 3-input gates						
Inputs			Output of each gate			
A	B	C	AND	NAND	OR	NOR
0	0	0	0	1	0	1
0	0	1	0	1	1	0
0	1	0	0	1	1	0
0	1	1	0	1	1	0
1	0	0	0	1	1	0
1	0	1	0	1	1	0
1	1	0	0	1	1	0
1	1	1	1	0	1	0

NAND Gate Equivalents

The table below shows the NAND gate equivalents of NOT, AND, OR and NOR gates:

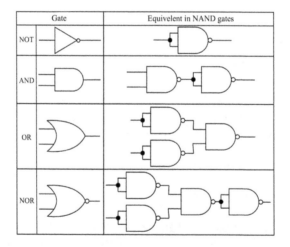

Gate	Equivelent in NAND gates
NOT	
AND	
OR	
NOR	

Low Order Thinking Questions: (Boolean Algebra)

a) State and verify absorption law in Boolean algebra.

Ans. Absorption Law states that :

a) X+XY=X b) X(X+Y)=X

b) Verify X'.Y+X.Y'=(X'+Y').(X+Y) algebraically.

Ans. LHS= X'Y + XY'

       = (X'+X) (X'+Y') (Y+X) (Y+Y')

$= 1.(X'+Y') (X+Y).1$

$= (X'+Y') (X+Y)$

= RHS, hence proved

c) Write the equivalent Boolean Expression F for the following circuit diagram :

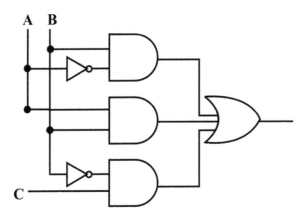

Ans.: A'B+AB+B'C

d) If F(P,Q,R,S) = Π (3,4,5,6,7,13,15) , obtain the simplified form using K-Map.

Ans.:

RS PQ	R+ S 0+ 0	R+ S 0+ 1	R+ S 1+ 1	R+ S 1+ 0
P+ Q 0+ 0	0	1	**0** 3	2
P+ Q' 0+ 1	4	**0** 5	**0** 7	**0** 6
P+ Q' 1+ 1	12	**0** 13	**0** 15	14
P+ Q 1+ 0	8	9	11	10

Reduction of groups following the reduction rule :

Quad1 = M4.M5.M6.M7

= P+Q'

Quad2 = M5.M7.M13.M15

= Q'+S'

Pair = M3.M7

= P+R'+S'

Therefore POS of F(P,Q,R,S) = (P+Q')(Q'+S')(P+R'+S')

e) $F(a,b,c,d)=\Sigma(0,2,4,5,7,8,10,12,13,15)$

F(a,b,c,d)=B1+B2+B3

B1=m0+m4+m12+m8==c'd'

B2=m5+m7+m13+m15=bd

B3=m0+m2+m8+m10=b'd'

F(a,b,c,d)=c'd'+bd+b'd'

f) Write the equivalent Boolean expression for the following logic circuit:

X	Y	Z	F
0	0	0	0
0	0	1	1
0	1	0	0
0	1	1	0
1	0	0	0
1	0	1	1
1	1	0	0
1	1	1	1

References

- What-is-binary, why-do-computers-use-it: howtogeek.com, Retrieved 5 February, 2019

- Basics_of_computers_number_system, basics_of_computers: tutorialspoint.com, Retrieved 10 June, 2019

- Octal-number-system: tutorialspoint.com, Retrieved 12 August, 2019

- Binary: electronics-tutorials.ws, Retrieved 4 July, 2019

- Number_system_conversion, computer_logical_organization: tutorialspoint.com, Retrieved 27 June, 2019

- Logic-gate-AND-OR-XOR-NOT-NAND-NOR-and-XNOR: techtarget.com, Retrieved 8 January, 2019

- Boolean: electronics-tutorials.ws, Retrieved 13 March, 2019

- Logic-circuits: teachcomputerscience.com, Retrieved 19 May, 2019

- Combination: electronics-tutorials.ws, Retrieved 17 April, 2019

- Boolean-Algebra: edurev.in, Retrieved 22 July, 2019

Operating System and Computer Architecture

An operating system is system software that provides common services for computer programs through the management of computer hardware and software resources. The set of rules and methods that describe the functionality, organization, and implementation of computer systems is termed as computer architecture. This chapter has been carefully written to provide an easy understanding of the varied facets of the operating systems and computer architecture.

Operating System

An operating system is a software which acts as an interface between the end user and computer hardware. Every computer must have at least one OS to run other programs. An application like Chrome, MS Word, Games, etc needs some environment in which it will run and perform its task.

The OS helps you to communicate with the computer without knowing how to speak the computer's language. It is not possible for the user to use any computer or mobile device without having an operating system.

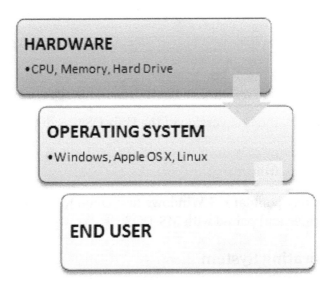

HARDWARE
•CPU, Memory, Hard Drive

OPERATING SYSTEM
•Windows, Apple OS X, Linux

END USER

Operating System with Market Share

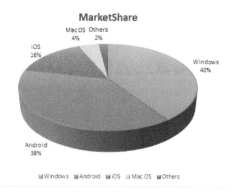

Here is a list of Operating Systems with the latest MarketShare

OS Name	Share
Windows	40.34
Android	37.95
iOS	15.44
Mac OS	4.34
Linux	0.95
Chrome OS	0.14
Windows Phone OS	0.06

History of OS

- Operating systems were first developed in the late 1950s to manage tape storage

- The General Motors Research Lab implemented the first OS in the early 1950s for their IBM 701

- In the mid-1960s, operating systems started to use disks

- In the late 1960s, the first version of the Unix OS was developed

- The first OS built by Microsoft was DOS. It was built in 1981 by purchasing the 86-DOS software from a Seattle company

- The present-day popular OS Windows first came to existence in 1985 when a GUI was created and paired with MS-DOS.

Features of Operating System

Here is a list commonly found important features of an Operating System:

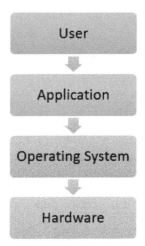

- Protected and supervisor mode

- Allows disk access and file systems Device drivers Networking Security

- Program Execution

- Memory management Virtual Memory Multitasking

- Handling I/O operations

- Manipulation of the file system

- Error Detection and handling

- Resource allocation

- Information and Resource Protection

Kernel

The kernel is the central component of a computer operating systems. The only job performed by the kernel is to the manage the communication between the software and the hardware. A Kernel is at the nucleus of a computer. It makes the communication between the hardware and software possible. While the Kernel is the innermost part of an operating system, a shell is the outermost one.

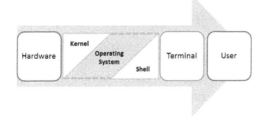

Features of Kennel

- Low-level scheduling of processes
- Inter-process communication
- Process synchronization
- Context switching

Types of Kernels

There are many types of kernels that exists, but among them, the two most popular kernels are:

1. Monolithic

A monolithic kernel is a single code or block of the program. It provides all the required services offered by the operating system. It is a simplistic design which creates a distinct communication layer between the hardware and software.

2. Microkernels

Microkernel manages all system resources. In this type of kernel, services are implemented in different address space. The user services are stored in user address space, and kernel services are stored under kernel address space. So, it helps to reduce the size of both the kernel and operating system.

Functions of an Operating System

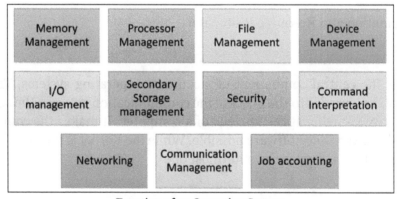

Function of an Operating System

In an operating system software performs each of the function:

1. Process management: Process management helps OS to create and delete processes. It also provides mechanisms for synchronization and communication among processes.

2. Memory management: Memory management module performs the task of allocation and de-allocation of memory space to programs in need of this resources.

3. File management: It manages all the file-related activities such as organization storage, retrieval, naming, sharing, and protection of files.

4. Device Management: Device management keeps tracks of all devices. This module also responsible for this task is known as the I/O controller. It also performs the task of allocation and de-allocation of the devices.

5. I/O System Management: One of the main objects of any OS is to hide the peculiarities of that hardware devices from the user.

6. Secondary-Storage Management: Systems have several levels of storage which includes primary storage, secondary storage, and cache storage. Instructions and data must be stored in primary storage or cache so that a running program can reference it.

7. Security: Security module protects the data and information of a computer system against malware threat and authorized access.

8. Command interpretation: This module is interpreting commands given by the and acting system resources to process that commands.

9. Networking: A distributed system is a group of processors which do not share memory, hardware devices, or a clock. The processors communicate with one another through the network.

10. Job accounting: Keeping track of time & resource used by various job and users.

11. Communication management: Coordination and assignment of compilers, interpreters, and another software resource of the various users of the computer systems.

Types of Operating system

- Batch Operating System
- Multitasking/Time Sharing OS
- Multiprocessing OS
- Real Time OS
- Distributed OS
- Network OS
- Mobile OS

Batch Operating System

Some computer processes are very lengthy and time-consuming. To speed the same process, a job with a similar type of needs are batched together and run as a group.

The user of a batch operating system never directly interacts with the computer. In this type of OS, every user prepares his or her job on an offline device like a punch card and submit it to the computer operator.

Multi-Tasking/Time-sharing Operating systems

Time-sharing operating system enables people located at a different terminal (shell) to use a single computer system at the same time. The processor time (CPU) which is shared among multiple users is termed as time sharing.

Real Time OS

A real time operating system time interval to process and respond to inputs is very small. Examples: Military Software Systems, Space Software Systems.

Distributed Operating System

Distributed systems use many processors located in different machines to provide very fast computation to its users.

Network Operating System

Network Operating System runs on a server. It provides the capability to serve to manage data, user, groups, security, application, and other networking functions.

Mobile OS

Mobile operating systems are those OS which is especially that are designed to power smartphones, tablets, and wearables devices.

Some most famous mobile operating systems are Android and iOS, but others include BlackBerry, Web, and watchOS.

Difference between Firmware and Operating System

Firmware	Operating System
Firmware is one kind of programming that is embedded on a chip in the device which controls that specific device.	OS provides functionality over and above that which is provided by the firmware.

Firmware is programs that been encoded by the manufacture of the IC or something and cannot be changed.	OS is a program that can be installed by the user and can be changed.
It is stored on non-volatile memory.	OS is stored on the hard drive.

Difference between 32-Bit vs. 64 Bit Operating System

Parameters	32. Bit	64. Bit
Architecture and Software	Allow 32 bit of data processing simultaneously.	Allow 64 bit of data processing simultaneously.
Compatibility	32-bit applications require 32-bit OS and CPUs.	64-bit applications require a 64-bit OS and CPU.
Systems Available	All versions of Windows 8, Windows 7, Windows Vista, and Windows XP, Linux, etc.	Windows XP Professional, Vista, 7, Mac OS X and Linux.
Memory Limits	32-bit systems are limited to 3.2 GB of RAM.	64-bit systems allow a maximum 17 Billion GB of RAM.

The advantage of using Operating System

- Allows you to hide details of hardware by creating an abstraction.
- Easy to use with a GUI.
- Offers an environment in which a user may execute programs/applications.
- The operating system must make sure that the computer system convenient to use.
- Operating System acts as an intermediary among applications and the hardware components.
- It provides the computer system resources with easy to use format.
- Acts as an intermediator between all hardware's and software's of the system.

Disadvantages of using Operating System

- If any issue occurs in OS, you may lose all the contents which have been stored in your system.
- Operating system's software is quite expensive for small size organization which adds burden on them. Example Windows.
- It is never entirely secure as a threat can occur at any time.

UNIX

Unix and Unix-like operating systems are a family of computer operating systems that are derived from the original Unix System from Bell Labs.

Initial proprietary derivatives included the HP-UX and the SunOS systems. However, growing incompatibility between these systems led to the creation of interoperability standards like POSIX. Modern POSIX systems include Linux, its variants, and Mac OS.

Unix is the most powerful and popular multi-user and multi-tasking Operating System. The basic concepts of Unix were originated in the Multics project of 1969. The Multics system was intended as a time-sharing system that would allow multiple users to simultaneously access a mainframe computer.

Ken Thompson, Dennis Ritchie, and others developed the basic building blocks of Unix including a hierarchical file system, i.e, the concepts of processes and a command line interpreter for the PDP-7. From there, multiple generations of Unix were developed for various machines.

Growing incompatibility between these systems led to the creation of interoperability standards like POSIX and Single Unix Specification.

Unix programs are designed around some core philosophies that include requirements like single purpose, interoperable, and working with a standardized text interface. Unix systems are built around a core kernel that manages the system and the other processes.

Kernel subsystems may include process management, file management, memory management, network management and others.

Salient Features of Unix

There are several prominent features of Unix, and few among them are stated below:

- It is a multi-user system where the same resources can be shared by different users.
- It provides multi-tasking, wherein each user can execute many processes at the same time.
- It was the first operating system that was written in a high-level language (C Language). This made it easy to port to other machines with minimum adaptations.
- It provides a hierarchical file structure which allows easier access and maintenance of data.
- Unix has built-in networking functions so that different users can easily exchange information.
- Unix functionality can be extended through user programs built on a standard programming interface.

The UNIX Operating System

The UNIX operating system is made up of three parts; the kernel, the shell and the programs.

The Kernel

The kernel of UNIX is the hub of the operating system: it allocates time and memory to programs and handles the filestore and communications in response to system calls.

As an illustration of the way that the shell and the kernel work together, suppose a user types rm myfile (which has the effect of removing the file myfile). The shell searches the filestore for the file containing the program rm, and then requests the kernel, through system calls, to execute the program rm on myfile. When the process rm myfile has finished running, the shell then returns the UNIX prompt % to the user, indicating that it is waiting for further commands.

The Shell

The shell acts as an interface between the user and the kernel. When a user logs in, the login program checks the username and password, and then starts another program called the shell. The shell is a command line interpreter (CLI). It interprets the commands the user types in and arranges for them to be carried out. The commands are themselves programs: when they terminate, the shell gives the user another prompt (% on our systems).

The adept user can customise his/her own shell, and users can use different shells on the same machine. Staff and students in the school have the tcsh shell by default.

The tcsh shell has certain features to help the user inputting commands.

Filename Completion - By typing part of the name of a command, filename or directory and pressing the [Tab] key, the tcsh shell will complete the rest of the name automatically. If the shell finds more than one name beginning with those letters you have typed, it will beep, prompting you to type a few more letters before pressing the tab key again.

History - The shell keeps a list of the commands you have typed in. If you need to repeat a command, use the cursor keys to scroll up and down the list or type history for a list of previous commands.

Files and Processes

Everything in UNIX is either a file or a process.

A process is an executing program identified by a unique PID (process identifier).

A file is a collection of data. They are created by users using text editors, running compilers etc.

Examples of Files

- A document (report, essay etc.);

- The text of a program written in some high-level programming language;

- Instructions comprehensible directly to the machine and incomprehensible to a casual user, for example, a collection of binary digits (an executable or binary file); and

- A directory, containing information about its contents, which may be a mixture of other directories (subdirectories) and ordinary files.

The Directory Structure

All the files are grouped together in the directory structure. The file-system is arranged in a hierarchical structure, like an inverted tree. The top of the hierarchy is traditionally called root (written as a slash /).

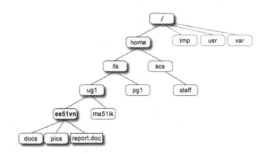

In the diagram above, we see that the home directory of the undergraduate student "ee51vn" contains two sub-directories (docs and pics) and a file called report.doc.

The full path to the file report.doc is "/home/its/ug1/ee51vn/report.doc".

Starting an UNIX Terminal

To open an UNIX terminal window, click on the "Terminal" icon from Applications/ Accessories menus.

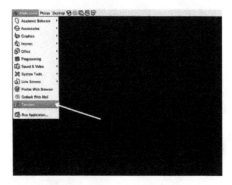

An UNIX Terminal window will then appear with a % prompt, waiting for you to start entering commands.

macOS

macOS is the newest name of the Unix-based operating system that runs on Mac hardware, including desktop and portable models. And while the name is new, the features and capabilities of the Mac operating system have a long history, as you'll read here.

The Macintosh started life using an operating system known simply as System, which produced versions ranging from System 1 to System 7. In 1996, the System was rebranded as Mac OS 8, with the final version, Mac OS 9, released in 1999.

Apple needed a modern operating system to replace Mac OS 9 and take the Macintosh into the future, so in 2001, Apple released OS X 10.0; Cheetah, as it was affectionately known. OS X was a new OS, built on a Unix-like kernel, that brought modern preemptive multitasking, protected memory, and an operating system that could grow with the new technology that Apple was envisioning.

In 2016, Apple changed the name of OS X to macOS, to better position the operating system's name with the rest of Apple's products (iOS, watchOS, and tvOS). Although the name changed, macOS retains its Unix roots, and its unique user interface and features.

If you've been wondering about the history of the macOS, or when features were added or removed, read on to look back to 2001, when OS X Cheetah was introduced, and learn what each subsequent version of the operating system brought with it.

macOS Mojave (10.14.x)

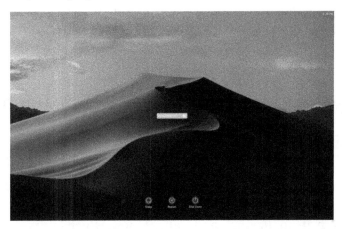

macOS Mojave gets its name from one of the deserts of Southern California. This is a bit of a departure for Mac operating system names, which had previously been inspired by the central Sierra Nevada mountain range.

Early rumors about Mojave suggested that Apple would be concentrating on security and performance issues, and that we wouldn't be seeing much in the way of new features. As usual, the rumors were both right, and wrong. Mojave provides security and privacy improvements, as well as a few new features:

- Dark Mode: Adds a new system-wide appearance option that changes the current Dock, menu bar, windows, and most UI elements to the dark side, or at least a dark gray in appearance. This is nothing new; apps have been using a dark theme for years, and Apple used a dark theme in its old Aperture image library application. There was even a dark UI option in the recent versions of macOS, but the effect was limited to the Dock and menu bar. With the new Dark Mode, you can carry the darkness throughout the system and most Apple apps. Third-party apps can also make use of the new UI, but aren't required to do so.

- New Mac App Store: The Mac App Store hasn't changed much since it was introduced with OS X Snow Leopard back in 2010. The new revisions to the store take their cue from the iOS App Store, which was revised in 2017. The new store provides easier to use categories designed to match up to how you use your Mac, a special Discover tool for finding hidden apps, and curated collections put together by Apple editors to assist in workflows of any type, including games.

- iOS Apps: Four popular iOS apps are making the transition to macOS: News, Stocks, Home, and Voice Memos. It was rumored that macOS would be able to run iOS apps, but that isn't what's happening here. These apps were recompiled, using new macOS APIs, as a showcase for developers that may want to redesign an iOS app for use with the Mac. It's a beginning, and it may point to some of the more popular iOS apps making their way to the Mac in the future.

- Dynamic Desktops: Desktops can now shift their appearance based on the time of day. The default Mojave sand dune images use the Dynamic Desktop feature to display sunrise over the dunes, shadows tracking the sun during the day, and sunset and a darkening sky in the evening.

- Desktop Stacks: Stacks have been a part of the Dock for a long time; now they've made their way to the desktop, where they can be used to automatically de-clutter your desktop by organizing files by type, date, tags, and various metadata items, such as project names or client names.

- Finder: The Finder gets some improvements, including a new metadata pane for viewing details about a file, Quick Actions that let you work on a file without opening it in an application, and Gallery View, which lets you scroll through file previews to find the one you're looking for.

- Safari Privacy: Enhanced Tracking Protection built into Safari can thwart the creation of user fingerprints that are used to track your browsing on the web. Additionally, Intelligent Tracking Prevention keeps social media Like buttons, Share buttons, and comment widgets from being used to track you as well.

- Personal Privacy: Access to your image (camera) or your voice (microphone) must now be explicitly granted to any app that wishes to use these devices. Explicit permission is also required for any app that wishes to use message histories or the mail database.

macOS High Sierra (10.13.x)

macOS High Sierra's main goal was to improve the performance and stability of the macOS platform. But that didn't stop Apple from adding new features and improvements to the operating system.

- APFS: The Apple File System (APFS) actually isn't new; it was first included in macOS Sierra. What makes its inclusion in macOS High Sierra an important feature is that now the APFS file system is the default; before this, it was just available as an alternative. Although APFS is now the norm, you can still make use of the older HFS+ file system, if you need to.

- HEVC: High Efficiency Video Encoding (HEVC) is a new compression standard that provides better quality compression compared to H.264, the default used in previous versions of the macOS.

- Metal 2: This new graphics technology provides Mac developers with near direct access to the Mac's graphics processing units. Removing the necessity to use intermediate programming layers to control the graphics should allow developers to radically improve performance of graphics-intensive applications. Metal 2 also allows the GPUs to be used for accelerated machine learning, opening up new capabilities to programmers and their apps. And if your current graphics card isn't up to snuff, Metal 2 supports external graphics cards connected via Thunderbolt 3.

- Safari: The default web browser, Safari sees new technology being introduced, including Intelligent Tracking Prevention to protect privacy and allow you to customize how privacy is enforced in general and site-by-site. Additionally, Safari gains the ability to block auto-playing videos, a great companion feature to its current ability to block auto-playing audio.

- Photos: Photos gets a number of new tools, including a persistent sidebar, editing of Live Photos, and a new Memory category for organizing your images. There's also improved facial recognition, new filters, and new editing tools for Curves and Selective Color.

macOS Sierra (10.12.x)

macOS Sierra was the first of the macOS series of operating systems. The main purpose of the name change from OS X to macOS was to unite the Apple family of operating systems into a single naming convention: iOS, tvOS, watchOS, and now macOS. In addition to the name change, macOS Sierra brought with it a number of new features and updates to existing services.

- Siri: Siri may be old news to iOS users, but macOS Sierra is the first time Siri has graced the Mac. The intelligent assistant is available from the Dock and the Menu Bar, and also from a keyboard shortcut. With a little work by the user, Siri can also be made to respond directly to voice commands without having to first invoke the Siri app.

- APFS: Apple included a preview of the new Apple File System as part of macOS Sierra. APFS wasn't turned on by default, and there were no apps other than Terminal that could be used to interact with the new file system. As a result, few Mac users knew a new modern file system was available at their fingertips.

- Night Shift: Night Shift was added to macOS Sierra with the 10.12.4 release. It mimics the feature found in iOS that allows the display to increase blue light as the evening progresses. The increase in blue light, along with the corresponding reduction in yellow light, is believed to aid sleep.

- Optimized Storage: This new feature of the macOS allows you to use smaller drives but still have access to a large amount of data. In conjunction with iCloud Drive, Optimized Storage can move some of your local data to the cloud, allowing you to free up space on your drive. The moved data still appears to be present locally, but when you need the information, it's retrieved from your iCloud Drive.

- Tabs Everywhere: Apps that include support for multiple windows gain the benefit of those windows being available from a tab bar generated by the operating system.

- Disk Utility: This venerable app regains the ability to create and manage RAID arrays, a feature it lost in OS X El Capitan.

OS X El Capitan (10.11.x)

The last version of the Mac operating system to use the OS X nomenclature, El Capitan saw a number of improvements, as well as the removal of some features, leading to an outcry from many users.

- Split View: Split View brought an iOS feature - the ability to see two full-screen apps side by side - to the Mac. The Mac has supported full-screen apps since OS X Lion, but Split View brought new capabilities to the feature.

- Multi-Touch Gestures: While the operating system has supported multi-touch gestures since the introduction of the Magic Mouse and Magic Trackpad, El Capitan brought direct support for gestures to various apps, including Mail and Messages.

- Maps: The Maps app saw public transit information added to regional maps. Initial support was limited to major metropolitan centers, but additional transit maps were added with subsequent updates.

- Disk Utility: Disk Utility saw a major redesign of the user interface, resulting in the loss of many features, including the ability to create and support RAID arrays.

- Spotlight: The Spotlight search engine saw the addition of weather, stock, news, and sports scores as searchable items.

- System Integrity Protection: SIP (System Integrity Protection) was a new security feature incorporated into the OS. With SIP, most system files and processes could not be modified by other apps or systems, even if the user had root access. SIP is very effective at preventing system tampering, by malware or by accident.

OS X Yosemite (10.10.x)

OS X Yosemite brought with it a major redesign of the user interface. While the basic functions of the interface remained the same, the look got a makeover, replacing the skeuomorph element philosophy of the original Mac, which made use of design cues that reflected the actual function of an item, with a flat graphic design that mimicked the user interface seen in iOS devices. In addition to changes to icons and menus, the use of blurred transparent window elements made their appearance.

Lucida Grande, the default system font, was replaced with Helvetica Neue, and the Dock lost its 3D glass shelf appearance, replaced with a translucent 2D rectangle.

- Continuity and Handoff: Yosemite included the ability for the operating system to integrate with iOS 8 or later devices. With the use of Handoff, a service that used Bluetooth LE and Wi-Fi, users could use their Macs to place or answer phone calls through their iPhones, as well as use their iPhones to establish hotspots, allowing their Macs to connect to their iPhone's data plan. Continuity used the same technology to allow users to work in an app on one device, say an iPad, and then pick up right where they left off in the equivalent app on their Mac.

- Notifications Center: The Notifications Center added a new Today view that displayed timely updates, such as weather, stocks, and calendar events.

- Photos: Yosemite 10.10.3 saw iPhotos and Aperture replaced by the new Photos image management app. The original implementation of Photos lacked many of the features of iPhotos or Aperture that users had come to rely on, and was seen as a step back by many. Over time, new versions of Photos addressed many user concerns.

- Dark Mode: A new system preference that darkened the menu bar and Dock in keeping with the trend in many apps to use dark backgrounds.

OS X Mavericks (10.9.x)

OS X Mavericks marked the end of naming the operating system after big cats; instead, Apple used California place names. Mavericks refers to one of the biggest large-wave surfing competitions held annually off the coast of California, near Pillar Point, outside the town of Half Moon Bay.

Changes in Mavericks concentrated on reducing power consumption and extending battery life.

- Timer Coalescing: This technique reduced CPU usage by synchronizing tasks. This allowed the CPU to always have tasks to perform when awake, and allowed CPU sleep to occur for longer periods of time. The end result was less waking from sleep, quicker overall task performance, and reduced battery use because of longer CPU sleep times.

- App Nap: Before App Nap, some applications were running but not performing any useful activity; for example, waiting for user input could keep processors active, wasting power and generating heat for no real gain. App Nap could put individual apps to sleep when they weren't active, or if their windows and dialog boxes were hidden by other apps on the screen.

- Compressed Memory: Mavericks saw the introduction of a new memory management system that helped prevent disk paging, and made better use of available memory. The end effect was that Compressed Memory increased app performance by making better use of RAM space. It also had the side effect of requiring smaller amounts of RAM to perform tasks, making a Mac with a small amount of RAM installed perform like it had more than it actually did.

- iCloud Keychain: Allowed users to store passwords, user names, and other ID information safely in iCloud, and then use the information on any of their Apple devices.

- Maps: The Maps application was introduced to the Mac, mimicking the Maps app available on iOS devices.

- Safari: A new JavaScript engine was introduced with Safari that significantly increased Safari's performance, beating out Chrome and Firefox in many tasks.

- Finder: The Finder added a tabbed user interface, as well as a new tagging system to organize files.

OS X Mountain Lion (10.8.x)

The last version of the operating system to be named after a big cat, OS X Mountain Lion continued the goal of uniting many Mac and iOS functions. To help bring the apps together, Mountain Lion renamed Address Book to Contacts, iCal to Calendar, and replaced iChat with Messages. Along with the app name changes, the new versions gained an easier system for syncing data between Apple devices.

- Notifications Center: New with Mountain Lion, the Notifications Center provided a unified method of receiving and organizing alerts issued by applications and web services.

- Notes: Once part of Mail, Notes was broken out as its own separate app; this matched the Notes implementation in iOS. Notes were synced across all of a user's Apple devices.

- Messages: The new Messages app replaced the well-regarded iChat app that was the default instant messaging app in previous generations of OS X. Messages supported Apple's iMessage protocol used in iOS devices, as well as XMPP (Jabber), AIM (AOL Instant Messaging), and OSCAR, as well as connections to Yahoo! Messenger and Google Talk.

- Game Center: Another new app making the crossover from iOS, Game Center allowed you to play against other Game Center players, keep track of scores and achievements, and follow a leader board for each game.

- AirPlay Mirroring: This new feature allowed the content of your display to appear on an Apple TV device on your local network.

OS X Lion (10.7.x)

Lion was the first version of the Mac operating system available as a download from the Mac App Store, and required a Mac with a 64-bit Intel processor. This requirement meant that some of the first Intel Macs that used 32-bit Intel processors couldn't be updated to OS X Lion. In addition, Lion dropped support for Rosetta, an emulation layer that was part of early versions of OS X. Rosetta allowed applications written for PowerPC Macs (non-Intel) to run on Macs that used Intel processors.

OS X Lion was also the first version of the Mac operating system to include elements from iOS; the convergence of OS X and iOS began with this release. One of Lion's goals was to start to create uniformity between the two OSes, so that a user could move between the two without any real training needs. To facilitate this, a number of new features and apps were added that mimicked how the iOS interface worked.

- Launchpad: This new application launcher looked and operated like the app launcher in iOS. Because Launchpad is an app, it didn't replace the existing Dock or Applications folder; instead, it just offered another method to start up applications.

- Scroll Bars: iOS uses a technique called natural scrolling, and OS X Lion incorporated it as the default scrolling method. For many Mac users, the result was very confusing, as the scrolling direction was reversed. Thankfully, the system preferences allowed you to select the method you wanted to use. In addition to natural scrolling, scroll bars also became invisible when not in use. This could also be changed in the system preferences.

- Auto Save and Versions: New with OS X Lion, Auto Save allowed apps to automatically save documents as you were working on them; Versions allowed you to access past revisions of a document.

- Address Space Layout Randomization: This security technique assigns system and app data to randomly selected locations in memory. This can help prevent malware from targeting a known location to inject itself into an app or service.

- File Vault 2: Updated File Vault to offer full disk encryption instead of just user space encryption.

OS X Snow Leopard (10.6.x)

Snow Leopard was the last version of the OS offered on physical media (DVD). It's also the oldest version of the Mac operating system you can still purchase directly from the Apple Store ($19.99).

Snow Leopard is thought of as the last native Mac operating system. After Snow Leopard, the operating system began incorporating bits and pieces of iOS to bring a more uniform platform to Apple mobile (iPhone) and desktop (Mac) systems.

Snow Leopard is a 64-bit operating system, but it was also the last version of the OS that supported 32-bit processors, such as Intel's Core Solo and Core Duo lines that were used in the first Intel Macs. Snow Leopard was also the last version of OS X that can make use of a Rosetta emulator to run apps written for PowerPC Macs.

- Mac App Store: Snow Leopard was the first version of the OS to incorporate the Mac App Store for purchasing, downloading, installing, and updating Mac apps, including the Mac operating system. The Mac App Store was added with the release of 10.6.6.

- Finder: The Finder was completely rewritten in Cocoa to help improve overall performance and take advantage of new technology built into the operating system.

- Multi-Touch Support: Snow Leopard was the first version of the OS that included complete support for multi-touch natively. Earlier versions of Macs that had multi-touch trackpads were limited by the number of multi-touch gestures supported.

- OS Footprint: The Snow Leopard footprint was reduced to less than 7 GB of drive space.

- AppleTalk: An early networking protocol used by Apple that is no longer supported.

- Boot Camp: Boot Camp gained the ability to read and copy files from HFS+ volumes.

OS X Leopard (10.5.x)

Leopard was a major upgrade from Tiger, the previous version of OS X. According to Apple, it contained over 300 changes and improvements. Most of those changes, however, were to core technology that end users wouldn't see, although developers were able to make use of them.

The launch of OS X Leopard was late, having originally been planned for a late 2006 release. The cause of the delay was believed to have been Apple diverting resources to the iPhone, which was shown to the public for the first time in January of 2007, and went on sale in June.

- Time Machine: One of the major new features in Leopard was the first inclusion of Time Machine, a then revolutionary backup application that was easy to set up and use, and even easier to find and restore individual files when needed.

- Boot Camp: Although users had already been messing around with ways to run Windows on the Mac's Intel-based hardware, Boot Camp was the first official method endorsed and even encouraged by Apple. Boot Camp provided tools for partitioning a Mac's startup drive to include a Windows volume, as well as the drivers needed to allow Windows to work with the Mac's hardware.

- Spaces: Allowed the creation of virtual desktops, each containing applications and windows used for specific tasks. You could create a space for working with emails and web browsing, another for gaming, and a third for productivity apps. You were only limited by how many "spaces" you could come up with.

- Quick Look: A built-in service that allowed documents to be quickly viewed without having to launch the applications that created them.

- User Interface Changes: Leopard included a number of minor user interface changes, including a 3D Dock and a transparent menu bar. The original multi-colored Apple icon in the menu bar was replaced with an all-black version.

- Application Signing: Leopard was the first version of the Mac operating system that used public key signing to ensure applications had not been tampered with, or that updates were indeed really the same app and not a piece of malware masquerading as one.

OS X Tiger (10.4.x)

OS X Tiger was the version of the operating system in use when the first Intel Macs were released. The original version of Tiger only supported the older PowerPC processor-based Macs; a special version of Tiger (10.4.4) was included with the Intel Macs. This led to a bit of confusion among users, many of whom attempted to reinstall Tiger on their Intel iMacs only to find the original version wouldn't load. Likewise, PowerPC users who bought discounted versions of Tiger off the Internet found that what they were really getting was the Intel-specific version that had come with someone's Mac.

The great Tiger confusion wasn't cleared up until OS X Leopard was released; it included universal binaries that could run on PowerPC or Intel Macs.

- Rosetta: This translation layer that was included with later versions of OS X Tiger allowed apps written for PowerPC processors to run on Intel Macs.

- Spotlight: This core search technology first appeared in Tiger, allowing Spotlight to be used to search all document types present on the Mac. Spotlight also introduced the concept of Smart Folders, special folders whose content was always updated based on search filters the user created. This allowed users to create Smart Folders that would contain, for example, all the documents they worked on in the last week.

- iChat AV: This addition to the iChat messaging system allowed up to four people to participate in a video conference.

- Dashboard: A special environment that allowed apps created with just HTML, CSS, and JavaScript to run. The apps were known as Widgets, and were thought of as the return of Desk Accessories, a type of application that was common in the earlier Mac OS.

- Automator: This scripting tool allowed users to link together apps and services that resided on their Macs, letting them create complex workflow automation with an easy-to-understand graphical interface.

- 64-bit User Space: Tiger supported both 32-bit and 64-bit processors. In addition, Tiger could support 64-bit userland addressing space, expanding the amount of memory that could be directly addressed.

OS X Panther (10.3.x)

Panther continued the tradition of OS X releases offering noticeable performance improvements. This occurred as Apple developers continued to refine and enhance the code used in the still relatively new operating system.

Panther also marked the first time OS X began dropping support for older Mac models, including the Beige G3 and Wall Street PowerBook G3. The models that were dropped all used Macintosh Toolbox ROM on the logic board. The Toolbox ROM contained code used to perform certain primitive processes that were used on the classic Mac architecture. More importantly, the ROM was used to control the boot process, a function that under Panther was now controlled by Open Firmware.

- Finder: The Finder made use of a new brushed-metal interface that included a new user customizable sidebar. Additionally, the Finder included direct support for zipping and unzipping files.

- Fast User Switching: This feature allowed a user to remain logged in while another user logged in and took control of the Mac.

- Exposé: A window manager that allowed all open windows to be shown as thumbnails, letting a user quickly switch between them.

OS X Jaguar (10.2.x)

Jaguar was one of my favorite versions of OS X, although that may be mainly because of how Steve Jobs pronounced the name during its introduction: jag-u-waarrr. This was also the first version of OS X where the cat-based name was officially used. Before Jaguar, the cat names were publicly known, but Apple always referred to them in publications by the version number.

OS X Jaguar included a hefty performance gain over the previous version. That's understandable as the OS X operating system was still being fine-tuned by developers. Jaguar also saw remarkable improvements in graphics performance, mostly because it included finely tuned drivers for the then-new ATI and NVIDIA series of AGP-based graphics cards.

- MPEG-4: Support for the MPEG-4 standard was built in to Jaguar via Quick-Time.

- Address Book: This was the first appearance of Address Book for storing contact information.

- iTunes: Although iTunes was available for the Mac earlier, this was the first version of OS X that included the iTunes app.

- Inkwell: Inkwell provided native handwriting recognition. This technology was originally developed for the Newton OS, and the short-lived Newton personal digital assistant.

- Rendezvous: This networking protocol allowed devices on a local network to self-discover other devices, making networking setup mostly a plug-and-play process. Rendezvous was renamed to Bonjour in later versions of OS X.

- Journaling: The HFS+ file system was updated with journaling support. Journaling increased reliability of the file system, and added data recovery features.

- Universal Access: This feature brought specialized access systems to the Mac to allow easier usage by individuals with various types of physical impairments.

- CUPS: The printing subsystem in OS X was upgraded to support CUPS (Common Unix Printing System). This allowed additional printer choices for Mac users, since easily available drivers could be used instead of custom ones designed for the Mac.

- SMB (Samba): Jaguar included support for Samba, an open source server that could work with Microsoft's SMB networking system. This allowed easy setup and use of file and printer sharing between Macs and Windows PCs.

- Happy Mac: Jaguar marked the end of the Happy Mac, a stylized splash screen showing a smiling face. In its place, Jaguar used a gray version of the Apple logo.

OS X Puma (10.1.x)

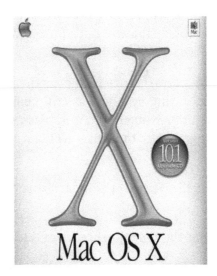

Puma was looked at mostly as a bug fix for the original OS X Cheetah that preceded it. Puma also provided some minor performance increases. Perhaps most telling was that the original release of Puma was not the default operating system for Macintosh computers; instead, the Mac booted up to Mac OS 9.x. Users could switch to OS X Puma, if they wished.

It wasn't until OS X 10.1.2 that Apple set Puma as the default operating system for new Macs.

- Better CD and DVD support: The Finder and iTunes included direct support for working with CDs and DVDs; DVDs could be played back in the Apple DVD player app.

- Additional Printer Drivers: Apple claimed that OS X Puma had over 200 printer drivers available. Even so, printing was still an issue with the new OS X as few printer manufacturers were including support for it.

- New OpenGL Drivers: The new OpenGL drivers improved graphics performance, especially for 3D elements used in the user interface and applications.

- ColorSync: ColorSync brought color management to OS X, allowing users to fine-tune the color seen on displays and in printed materials.

- Image Capture: This standalone utility was added to Puma to allow images from digital cameras and scanners to be downloaded to the Mac without requiring a specialized app from third-party manufacturers.

OS X Cheetah (10.0.x)

Cheetah was the first official release of OS X, although there was an earlier public beta of OS X available. OS X was quite a change from the Mac OS that preceded Cheetah. It represented a brand-new operating system completely separate from the earlier OS that powered the original Macintosh.

OS X was built on a Unix-like core made up of code developed by Apple, NeXTSTEP, BSD, and Mach. The kernel (technically a hybrid kernel) used Mach 3 and various elements of BSD, including the network stack and file system. Combined with the code from NeXTSTEP (owned by Apple) and Apple, the operating system was known as Darwin, and was released as open source software under the Apple Public Source License.

Higher levels of the operating system, including the Cocoa and Carbon frameworks used by Apple developers to build apps and services, remained closed source.

Cheetah had a few problems when released, including a tendency to produce kernel panics at the drop of a hat. It seems many of the problems were from the memory management system that was brand new to Darwin and OS X Cheetah.

Other new features found in Cheetah included: The Dock-

- The Dock was an application launcher that was presented as a band along the bottom or sides of the display. Icons representing applications and documents could be placed (docked) in the Dock, making them easy to access and launch.

- Terminal: The Terminal app allowed access to the Darwin operating system using a standard command line interface. Until Terminal, the Mac OS was one of the few operating systems that did not have a command line interface available.

- Mail: OS X came with a built-in email client.Preemptive Multitasking: While the Mac OS was capable of multitasking, it used a cooperative system, with each app's tasks asking for, and hopefully being granted, use of system resources. Preemptive multitasking ensures access to the system when needed.

- Aqua UI: The new user interface was known as Aqua. During the rollout of Cheetah, Steve Jobs mentioned the three buttons on the top of most windows, claiming they had spent a great deal of time making them look so good that they were "lick-able."

- PDF Support: Applications were able to generate PDFs using the printing services built into OS X.

- Quartz: Originally, Apple looked at using Display PostScript to drive the display graphics of OS X; the idea was based on how NeXTSTEP made use of Display PostScript in its products. Instead, Apple developed its own display rendering technology known as Quartz, which used PostScript to cache intermediate window graphics as PDF-rendered models.

- AppleScript: OS X included the AppleScript scripting language that had been included with the Mac since System 7 (Mac OS).

- Sherlock: A search system for finding data residing on the Mac or the web.

- Protected Memory: Applications are assigned memory segments that prevent an app that corrupts its own memory location from being able to cascade into other memory locations used by other apps and system services.

Linux

From smartphones to cars, supercomputers and home appliances, the Linux operating system is everywhere.

Linux. It's been around since the mid '90s, and has since reached a user-base that spans industries and continents. For those in the know, you understand that Linux is actually everywhere. It's in your phones, in your cars, in your refrigerators, your Roku devices. It runs most of the Internet, the supercomputers making scientific breakthroughs, and the world\'s stock exchanges. But before Linux became the platform to run desktops, servers, and embedded systems across the globe, it was (and still is) one of the most reliable, secure, and worry-free operating systems available.

Just like Windows XP, Windows 7, Windows 8, and Mac OS X, Linux is an operating system. An operating system is software that manages all of the hardware resources associated with your desktop or laptop. To put it simply – the operating system manages the communication between your software and your hardware. Without the operating system (often referred to as the "OS"), the software wouldn't function.

The OS is comprised of a number of pieces:

- The Bootloader: The software that manages the boot process of your computer. For most users, this will simply be a splash screen that pops up and eventually goes away to boot into the operating system.

- The kernel: This is the one piece of the whole that is actually called "Linux". The kernel is the core of the system and manages the CPU, memory, and peripheral devices. The kernel is the "lowest" level of the OS.

- Daemons: These are background services (printing, sound, scheduling, etc) that either start up during boot, or after you log into the desktop.

- The Shell: You've probably heard mention of the Linux command line. This is the shell – a command process that allows you to control the computer via commands typed into a text interface. This is what, at one time, scared people away from Linux the most (assuming they had to learn a seemingly archaic command line structure to make Linux work). This is no longer the case. With modern desktop Linux, there is no need to ever touch the command line.

- Graphical Server: This is the sub-system that displays the graphics on your monitor. It is commonly referred to as the X server or just "X".

- Desktop Environment: This is the piece of the puzzle that the users actually interact with. There are many desktop environments to choose from (Unity, GNOME, Cinnamon, Enlightenment, KDE, XFCE, etc). Each desktop environment includes built-in applications (such as file managers, configuration tools, web browsers, games, etc).

- Applications: Desktop environments do not offer the full array of apps. Just like Windows and Mac, Linux offers thousands upon thousands of high-quality software titles that can be easily found and installed. Most modern Linux distributions (more on this in a moment) include App Store-like tools that centralize and simplify application installation. For example: Ubuntu Linux has the Ubuntu Software Center (Figure) which allows you to quickly search among the thousands of apps and install them from one centralized location.

The Ubuntu software center is a Linux app store that carries thousands of free and commerical applications for Linux.

Reasons for using Linux

This is the one question that most people ask. Why bother learning a completely different computing environment, when the operating system that ships with most desktops, laptops, and servers works just fine? To answer that question, I would pose another question. Does that operating system you're currently using really work "just fine"? Or are you constantly battling viruses, malware, slow downs, crashes, costly repairs, and licensing fees?

If you struggle with the above, and want to free yourself from the constant fear of losing data or having to take your computer in for the "yearly clean up," Linux might be the perfect platform for you. Linux has evolved into one of the most reliable computer ecosystems on the planet. Combine that reliability with zero cost of entry and you have the perfect solution for a desktop platform.

You can install Linux on as many computers as you like without paying a cent for software or server licensing (including costly Microsoft Client Access License – CALs).

Let's take a look at the cost of a Linux server, in comparison to Windows Server 2012. The price of the Windows Server 2012 software alone can run up to $1,200.00 USD. That doesn't include CALs, and licenses for other software you may need to run (such as a database, a web server, mail server, etc). With the Linux server...it's all free and easy to install. In fact, installing a full blown web server (that includes a database server), is just a few clicks or commands away.

If you're a system administrator, working with Linux is a dream come true. No more daily babysitting servers. In fact, Linux is as close to "set it and forget it" as you will ever find. And, on the off chance, one service on the server requires restarting, re-configuring, upgrading, etc., most likely the rest of the server won't be affected.

Be it the desktop or a server, if zero cost isn't enough to win you over – what about having an operating system that will work, trouble free, for as long as you use it? I've personally used Linux for nearly twenty years (as a desktop and server platform) and have not once had an issue with malware, viruses, or random computer slow-downs. It's that stable. And server reboots? Only if the kernel is updated. It is not out of the ordinary for a Linux server to go years without being rebooted. That's stability and dependability.

Linux is also distributed under an open source license. Open source follows the following key philosophies:

- The freedom to run the program, for any purpose.

- The freedom to study how the program works, and change it to make it do what you wish.

- The freedom to redistribute copies so you can help your neighbor.

- The freedom to distribute copies of your modified versions to others.

The above are crucial to understanding the community that comes together to create the Linux platform. It is, without a doubt, an operating system that is "by the people, for the people". These philosophies are also one of the main reasons a large percentage of people use Linux. It's about freedom and freedom of choice.

Linux Distribution

Linux has a number of different versions to suit nearly any type of user. From new users to hard-core users, you'll find a "flavor" of Linux to match your needs. These versions are called distributions (or, in the short form, "distros."). Nearly every distribution of Linux can be downloaded for free, burned onto disk (or USB thumb drive), and installed (on as many machines as you like).

The most popular Linux distributions are:

- Ubuntu Linux
- Linux Mint
- Arch Linux
- Deepin
- Fedora
- Debian
- openSUSE

Each distribution has a different take on the desktop. Some opt for very modern user interfaces (such as Ubuntu's Unity, above, and Deepin's Deepin Desktop), whereas others stick with a more traditional desktop environment (openSUSE uses KDE).

And don't think the server has been left behind. For this arena, you can turn to:

- Red Hat Enterprise Linux
- Ubuntu Server
- CentOS
- SUSE Enterprise Linux

Some of the above server distributions are free (such as Ubuntu Server and CentOS) and some have an associated price (such as Red Hat Enterprise Linux and SUSE Enterprise Linux). Those with an associated price also include support.

Choosing the Right Distribution for yourself

Which distribution you use will depend upon the answer to three simple questions:

- How skilled of a computer user are you?

- Do you prefer a modern or a standard desktop interface?

- Server or desktop?

If your computer skills are fairly basic, you'll want to stick with a newbie-friendly distribution such as Linux Mint, Ubuntu, or Deepin. If you're skill set extends into the above-average range, you could go with a distribution like Debian or Fedora. If, however, you've pretty much mastered the craft of computer and system administration, use a distribution like Gentoo.

If you're looking for a server-only distribution, you will also want to decide if you need a desktop interface, or if you want to do this via command-line only. The Ubuntu Server does not install a GUI interface. This means two things – your server won't be bogged down loading graphics and you'll need to have a solid understanding of the Linux command line. However (there is always an "however" with Linux), you can install a GUI package on top of the Ubuntu Server with a single command like sudo apt-get install ubuntu-desktop. System administrators will also want to view a distribution with regards to features. Do you want a server-specific distribution that will offer you, out of the box, everything you need for your server? If so, CentOS might be the best choice. Or, do you want to take a desktop distribution and add the pieces as you need them? If so, Debian or Ubuntu Linux might serve you well.

Installing Linux

For most, the idea of installing an operating system might seem like a very daunting task. Believe it or not, Linux offers one of the easiest installations of all operating systems. In fact, most versions of Linux offer what is called a Live distribution – which means you run the operating system from either a CD/DVD or USB flash drive without making any changes to your hard drive. You get the full functionality without having to commit to the installation. Once you've tried it out, and decided you wanted to use it, you simply double-click the "Install" icon and walk through the simple installation wizard.

Preparing for your Linux installation

Typically, the installation wizards walk you through the process with the following steps:

- Preparation: Make sure your machine meets the requirements for installation. This also may ask you if you want to install third-party software (such as plugins for MP3 playback, video codecs, and more).

- Wireless Setup (If necessary): If you are using a laptop (or machine with wireless), you'll need to connect to the network, in order to download third-party software and updates.

- Hard drive allocation: This step allows you to select how you want the operating system to be installed. Are you going to install Linux alongside another operating system (called "dual booting"), use the entire hard drive, upgrade an existing Linux installation, or install over an existing version of Linux.

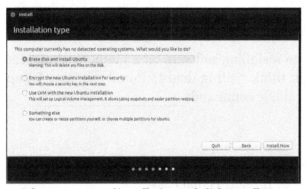

Select your type of installation and click Install Now

- Location: Select your location from the map.

- Keyboard layout: Select the keyboard layout for your system.

- User setup: Set up your username and password.

That's it. Once the system has completed the installation, reboot and you're ready to go.

Installing Software on Linux

Just as the operating system itself is easy to install, so too are applications. Most modern Linux distributions include what most would consider an "app store". This is a centralized location where software can be searched and installed. Ubuntu Linux has the Ubuntu Software Center, Deepin has the Deepin Software Center, some distributions rely on Synaptic, while others rely on GNOME Software.

Regardless of the name, each of these tools do the same thing – a central place to search for and install Linux software. Of course, these pieces of software depend upon the presence of a GUI. For GUI-less servers, you will have to depend upon the command line interface for installation.

Let's look at two different tools to illustrate how easy even the command line installation can be. Our examples are for Debian-based distributions and Fedora-based distributions. The Debian-based distros will use the apt-get tool for installing software and Fedora-based distros will require the use of the yum tool. Both work very similarly. I'll illustrate using the apt-get command. Let's say you want to install the wget tool (which is a handy tool used to download files from the command line). To install this using apt-get, the command would like like this:

Sudo apt-get Install Wget

The sudo command is added because you need super user privileges in order to install software. Similarly, to install the same software on a Fedora-based distribution, you would first su to the super user (literally issue the command su and enter the root password), and issue this command:

Yum Install Wget

That's it all there is to installing software on a Linux machine. It's not nearly as challenging as you might think. Still in doubt? Recall the Easy Lamp Server Installation from earlier? With a single command:

Sudo Tasksel

You can install a complete LAMP (Linux Apache MySQL PHP) server on either a server or desktop distribution. It really is that easy.

Microsoft Windows

Windows is Microsoft's flagship operating system (OS), the de facto standard for home and business computers. The graphical user interface (GUI)-based OS was introduced in 1985 and has been released in many versions since then, as described below. Microsoft got its start with the partnership of Bill Gates and Paul Allen in 1975. Gates and Allen co-developed Xenix (a version of Unix) and also collaborated on a BASIC interpreter for the Altair 8800. The company was incorporated in 1981.

Development of Microsoft and Windows

Microsoft gained prominence in the tech field with the release of MS-DOS, a text-based command-line-driven operating system. DOS was mostly based on a purchased intellectual property, QDOS. GUI-based operating systems of that time included Xerox's Alto, released in 1979, and Apple's LISA and Macintosh systems, which came later. Die-hard fans of MS-DOS referred to such systems as WIMPs, which stood for "windows, icons, mouse and pull-down menus (or pointers)."

However, Gates saw the potential in GUI-based systems and started a project he called

Interface Manager. Gates thought he could bring the GUI to a wider audience at a lower cost than the $9,000 LISA. The rest of Microsoft supported this idea, and, in a somewhat ironic move, the project team selected "Windows" as the name of the new operating system.

Microsoft announced the impending release of Windows 1.0 in 1983. The company used some features it licensed from Apple for portions of its interface. Microsoft released Windows 1.0 in 1985. Apple sued Microsoft and Hewlett-Packard for $5.5 billion in 1988 claiming it did not give the companies authorization to use certain GUI elements. In 1992, a federal court concluded Microsoft and Hewlett-Packard did not go beyond the 1985 agreement. Apple appealed that decision, which was upheld in 1994.

Competitors to Windows include Apple's macOS and the open source Linux operating system from Linus Torvalds. The free price gives Linux an edge in availability, while macOS is known for its stability and user experience. However, Microsoft Windows continues to maintain its dominance -- a June 2018 report from the NetMarketShare site shows Windows installed on nearly 88% of desktops and laptops -- with a steady rollout of new versions to support advances in hardware.

Windows Versions through the Years

1985: Windows 1.0

Like many early versions of Microsoft's GUI operating systems, Windows 1.0 was essentially a program that ran on top of DOS. Microsoft did not release the system until two years after its first announcement, leading to suggestions that Windows was vaporware. The release was a shaky start for the tech giant. Users found the software unstable. However, the point-and-click interface made it easier for new users to operate a computer. The user-friendly nature of Windows also drew interest from customers who might have been intimidated by a command-line interface. Windows 1.0 offered many of the common components found in today's graphical user interface, such as scroll bars and "OK" buttons.

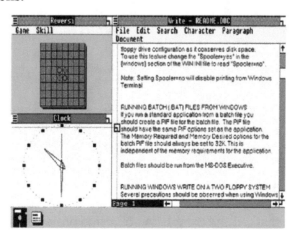

1987: Windows 2.0 and 2.11

Windows 2.0 was faster, more stable and had more GUI features in common with the Apple LISA. The system introduced the control panel and ran the first versions of Excel and Word. Windows 2.0 supported extended memory, and Microsoft updated it for compatibility with Intel's 80386 processor. It was during this time that Microsoft became the largest software vendor in the world, just as computers were becoming more commonplace. The fact that Windows systems were user-friendly and relatively affordable was a contributing factor to the growing PC market.

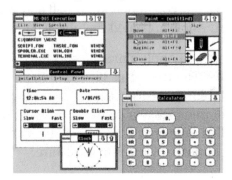

1990: Windows 3.0

Microsoft optimized the Windows 3.0 operating system, which still ran on top of DOS, for the 386 processor for a more responsive system. Windows 3.0 supported 16 colors and included the casual games familiar to most Windows users: Solitaire, Minesweeper and Hearts. Games that required more processing power still ran directly on MS-DOS. Exiting to DOS gave games direct hardware access made more system resources available that otherwise would have gone to Windows. Microsoft offered Windows 3.1 as a paid sub-release in 1993. Windows 3.1 features included support for TrueType fonts and peer-to-peer networking.

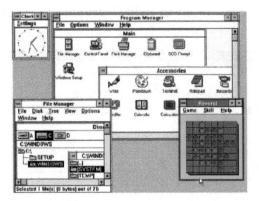

1993: Windows NT

Windows NT's release marked the completion of a side project to build a new, advanced

OS. NT was 32-bit and had a hardware abstraction layer. DOS was available through the command prompt, but it did not run the Windows OS. Microsoft designed NT as a workstation OS for businesses rather than home users. The system introduced the Start button.

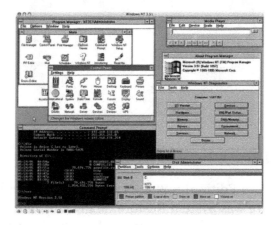

1995: Windows 95

Windows 95 introduced the Windows operating system to a wider audience with a marketing campaign that featured The Rolling Stones song "Start Me Up" to celebrate the Start button's arrival to the masses. Windows 95 facilitated hardware installation with its Plug and Play feature. Microsoft also unveiled 32-bit color depth, enhanced multimedia capabilities and TCP/IP network support.

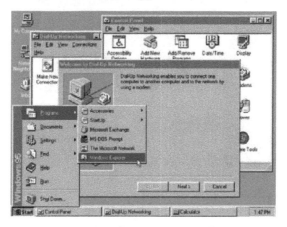

1998: Windows 98

Microsoft improved speed and Plug and Play hardware support in Windows 98. The company also debuted USB support and the Quick Launch bar in this release. DOS gaming began to wane as Windows gaming technology improved. The popularity of the OS made it an attractive target for malware. Microsoft integrated web technology into the Windows user interface and built its own web browser into the desktop. This feature was one of the defining issues in the U.S. Justice Department's antitrust suit against Microsoft in the 1990s.

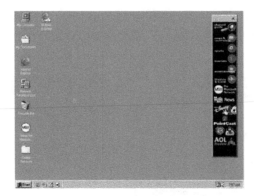

2000: Windows ME

Windows ME (Millennium Edition) was the last use of the Windows 95 codebase. Its most notable new feature was System Restore. Many customers found this release to be unstable, and it was acknowledged as a poor release by Steve Ballmer and Microsoft. Some critics said ME stood for "mistake edition."

Microsoft released the professional desktop OS Windows 2000 the same year. Microsoft based this OS on the more stable Windows NT code. Some home users installed Windows 2000 for its greater reliability. Microsoft updated Plug and Play support, which spurred home users to switch to this OS.

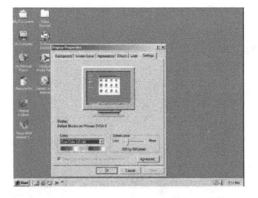

2001: Windows XP

Microsoft delivered Windows XP as the first NT-based system with a version aimed squarely at the home user. Home users and critics rated XP highly. The system improved Windows appearance with colorful themes and provided a more stable platform.

Microsoft virtually ended gaming in DOS with this release. DirectX-enabled features in 3D gaming that OpenGL had difficulties with. XP offered the first Windows support for 64-bit computing, but it was not very well supported, lacking drivers and applications to run.

2006: Windows Vista

Microsoft hyped Windows Vista after the company spent a lot of resources to develop a more polished appearance. Vista had interesting visual effects but the OS was slow to start and run. The 32-bit version, in particular, didn't enable enough RAM for the memory-hungry OS to operate properly.

Microsoft tightened licensing rights and made it more work to activate Windows. The company also peeled back user control of the operating system's internal workings.

Microsoft lost market share to Apple and Linux variants. Vista's flaws -- coupled with the fact that many older computers lacked the resources to run the system -- led to many home and business users staying with XP.

2009: Windows 7

Microsoft built Windows 7 on the Vista kernel. Windows 7 picked up Vista's visual capabilities but featured more stability. To many end users, the biggest changes between Vista and Windows 7 were faster boot times, new user interface and the addition of Internet Explorer 8.

With true 64-bit support and more Direct X features, Windows 7 proved to be a popular release for Windows users.

2012: Windows 8

Microsoft released Windows 8 with a number of enhancements and debuted its tile-based Metro user interface. Windows 8 took better advantage of multicore processing, solid-state drives (SSD), touchscreens and other alternate input methods. Users found the switching from the traditional desktop to the tile-based interface awkward. Even after Microsoft's UI and other updates in 8.1, Windows 8 trailed not just Windows 7 but XP in user numbers into 2014.

2015: Windows 10

Microsoft announced Windows 10 in September 2014, skipping Windows 9. Version 10 includes the Start menu, which was absent from Windows 8. A responsive design feature called Continuum adapts the interface depending on whether the user works with a touchscreen or a keyboard and mouse for input. New features like an onscreen back button simplified touch input. Microsoft designed the OS to have a consistent interface across devices including PCs, laptops and tablets.

Changes in Security

Microsoft did not implement many security methods in its operating systems until Windows NT and XP. For example, the default user on a Windows computer received administrator privileges until Vista.

Consumer editions of early versions of Windows did not have security measures built in since Microsoft designed the OS for single users without network connections. The company integrated security features in Windows NT, but they weren't in the forefront of Microsoft's design.The combination of lack of security and widespread popularity made Windows systems a target for malicious programs, such as viruses or system exploits.

Microsoft began to release monthly patches every second Tuesday of the month, known as Patch Tuesday, in 2003. Patches to update critical issues may be released on a faster schedule, known as out-of-band patches.

Windows Vista added User Account Control, a privilege evaluation feature based on a token system. The token allowed users only the most basic privileges, such as the ability to execute tasks that may modify system data. When an administrator logged on, they received two tokens -- one that a standard user would receive and another that allowed administrator-level tasks.

Microsoft released its Windows Defender security application as a beta program for Windows XP in 2005. Windows Defender protects systems from spyware threats. Microsoft included Defender in later versions of Windows, such as Windows 10. Microsoft further buttressed system security with Windows Defender Credential Guard for virtualization-based security, System Guard to protect firmware components and configurations and Application Guard to protect against malware and hacking threats in the Microsoft Edge browser.

Differences in Windows Operating System Editions

Starting with Windows XP, Microsoft separated Windows to give different features to distinct audiences. Windows 10, for example, has multiple editions including Windows 10 Home, Pro and Enterprise editions.

Microsoft makes its consumer operating systems for users in an ordinary household setting. Enterprise operating system is designed for large organizations in a business setting. The enterprise software tends to have more customization abilities and features that an organization can utilize, such as security or language packs.

Microsoft designed Windows 10 Home for consumers and tailored to operate on PCs, tablets and 2-in-1 devices. Microsoft built Windows 10 Pro as a baseline OS for any business, while it developed Windows 10 Enterprise for businesses with higher security needs.

Security features differ from Windows 10 Home, Pro and Enterprise editions. Windows 10 Home includes basic security features such as Windows Defender, Device Encryption and Windows Information Protection. Windows 10 Pro adds more security features such as Bitlocker, Windows Defender System Guard, Windows Defender Exploit Guard and Windows Defender Antivirus. Windows 10 Enterprise is identical in features and functionality to Pro but adds more security features such as Windows Defender Credential Guard, Windows Defender Application Guard and Windows Defender Application Control.

Windows Versus macOS

MacOS is a GUI-based OS developed and owned by Apple. MacOS is the primary OS for Apple computers. Apple introduced macOS in 1984. The company released a consumer version in 2001 with macOS X 10.0, which drew praise for its user interface, but criticism for its performance.

After macOS X 10.0, Apple developed newer versions of macOS X from 10.0-10.14. Earlier versions were named after big cats, such as Tiger, Puma, Snow Leopard and Mountain Lion. MacOS 10.4.4, or Tiger, was a notable update, which improved performance with graphics processing and file searching. Later versions of MacOS X were then named after California landmarks such as Yosemite, Sierra or Mojave.

Windows Versus Linux

Linux is an open source OS built on a Linux kernel. Released in 1991, Linux loads and unloads its kernel at runtime, meaning the user can add software or hardware to a Linux system without rebooting.

Linux is used in consumer and enterprise settings. A well-known consumer-based Linux OS, for example, is Android, which has a large install base on mobile devices. Enterprises can use server versions of Linux for enterprise use, such as virtual machines.

Multi Programming, Multiprocessing, Multitasking and Multi Threading

Multi Programming

In a modern computing system, there are usually several concurrent application processes which want to execute. Now it is the responsibility of the Operating System to manage all the processes effectively and efficiently.

One of the most important aspects of an Operating System is to multi program. In a computer system, there are multiple processes waiting to be executed, i.e. they are waiting when the CPU will be allocated to them and they begin their execution. These processes are also known as jobs. Now the main memory is too small to accommodate all of these processes or jobs into it. Thus, these processes are initially kept in an area called job pool. This job pool consists of all those processes awaiting allocation of main memory and CPU.

CPU selects one job out of all these waiting jobs, brings it from the job pool to main memory and starts executing it. The processor executes one job until it is interrupted by some external factor or it goes for an I/O task.

Non-multi Programmed System's Working

- In a non multi programmed system, As soon as one job leaves the CPU and goes for some other task (say I/O), the CPU becomes idle. The CPU keeps waiting and waiting until this job (which was executing earlier) comes back and resumes its execution with the CPU. So CPU remains free for all this while.

- Now it has a drawback that the CPU remains idle for a very long period of time. Also, other jobs which are waiting to be executed might not get a chance to execute because the CPU is still allocated to the earlier job. This poses a very serious problem that even though other jobs are ready to execute, CPU is not allocated to them as the CPU is allocated to a job which is not even utilizing it (as it is busy in I/O tasks).

- It cannot happen that one job is using the CPU for say 1 hour while the others have been waiting in the queue for 5 hours. To avoid situations like this and come up with efficient utilization of CPU, the concept of multi programming came up.

The main idea of multi programming is to maximize the CPU time.

Multi Programmed System's Working

- In a multi-programmed system, as soon as one job goes for an I/O task, the Operating System interrupts that job, chooses another job from the job pool (waiting queue), gives CPU to this new job and starts its execution. The previous job keeps doing its I/O operation while this new job does CPU bound tasks. Now say the second job also goes for an I/O task, the CPU chooses a third job and starts executing it. As soon as a job completes its I/O operation and comes back for CPU tasks, the CPU is allocated to it.

- In this way, no CPU time is wasted by the system waiting for the I/O task to be completed. Therefore, the ultimate goal of multi programming is to keep the CPU busy as long as there are processes ready to execute. This way, multiple programs can be executed on a single processor by executing a part of a program at one time, a part of another program after this, then a part of another program and so on, hence executing multiple programs. Hence, the CPU never remains idle.

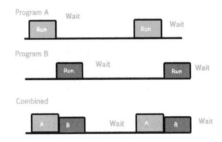

In the image above, program A runs for some time and then goes to waiting state. In the mean time program B begins its execution. So the CPU does not waste its resources and gives program B an opportunity to run.

Multiprocessing

In a uni-processor system, only one process executes at a time. Multiprocessing is the use of two or more CPUs (processors) within a single Computer system. The term also refers to the ability of a system to support more than one processor within a single computer system. Now since there are multiple processors available, multiple processes can be executed at a time. These multi processors share the computer bus, sometimes the clock, memory and peripheral devices also.

Multi Processing system's working

- With the help of multiprocessing, many processes can be executed simultaneously. Say processes P1, P2, P3 and P4 are waiting for execution. Now in a single processor system, firstly one process will execute, then the other, then the other and so on.

- But with multiprocessing, each process can be assigned to a different processor for its execution. If its a dual-core processor (2 processors), two processes can be executed simultaneously and thus will be two times faster, similarly a quad core processor will be four times as fast as a single processor.

Why use Multi Processing

- The main advantage of multiprocessor system is to get more work done in a shorter period of time. These types of systems are used when very high speed is required to process a large volume of data. Multi processing systems can save money in comparison to single processor systems because the processors can share peripherals and power supplies.

- It also provides increased reliability in the sense that if one processor fails, the work does not halt, it only slows down. e.g. if we have 10 processors and 1 fails, then the work does not halt, rather the remaining 9 processors can share the work of the 10th processor. Thus the whole system runs only 10 percent slower, rather than failing altogether.

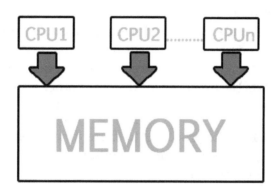

Multiprocessing refers to the hardware (i.e., the CPU units) rather than the software (i.e., running processes). If the underlying hardware provides more than one processor then that is multiprocessing. It is the ability of the system to leverage multiple processors' computing power.

Difference between Multi programming and Multi Processing

- A System can be both multi programmed by having multiple programs running at the same time and multiprocessing by having more than one physical processor. The difference between multiprocessing and multi programming is that Multiprocessing is basically executing multiple processes at the same time on multiple processors, whereas multi programming is keeping several programs in main memory and executing them concurrently using a single CPU only.

- Multiprocessing occurs by means of parallel processing whereas Multi programming occurs by switching from one process to other (phenomenon called as context switching).

Multitasking

As the name itself suggests, multi tasking refers to execution of multiple tasks (say processes, programs, threads etc.) at a time. In the modern operating systems, we are able to play MP3 music, edit documents in Microsoft Word, surf the Google Chrome all simultaneously, this is accomplished by means of multi tasking.

Multitasking is a logical extension of multi programming. The major way in which multitasking differs from multi programming is that multi programming works solely on the concept of context switching whereas multitasking is based on time sharing along-side the concept of context switching.

Multi Tasking System's Working

- In a time sharing system, each process is assigned some specific quantum of time for which a process is meant to execute. Say there are 4 processes P1, P2, P3, P4 ready to execute. So each of them are assigned some time quantum for which they will execute e.g time quantum of 5 nanoseconds (5 ns). As one process begins execution (say P2), it executes for that quantum of time (5 ns). After 5 ns the CPU starts the execution of the other process (say P3) for the specified quantum of time.

- Thus the CPU makes the processes to share time slices between them and execute accordingly. As soon as time quantum of one process expires, another process begins its execution.

- Here also basically a context switch is occurring but it is occurring so fast that the user is able to interact with each program separately while it is running. This way, the user is given the illusion that multiple processes/ tasks are executing simultaneously. But actually only one process/ task is executing at a particular instant of time. In multitasking, time sharing is best manifested because each running process takes only a fair quantum of the CPU time.

In a more general sense, multitasking refers to having multiple programs, processes, tasks, threads running at the same time. This term is used in modern operating systems when multiple tasks share a common processing resource (e.g., CPU and Memory).

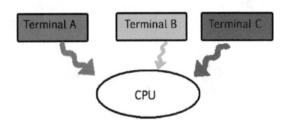

- As depicted in the above image, At any time the CPU is executing only one task while other tasks are waiting for their turn. The illusion of parallelism is achieved when the CPU is reassigned to another task. i.e all the three tasks A, B and C are appearing to occur simultaneously because of time sharing.

- So for multitasking to take place, firstly there should be multiprogramming i.e. presence of multiple programs ready for execution. And secondly the concept of time sharing.

Multi Threading

A thread is a basic unit of CPU utilization. Multi threading is an execution model that allows a single process to have multiple code segments (i.e., threads) running concurrently within the "context" of that process.

e.g. VLC media player, where one thread is used for opening the VLC media player, one thread for playing a particular song and another thread for adding new songs to the playlist.

Multi threading is the ability of a process to manage its use by more than one user at a time and to manage multiple requests by the same user without having to have multiple copies of the program.

Multi Threading System's Working

Example–

- Say there is a web server which processes client requests. Now if it executes as a single threaded process, then it will not be able to process multiple requests at a time. Firstly one client will make its request and finish its execution and only then, the server will be able to process another client request. This is really costly, time consuming and tiring task. To avoid this, multi threading can be made use of.

- Now, whenever a new client request comes in, the web server simply creates a new thread for processing this request and resumes its execution to hear more client requests. So the web server has the task of listening to new client requests and creating threads for each individual request. Each newly created thread processes one client request, thus reducing the burden on web server.

Example-

- We can think of threads as child processes that share the parent process resources but execute independently. Now take the case of a GUI. Say we are performing a calculation on the GUI (which is taking very long time to finish). Now we can not interact with the rest of the GUI until this command finishes its execution. To be able to interact with the rest of the GUI, this command of calculation should be assigned to a separate thread. So at this point of time, 2 threads will be executing i.e. one for calculation, and one for the rest of the GUI. Hence here in a single process, we used multiple threads for multiple functionality.

The image below completely describes the VLC player example:

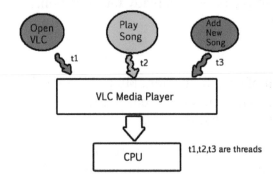

Advantages of Multi Threading

- Benefits of Multi threading include increased responsiveness. Since there are multiple threads in a program, so if one thread is taking too long to execute or if it gets blocked, the rest of the threads keep executing without any problem. Thus the whole program remains responsive to the user by means of remaining threads.

- Another advantage of multi threading is that it is less costly. Creating brand new processes and allocating resources is a time consuming task, but since threads share resources of the parent process, creating threads and switching between them is comparatively easy. Hence multi threading is the need of modern Operating Systems.

Computer Architecture

Computer is an electronic machine that makes performing any task very easy. In computer, the CPU executes each instruction provided to it, in a series of steps, this series of steps is called Machine Cycle, and is repeated for each instruction. One machine cycle involves fetching of instruction, decoding the instruction, transferring the data, executing the instruction.

Computer system has five basic units that help the computer to perform operations, which are given below:

1. Input Unit

2. Output Unit

3. Storage Unit

4. Arithmetic Logic Unit

5. Control Unit

Input Unit

Input unit connects the external environment with internal computer system. It provides data and instructions to the computer system. Commonly used input devices are keyboard, mouse, magnetic tape etc.

Input unit performs following tasks:

1. Accept the data and instructions from the outside environment.

2. Convert it into machine language.

3. Supply the converted data to computer system.

Output Unit

It connects the internal system of a computer to the external environment. It provides the results of any computation, or instructions to the outside world. Some output devices are printers, monitor etc.

Storage Unit

This unit holds the data and instructions. It also stores the intermediate results before these are sent to the output devices. It also stores the data for later use.

The storage unit of a computer system can be divided into two categories:

- Primary Storage: This memory is used to store the data which is being currently executed. It is used for temporary storage of data. The data is lost, when the computer is switched off. RAM is used as primary storage memory.

- Secondary Storage: The secondary memory is slower and cheaper than primary memory. It is used for permanent storage of data. Commonly used secondary memory devices are hard disk, CD etc.

Arithmetic Logical Unit

All the calculations are performed in ALU of the computer system. The ALU can perform basic operations such as addition, subtraction, division, multiplication etc. Whenever calculations are required, the control unit transfers the data from storage unit to ALU. When the operations are done, the result is transferred back to the storage unit.

Control Unit

It controls all other units of the computer. It controls the flow of data and instructions to and from the storage unit to ALU. Thus it is also known as central nervous system of the computer.

CPU

It is Central Processing Unit of the computer. The control unit and ALU are together known as CPU. CPU is the brain of computer system. It performs following tasks:

- It performs all operations.

- It takes all decisions.

- It controls all the units of computer.

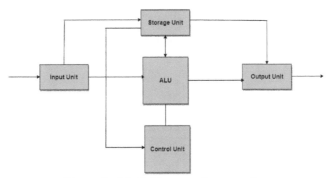

Shows the block diagram of a computer

Input/Output Devices

An input device sends information to a computer system for processing, and an output device reproduces or displays the results of that processing. Input devices only allow for input of data to a computer and output devices only receive the output of data from another device.

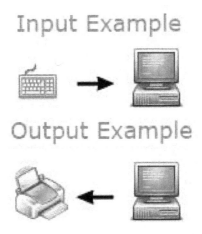

Most devices are only input devices or output devices, as they can only accept data input from a user or output data generated by a computer. However, some devices can accept input and display output, and they are referred to as I/O devices (input/output devices).

For example, as you can see in the top half of the image to the right, a keyboard sends electrical signals, which are received by the computer as input. Those signals are then interpreted by the computer and displayed, or output, on the monitor as text or images. In the lower half of the image, the computer sends, or outputs, data to a printer, which will print the data onto a piece of paper, also considered output.

Input Devices

An input device can send data to another device, but it cannot receive data from another device. Examples of input devices include the following.

- Keyboard and Mouse - Accepts input from a user and sends that data (input) to the computer. They cannot accept or reproduce information (output) from the computer.

- Microphone - Receives sound generated by an input source, and sends that sound to a computer.

- Webcam - Receives images generated by whatever it is pointed at (input) and sends those images to a computer.

Output Devices

An output device can receive data from another device and generate output with that data, but it cannot send data to another device. Examples of output devices include the following.

- Monitor - Receives data from a computer (output) and displays that information as text and images for users to view. It cannot accept data from a user and send that data to another device.

- Projector - Receives data from a computer (output) and displays, or projects, that information as text and images onto a surface, like a wall or a screen. It cannot accept data from a user and send that data to another device.

- Speakers - Receives sound data from a computer and plays the sounds for users to hear. It cannot accept sound generated by users and send that sound to another device.

Input/output Devices

An input/output device can receive data from users, or another device (input), and send data to another device (output). Examples of input/output devices include the following.

- CD-RW drive and DVD-RW drive - Receives data from a computer (input), to copy onto a writable CD or DVD. Also, the drive sends data contained on a CD or DVD (output) to a computer.

- USB flash drive - Receives, or saves, data from a computer (input). Also, the drive sends data to a computer or another device (output).

References

- Operating-system: guru99.com, Retrieved 12 April, 2019

- Unix-introduction: softwaretestinghelp.com, Retrieved 7 August, 2019

- Unixintro, Unix: surrey.ac.uk, Retrieved 16 July, 2019

- What-is-macos: lifewire.com, Retrieved 21 January, 2019

- What-is-linux: linux.com, Retrieved 25 March, 2019

- Windows: searchwindowsserver.techtarget.com, Retrieved 6 July, 2019

- Operating-system, difference-multitasking-multithreading-multiprocessing: geeksforgeeks.org, Retrieved 19 August, 2019

- Architecture-of-computer-system, computer-architecture: studytonight.com, Retrieved 18 February, 2019

- Issues: computerhope.com, Retrieved 3 June, 2019

Data Storage and Data Manipulation

4

The recording of information in a storage medium is known as data storage. Computer data storage is a technology that comprises of recording media and computer components via which digital data are retained. Computer data storage includes primary, secondary, tertiary and off-line storage. The chapter closely examines the key concepts of data storage and manipulation to provide an extensive understanding of the subject.

Data Storage

Data storage is the collective methods and technologies that capture and retain digital information on electromagnetic, optical or silicon-based storage media. Storage is a key component of digital devices, as consumers and businesses have come to rely on it to preserve information ranging from personal photos to business-critical information.

Storage is frequently used to describe the devices and data connected to the computer through input/output (I/O) operations, including hard disks, flash devices, tape systems and other media types.

Importance of Data Storage

Underscoring the importance of storage is a steady climb in the generation of new data, which is attributable to big data and the profusion of internet of things (IoT) devices. Modern storage systems require enhanced capabilities to allow enterprises to apply machine learning-enabled artificial intelligence (AI) to capture this data, analyze it and wring maximum value from it.

Larger application scripts and real-time database analytics have contributed to the advent of highly dense and scalable storage systems, including high-performance computing storage, converged infrastructure, composable storage systems, hyper-converged storage infrastructure, scale-out and scale-up network-attached storage (NAS) and object storage platforms.

By 2025, it is expected that 163 zettabytes (ZB) of new data will be generated, according to a report by IT analyst firm IDC. That estimate represents a potential tenfold increase from the 16 ZB produced through 2016.

How Data Storage Works

The term storage may refer both to a user's data generally and, more specifically, to the integrated hardware and software systems used to capture, manage and prioritize the data. This includes information in applications, databases, data warehouses, archiving, backup appliances and cloud storage.

Digital information is written to target storage media through the use of software commands. The smallest unit of measure in a computer memory is a bit, described with a binary value of 0 or 1, according to the level of electrical voltage contained in a single capacitor. Eight bits make up one byte.

Other capacity measurements to know are:

- kilobit (Kb)
- megabit (Mb)
- gigabit (Gb)
- terabit (Tb)
- petabit (Pb)
- exabit (Eb)

Larger measures include:

- kilobyte (KB) equal to 1,024 bytes
- megabyte (MB) equal to 1,024 KB
- gigabyte (GB) equal to 1,024 MB
- terabyte (TB) equal to 1,024 GB
- petabyte (PB) equal to 1,024 TB
- exabyte (EB) equal to 1,024 PB

Few organizations require a single storage system or connected system that can reach an exabyte of data, but there are storage systems that scale to multiple petabytes.

Data storage capacity requirements define how much storage is needed to run an application, a set of applications or data sets. Capacity requirements take into account the types of data. For instance, simple documents may only require kilobytes of capacity, while graphic-intensive files, such as digital photographs, may take up megabytes, and a video file can require gigabytes of storage. Computer applications commonly list the minimum and recommended capacity requirements needed to run them.

On an electromechanical disk, bytes store blocks of data within sectors. A hard disk is a circular platter coated with a thin layer of magnetic material. The disk is inserted on a spindle and spins at speeds of up to 15,000 revolutions per minute (rpm). As it rotates, data is written on the disk surface using magnetic recording heads. A high-speed actuator arm positions the recording head to the first available space on the disk, allowing data to be written in a circular fashion.

A sector on a standard disk is 512 bytes. Recent advances in disk include shingled magnetic recording, in which data writes occur in overlapping fashion to boost the platter's areal density.

On solid-state drives (SSDs), data is written to pooled NAND flash, designed with floating gate transistors that enable the cell to retain an electrical charge. An SSD is not technically a drive, but it exhibits design characteristics similar to an integrated circuit, featuring potentially millions of nanotransistors placed on millimeter-sized silicon chips.

Backup data copies are written to disk appliances with the aid of a hierarchical storage management system. And although less commonly practiced than in years past, the tactic of some organizations remains to write disk-based backup data to magnetic tape as a tertiary storage tier. This is a best practice in organizations subject to legal regulations.

A virtual tape library (VTL) uses no tape at all. It is a system in which data is written sequentially to disks, but retains the characteristics and properties of tape. The value of a VTL is its quick recovery and scalability.

Evaluating the Storage Hierarchy

Organizations increasingly use tiered storage to automate data placement on different storage media, based on an application's capacity, compliance and performance requirements.

Enterprise data storage is often classified as primary and secondary storage, depending on how the data is used and the type of media it requires. Primary storage handles application workloads central to a company's day-to-day production and main lines of business.

Primary storage is occasionally referred to as main storage or primary memory. Data is held in random access memory (RAM) and other built-in devices, such as the processor's L1 cache. Secondary storage encompasses data on flash, hard disk, tape and other devices requiring I/O operations. Secondary storage media is often used in backup and cloud storage.

Primary storage generally provides faster access than secondary storage due to the proximity of storage to the computer processor. On the other hand, secondary storage can hold much more data than primary storage. Secondary storage also replicates inactive data to a backup storage device, yet keeps it highly available in case it is needed again.

Digital transformation of business has prompted more and more companies to deploy multiple hybrid clouds, adding a remote tier to buttress local storage.

Enterprise Storage Networks and Server-side Flash

Enterprise storage vendors provide integrated NAS systems to help organizations collect and manage large volumes of data. The hardware includes storage arrays or storage servers equipped with hard drives, flash drives or a hybrid combination, and storage OS software to deliver array-based data services.

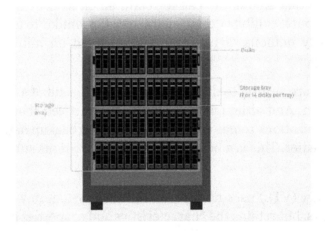

The storage management software offers data protection tools for archiving, clones, copy data management, replication and snapshots. Data reduction features, including compression, data deduplication and thin provisioning, are becoming standard features of most storage arrays. The software also provides policy-based management to govern data placement for tiering to secondary data storage or a hybrid cloud to support a disaster recovery plan or long-term retention.

Since 2011, an increasing number of enterprises have implemented all-flash arrays outfitted only with NAND flash-based SSDs, either as an adjunct or replacement to disk arrays.

Unlike disk, flash storage devices do not rely on moving mechanical parts to store data, thus offering faster access to data and lower latency than HDDs. Flash is nonvolatile, allowing data to persist in memory even if the storage system loses power. Disk-based storage systems require onboard battery backup or capacitors to keep data persistent. However, flash has not yet achieved an endurance equivalent to disk, leading to hybrid arrays that integrate both types of media.

There are three basic designs of networked storage systems. In its simplest configuration, direct-attached storage (DAS) involves the internal hard drive in an individual computer. In the enterprise, DAS can be a cluster of drives in a server or a group of external drives that attach directly to the server though the Small Computer System Interface (SCSI), Serial Attached SCSI (SAS), Fibre Channel (FC) or internet SCSI (iSC-SI).

NAS is a file-based architecture in which multiple file nodes are shared by users, typically across an Ethernet-based local area network (LAN) connection. The advantage of NAS is that filers do not require a full-featured enterprise storage operating system. NAS devices are managed with a browser-based utility, and each node on the network is assigned a unique IP address.

Closely related to scale-out NAS is object storage, which eliminates the necessity of a file system. Each object is represented by a unique identifier. All the objects are presented in a single flat namespace.

A storage area network (SAN) can be designed to span multiple data center locations that need high-performance block storage. In a SAN environment, block devices appear to the host as locally attached storage. Each server on the network is able to access shared storage as though it were a direct-attached drive.

Advances in NAND flash, coupled with falling prices in recent years, have paved the way for software-defined storage. Using this configuration, an enterprise installs commodity-priced SSDs in an x86-based server, using third-party storage software or custom open source code to apply storage management.

Nonvolatile memory express (NVMe) is a developing industry protocol for flash. Industry observers expect NVMe to emerge as the de facto standard for flash storage. NVMe flash will allow applications to communicate directly with a central processing unit (CPU) via Peripheral Component Interconnect Express (PCIe) links, bypassing SCSI command sets transported to a network host bus adapter. NVMe over Fabrics (NVMe-oF) is intended to speed the transfer of data between a host computer and flash target, using established Ethernet, FC or InfiniBand network connectivity.

A nonvolatile dual inline memory module (NVDIMM) is hybrid NAND and DRAM with integrated backup power that plugs into a standard DIMM slot on a memory bus. NVDIMMs only use flash for backup, processing normal calculations in the DRAM. An NVDIMM puts flash closer to the motherboard, presuming the computer's manufacturer has modified the server and developed basic input-output system (BIOS) drivers to recognize the device. NVDIMMs are a way to extend system memory or add a jolt of high-performance storage, rather than to add capacity. Current NVDIMMs on the market top out at 32 GB, but the form factor has seen density increases from 8 GB to 16 GB in just a few years.

Primary

Primary storage is the collective methods and technologies used to capture and retain digital information that is in active use and critical for an organization's operations. Primary storage data is frequently accessed by applications or other hardware systems and business users.

In contrast, secondary storage is used for data that is less frequently accessed, or no longer accessed at all. Examples of secondary storage include devices or systems use to store backup data (a second copy of current primary data) and archival data which is rarely if ever, accessed. Since secondary data has limited immediate usefulness and is infrequently accessed, it is often referred to as data at rest. Primary and secondary storage are components of a tiered-storage architecture which comprises at least the two primary and secondary levels of storage, although some environments have additional storage tiers. Regardless of the number of tiers storage, the primary tier is typically reserved for transactional data or mission-critical application data that requires high performance.

Types of Primary Storage

Depending on the computing environment, primary storage might consist of hard disks or flash-based solid-state drives installed locally on an application server or file server. Alternatively, the primary storage tier might be a centralized and shared storage-area network (SAN) or network-attached storage (NAS) array. Its how the storage resource is used rather than the type of storage architecture that determines it is primary storage or some other tier of data storage.

If an organization's primary storage is used for high-transaction, random access applications such as database management systems, the tier will often be a SAN device (or set of devices). SAN systems are block oriented, which means they store and access data in chunks of a predetermined size. Block access operates similarly to the way the storage media—hard disk drives or solid-state drives—stores, catalogs and accesses the data it hosts, so it typically provides the high performance that database systems require.

A NAS array may also be used as primary storage, but it uses a different method of storing and accessing data than a SAN. NAS storage is also often referred to as file storage, as it overlays the storage media system with a directory and metadata that more closely aligns with how applications store their related data. Applications such as Microsoft Word or Excel find their documents or spreadsheets via the NAS directory which collects that various pieces of a file that may be scattered across a drive or multiple drives and presents the file to the application as a single unit. Because of this added layer, file-based systems like NAS tend to be slower than SANs, but if a NAS meets an organization's requirements for primary storage, it can certainly function at that level.

Cloud-based storage may also serve as primary storage, but because it is remote, the circumstances under which it would be used as a primary storage resource are very different from those related to SAN or NAS. If an application is locally hosted in an organization's data center, it will have to access its stored in a cloud service via a private or public network such as the Internet. The relative slowness of telecommunications-based data, which would yield performance and responsiveness that wouldn't meet primary storage standards. However, if the application also resided in the same cloud system as the data, then performance might be adequate.

Types of Storage Media used for Primary Storage

A primary storage system, whether it's installed locally in a server, is networked and shared like a SAN or NAS, or is cloud-based, may be composed of various types of media. Hard-disk media is still the most prevalent type of data storage, but because high performance is typically required of primary storage, solid-state drives (SSDs) are increasingly replaced hard disks. In some cases, primary storage systems may employ both types of storage media, using the solid-state devices for fast access and processing of data and hard-disk drives for mass storage of the required data.

A more recent development in storage technology, storage-class memory, may also be used for primary storage if performance demands are particularly rigorous. Storage-class memory combines some of the features of solid-state storage with those of random-access memory (RAM) which works closely with a server's CPU to feed data to an application as rapidly as possible. Unlike RAM, storage-class memory is persistent, which means it retains data even when power is cut off. And while storage-class memory is somewhat slower than RAM, it's much faster than standard solid-state drives, which makes it ideal for use as primary storage for applications such as in-memory databases. It's also considerably more expensive than conventional solid-state storage.

Legacy References of Primary Storage

Back when mainframe computers ruled the data center, the term primary storage often referred to the volatile memory in the computer, much like RAM in modern servers, rather than the media that provided a permanent, persistent home for the data which might've been called secondary storage at that time. That storage would've ranged from the earliest punch card technologies to tape to hard-disk drives.

Secondary

Secondary Storage Devices are essential as the size of Primary storage or main memory in every computer is limited. With this, the computer can only accommodate a limited sized program and data. To carry out big jobs like commercial data processing, it becomes essential that data be held in some expansive form of storage. This is achieved through secondary storage Devices. It is also called as external storage, and can hold data either sequentially or at random. You should always keep in in mind that data in secondary storage devices is not directly accessible and has to be routed through the main storage for processing.

Types of Secondary Storage Devices in Computers are:

- Magnetic tape

- Magnetic disk and

- Magnetic drum.

Magnetic Tape

- Tapes are used for recording and storing data for computer processing. It is plastic reel similar to long lengths of movie film. A tape is usually ½" wide and 2400 feet in length and it is coated with particles of ferric oxide on which data can be recorded magnetically.

- The process of reading and writing of data is carried out on a device called Tape Drive and the records on magnetic tape are stored in sequential order. For example: if the payroll file is to be stored on a magnetic tape, the records would likely to be stored in the sequence of employee numbers. Hence, magnetic tapes are referred to as sequential access device.

Magnetic Disk

- Magnetic disk is another type of secondary storage device known as random (direct) access as it permits direct accessing of data. An individual disk is a circular metal plate coated on both side by ferrous oxide material.

- Data is recorded in the form of magnetized spots on the tracks of the disk, a spot representing the presence by "1" and its absence by "0" enabling representing of data in binary form.

- The surface of the magnetic disk is divided into number of invisible concentric circles called "tracks" and these tracks are further subdivided into "sectors", "blocks" etc. each its own unique addresses to facilitate the location of data and the Disk moves on a vertical rotating spindle.

- Reading /writing on the disks is accomplished by means of series of read/write heads which are placed close to the surfaces of the disks.

- It is good to know that data on the magnetic disk can be accessed again and again. It can also be recorded erasing the older information.

Magnetic Drum

- It is a metallic cylinder coated with a special magnetic alloy.

- Data is stored in this surface as minute magnetized spoke arranged in binary form in a series of parallel circular tracks.

- The drum rotates at a constant speed and data is recorded (or) retrieved by the read/write head. One for each track.

- The magnetic drum provides random access storage.

Advantages

- Very fast access.

- Random access capability.

- Stored data is not destroyed until new data is written in the same location.

Disadvantages

- Drums cannot be removed from the unit and stored.

- Storage capacity is limited.

- Requires machine interpretation to read the information as it is not humanly readable.

CD-ROM

- CD-ROM (Compact Disc Read Only Memory) is a Compact Disc contains data accessible by a computer. While the Compact Disc format was originally designed for music storage and play back, the format was later adapted to hold any form of binary data.

- The CR-ROM is also known as a laser disc, which is shiny metal like disk. The diameter of the disk is 5.25 inches or 12 cm disk. Information of 650 MB can be stored which is equal to nearly 2, 50,000 pages of printed text.

- The data is recorded as deep holes on the disk surface or burning microscopic bits.

- The plain and shiny disk surface and the microscopic bits help to represent the binary numbers 0 and 1, as required by the concentric tracks.

- CD-ROMs are popularly used to distribute computer software, including games and multimedia applications, though any data can be stored.

- Some CDs hold both computer data and audio with the latter capable of being played on a CD player, while data is only usable on a computer. These are called Enhanced CDs.

- The CD-ROMs are pre-recorded disks used for storing a large amount of data and information. Hence, the CD-ROM drive has become a standard peripheral device used for retrieval of stored data on the CD-ROM.

- A CD-ROM sector contains 2352 bytes, divided into 98 [ninety-eight], 24-byte frames.

- A mode-1 CD-ROM, which has the full three layers of error correction data, contains a net 2048 bytes of the available 2352 per sector.

- On a mode-2 CD-ROM, which is mostly used for video files, there are 2336 user available bytes per sector. A device called CD-Writer is necessary to record information onto a CD-ROM.

Hard Disk

- A hard disk drive [HDD], commonly referred to as a hard drive, hard disk or fixed disk drive. It is a non-volatile secondary storage device which stores digitally encoded data on rapidly rotating platters with magnetic surfaced. The hard disk is an electro mechanical device. The hard disk is also known as Winchester disk. HDDs record data by magnetizing a ferromagnetic material directionally to represent either a "0" or "1" binary digit. They read the data by detecting the magnetization of the material.

- The magnetic hard disk is an electro-mechanical device which consists of some smooth metal plates and disks coated on either sides or surfaces with a thin-film of magnetic material. The set of such magnetic disks are fixed on one spindle, one above the other, like a stack of disks. This is called a disk pack, which is sealed into one unit and mounted on a disk drive.

- The hard disk drive has a set of magnetic heads or read/write heads for both surfaces of each disk, on the spindle.

- The disk drive consists of a motor to rotate the disk pack at a speed of about 3600 revolutions per minute [rpm] about a spindle.

- Each magnetic head (or) magnetic read/write heads mounted on arm can move in and out rapidly on the disk surface to perform read and write operations. The information is recorded and stored or retrieved that is read from the magnetic recording surface, while the disk rotates about the spindle at high-speed.

- The information is stored on the magnetic surfaces as bits 0's and 1's on the concentric circles as tracks.

- Each track is divided into sectors of the same density.

- The set of corresponding tracks of all the surfaces of all the disks constitute a cylinder.

- The magnetic disk pack is connected to controller by an electronic circuit called as a disk controller (or) hard disk controller HDC. The controllers accept control signals from the control unit of the computer for specific read and write operation.

- Now days the capacity of hard disk begins from 20 GB, 40 GB and so on, to fulfill the need of large data information storage.

- Hard disk drives are sealed to prevent dust and other sources of contamination from interfering with the operation of the hard disk heads.

- The hard drives are not air tight, but rather utilize an extremely fine air filter, to allow for air inside the hard drive enclosure. The spinning of the disks causes the air to circulate forcing any particulars to become trapped on the filter. The same air currents also as a gas bearing which enables the heads to float on a cushion of air above the surfaces of the disks.

Floppy Disks

These are also called as flexible disks. These are used in the smallest micro computer systems as well as mini computers. Floppy disks have higher storage capacity and offer direct access capability. The floppy disk is permanently sealed in a plastic coated jacket and the whole package is inserted the floppy drive for data recording and retrieval.

The jacket of the disk has a small slot to permit the read/write head to contact the disk. They are 5.25 inch (or) 3.5 inch in diameter. They come in single and double density and recorded on one or both surface of the diskette. The capacity of a 5.25 inch floppy is 1.2 mega bytes whereas for 3.5 inch floppy it is 1.44 mega bytes.

It is cheaper than that of any other secondary storage devices and is portable too. The floppy is a low-cost device particularly suitable for personal computer system. Once data has been recorded, a floppy disk reader can be used to enter data into CPU. Again, the disk is loaded and rotated at a constant speed inside its envelope. Tiny magnetic heads in the disk reader access data through the slot in the jacket.

Characteristics of Storage

Storage devices can be described by their physical storage characteristics. These characteristics include whether or not the device can store data permanently; how the computer system locates data in the device; and whether or not it needs constant electric power to store data.

Permanent and Non-permanent

Permanent means 'protected against any alterations'. No data storage device will last forever, but it is possible to protect it against data changes during its life. A device is non-permanent if it can be altered.

Random and Sequential

Sequential access means that the storage locations have to be read or written in their correct order, starting with the first location. For example, if you need to restore just one file from a tape backup the only way you (or the backup software) can find the file is to start at the beginning of the tape and search it byte by byte.

Sequential access is the slowest. This speed problem means that it is used almost entirely for long-term data storage and for data backups.

Random access means that any storage location can be directly read or written. Random access is also called 'direct access'. It is much faster and more efficient than sequential access devices. If the starting address or location of the file is known then you can move directly to it. Random access relies on knowing the exact position of the stored data.

Volatile and non-volatile

Volatile refers to storage devices that will lose all their data if the power is switched off. Less common. RAM is the only storage device that needs constant power supply to keep its data, making it volatile.

Volatility is a term used in information processing. It refers to the percentage of records that are added to or deleted from a file during a single processing operation. A data file that has a high percentage of changes would be described as having a high volatility.

DEVICE	ACCESS	VOLATILE	PERMANENT
RAM	Random	Yes	No
ROM	Random	No	ROM and PROM only
Floppy Disk	Random	No	No
Hard Disk	Random	No	No
CD	Random	No	CD-A, CD-ROM, CD-R and non-recordable DVD
Zip and Jaz Disks	Random	No	No
Tape	Sequential	No	No
Flash RAM	Random	Yes	No
Flash memory	Random	No	No

Data Compression

Data compression, also called data compaction is the process of reducing the amount of data needed for the storage or transmission of a given piece of information, typically by the use of encoding techniques. Compression predates digital technology, having been used in Morse Code, which assigned the shortest codes to the most common characters, and in telephony, which cuts off high frequencies in voice transmission. Today, when an uncompressed digital image may require 20 megabytes, data compression is important in storing information digitally on computer disks and in transmitting it over communications networks.

Shannon's communication modelConsider a simple telephone conversation: A person (message source) speaks into a telephone receiver (encoder), which converts the sound of the spoken word into an electrical signal. This electrical signal is then transmitted over telephone lines (channel) subject to interference (noise). When the signal reaches the telephone receiver (decoder) at the other end of the line it is converted back into vocal sounds. Finally, the recipient (message receiver) hears the original message.

Information is digitally encoded as a pattern of 0s and 1s, or bits (binary digits). A four-letter alphabet (a, e, r, t) would require two bits per character if all characters were equally probable. All the letters in the sentence "A rat ate a tart at a tea," could thus be encoded with $2 \times 18 = 36$ bits. Because a is most frequent in this text, with t the second most common, assigning a variable-length binary code—a: 0, t: 10, r: 110, e: 111—would result in a compressed message of only 32 bits. This encoding has the important property that no code is a prefix of any other. That is, no extra bits are required to separate letter codes: 010111 decodes unambiguously as ate.

Data compression may be lossless (exact) or lossy (inexact). Lossless compression can be reversed to yield the original data, while lossy compression loses detail or introduces small errors upon reversal. Lossless compression is necessary for text, where every character is important, while lossy compression may be acceptable for images or voice (the limitation of the frequency spectrum in telephony being an example of lossy compression). The three most common compression programs for general data are Zip (on computers using Windows operating system), StuffIt (on Apple computers), and gzip (on computers running UNIX); all use lossless compression. A common format for compressing static images, especially for display over the Internet, is GIF (graphics interchange format), which is also lossless except that its images are limited to 256 colours. A greater range of colours can be used with the JPEG (joint photographic experts group) formatting standard, which uses both lossless and lossy techniques, as do various standards of MPEG (moving picture expert group) for videos.

For compression programs to work, they must have a model of the data that describes the distribution of characters, words, or other elements, such as the frequency with which individual characters occur in English. Fixed models such as the simple example of the four-character alphabet, above, may not characterize a single text very well, particularly if the text contains tabular data or uses a specialized vocabulary. In these cases, adaptive models, derived from the text itself, may be superior. Adaptive models estimate the distribution of characters or words based on what they have processed so far. An important property of adaptive modeling is that if the compression and decompression programs use precisely the same rules for forming the model and the same table of codes that they assign to its elements, then the model itself need not be sent to the decompression program. For example, if the compressing program gives the next available code to the when it is seen for the third time, decompression will follow the same rule and expect that code for the after its second occurrence.

Coding may work with individual symbols or with words. Huffman codes use a static model and construct codes like that illustrated earlier in the four-letter alphabet. Arithmetic coding encodes strings of symbols as ranges of real numbers and achieves more nearly optimal codes. It is slower than Huffman coding but is suitable for adaptive models. Run-length encoding (RLE) is good for repetitive data, replacing it by a count and one copy of a repeated item. Adaptive dictionary methods build a table of strings and then replace occurrences of them by shorter codes. The Lempel-Ziv algorithm, invented by Israeli computer scientists Abraham Lempel and Jacob Ziv, uses the text itself as the dictionary, replacing later occurrences of a string by numbers indicating where it occurred before and its length. Zip and gzip use variations of the Lempel-Ziv algorithm.

Lossy compression extends these techniques by removing detail. In particular, digital images are composed of pixels that represent gray-scale or colour information. When a pixel differs only slightly from its neighbours, its value may be replaced by theirs, after which the "smoothed" image can be compressed using RLE. While smoothing out a large section of an image would be glaringly evident, the change is far less noticeable when spread over small scattered sections. The most common method uses the discrete cosine transform, a mathematical formula related to the Fourier transform, which breaks the image into separate parts of differing levels of importance for image quality. This technique, as well as fractal techniques, can achieve excellent compression ratios. While the performance of lossless compression is measured by its degree of compression, lossy compression is also evaluated on the basis of the error it introduces. There are mathematical methods for calculating error, but the measure of error also depends on how the data are to be used: discarding high-frequency tones produces little loss for spoken recordings, for example, but an unacceptable degradation for music.

Video images may be compressed by storing only the slight differences between successive frames. MPEG-1 is common in compressing video for CD-ROMs; it is also the basis for the MP3 format used to compress music. MPEG-2 is a higher "broadcast" quality format used for DVDs and some television networking devices. MPEG-4 is designed for "low bandwidth" applications and is common for broadcasting video over the World Wide Web (WWW). (MPEG-3 was subsumed into MPEG-2.) Video compression can achieve compression ratios approaching 20-to-1 with minimal distortion.

There is a trade-off between the time and memory that compression algorithms require and the compression that they achieve. English text can generally be compressed to one-half or one-third of its original size. Images can often be compressed by factors of 10 to 20 or more. Despite the growth of computer storage capacity and network speeds, data compression remains an essential tool for storing and transmitting ever-larger collections of data.

Compression vs. data Deduplication

Compression is often compared to data deduplication, but the two techniques operate differently. Deduplication is a type of compression that looks for redundant chunks of data across a storage or file system and then replaces each duplicate chunk with a pointer to the original. Data compression algorithms reduce the size of the bit strings in a data stream that is far smaller in scope and generally remembers no more than the last megabyte or less of data.

File-level deduplication eliminates redundant files and replaces them with stubs pointing to the original file. Block-level deduplication identifies duplicate data at the subfile level. The system saves unique instances of each block, uses a hash algorithm to process them and generates a unique identifier to store them in an index. Deduplication typically looks for larger chunks of duplicate data than compression, and systems can deduplicate using a fixed or variable-sized chunk.

Deduplication is most effective in environments that have a high degree of redundant data, such as virtual desktop infrastructure or storage backup systems. Data compression tends to be more effective than deduplication in reducing the size of unique information, such as images, audio, videos, databases and executable files. Many storage systems support both compression and deduplication.

Data Compression and Backup

Compression is often used for data that's not accessed much, as the process can be intensive and slow down systems. Administrators, though, can seamlessly integrate compression in their backup systems.

Backup is a redundant type of workload, as the process captures the same files frequently. An organization that performs full backups will often have close to the same data from backup to backup.

There are major benefits to compressing data prior to backup:

- Data takes up less space, as a compression ratio can reach 100:1, but between 2:1 and 5:1 is common.

- If compression is done in a server prior to transmission, the time needed to transmit the data and the total network bandwidth are drastically reduced.

- On tape, the compressed, smaller file system image can be scanned faster to reach a particular file, reducing restore latency.

- Compression is supported by backup software and tape libraries, so there is a choice of data compression techniques.

Pros and Cons of Compression

The main advantages of compression are a reduction in storage hardware, data transmission time and communication bandwidth -- and the resulting cost savings. A compressed file requires less storage capacity than an uncompressed file, and the use of compression can lead to a significant decrease in expenses for disk and/or solid-state drives. A compressed file also requires less time for transfer, and it consumes less network bandwidth than an uncompressed file.

The main disadvantage of data compression is the performance impact resulting from the use of CPU and memory resources to compress the data and perform decompression. Many vendors have designed their systems to try to minimize the impact of the processor-intensive calculations associated with compression. If the compression runs inline, before the data is written to disk, the system may offload compression to preserve system resources. For instance, IBM uses a separate hardware acceleration card to handle compression with some of its enterprise storage systems.

If data is compressed after it is written to disk, or post-process, the compression may run in the background to reduce the performance impact. Although post-process compression can reduce the response time for each input/output (I/O), it still consumes memory and processor cycles and can affect the overall number of I/Os a storage system can handle. Also, because data initially must be written to disk or flash drives in an uncompressed form, the physical storage savings are not as great as they are with inline compression.

Data Compression Techniques: File system Compression

File system compression takes a fairly straightforward approach to reducing the storage footprint of data by transparently compressing each file as it is written.

Many of the popular Linux file systems -- including Reiser4, ZFS and btrfs -- and Microsoft NTFS have a compression option. The server compresses chunks of data in a file and then writes the smaller fragments to storage.

Read-back involves a relatively small latency to expand each fragment, while writing adds substantial load to the server, so compression is usually not recommended for data that is volatile. File system compression can weaken performance, so it should be deployed selectively on files that are not accessed frequently.

Historically, with the expensive hard drives of early computers, data compression software, such as DiskDoubler and SuperStor Pro, were popular and helped establish mainstream file system compression.

Storage administrators can also apply the technique of using compression and deduplication for improved data reduction.

Technologies and Products that use Data Compression

Compression is built into a wide range of technologies, including storage systems, databases, operating systems and software applications used by businesses and enterprise organizations. Compressing data is also common in consumer devices, such as laptops, PCs and mobile phones.

Many systems and devices perform compression transparently, but some give users the option to turn compression on or off. It can be performed more than once on the same file or piece of data, but subsequent compressions result in little to no additional compression and may even increase the size of the file to a slight degree, depending on the data compression algorithms.

WinZip is a popular Windows program that compresses files when it packages them in an archive. Archive file formats that support compression include ZIP and RAR. The BZIP2 and GZIP formats see widespread use for compressing individual files.

Other vendors that offer compression include Dell EMC with its XtremIO all-flash array, Kaminario with its K2 all-flash array and RainStor with its data compression software.

Data Differencing

Data differencing is a general term for comparing the contents of two data objects. In the context of compression, it involves repetitively searching through the target file to find similar blocks and replacing them with a reference to a library object. This process repeats until it finds no additional duplicate objects. Data differencing can result in many compressed files with just one element in the library representing each duplicated object.

In virtual desktops, this technique can feature a compression ratio of as much as 100:1. The process is often more closely aligned with deduplication, which looks for identical files or objects, rather than within the content of each object.

Data differencing is sometimes referred to as deduplication.

Data Manipulation

Programmers must also ensure that the programs manipulate the binary codes in an appropriate way for the particular application. But what sorts of manipulation are possible inside a computer?

Perhaps surprisingly, a great deal of data manipulation in a computer is simply moving data around without changing it at all.

Not so surprisingly, a fair amount of the data manipulation takes the form of arithmetic: addition, subtraction, multiplication and division.

Another common manipulation is comparing data (with a view to taking an action that depends on the result of the comparison). This is usually referred to as testing. Think for example about a spell-check program that is checking whether a word in the email you have just typed is in its dictionary. The letters in your word and the letters in the word in the dictionary will all be in ASCII format. Pairs of ASCII codes can then be compared systematically, and if the codes in each pair are identical then your word is identical to the word in the dictionary and the spell checker can move on to the next word in your email. If all the codes are not identical then either the computer has yet to find the word you are using, or possibly you have a made spelling mistake, or the word is not in its dictionary. Either way, what the computer does next depends on the outcome of the comparison test.

The fourth sort of data manipulation, not so common but still used, is logic operations on the data. So there are four basic types of data manipulation carried out in computers:

- Moving data around unchanged;

- Carrying out arithmetic operations on data;

- Testing data; and

- Carrying out logic operations on data.

References

- Storage, definition: searchstorage.techtarget.com, Retrieved 6 February, 2019

- Primary-storage: searchstorage.techtarget.com, Retrieved 12 June, 2019

- Types, secondary-storage-devices-computers: jotuts.com, Retrieved 18 July, 2019

- Storage-characteristics: tracipt11.wikidot.com, Retrieved 13 August, 2019

- Data-compression, technology: britannica.com, Retrieved 25 January, 2019

- Compression, definition: searchstorage.techtarget.com, Retrieved 23 March, 2019

- Representing-and-manipulating-data-computers, computing, computing-and-ict, science-maths-technology: open.edu, Retrieved 29 April, 2019

5

Algorithms and Programming Languages

Algorithm is a set of instruction that is primarily used to solve a problem and to perform a computation. It includes algorithm design, algorithm implementation and algorithm analysis. A formal language that consists of a set of instructions to produce various kinds of outputs is known as a programming language. It is majorly used in computer programming in order to implement algorithms. The diverse applications of algorithms and programming language in the current scenario have been thoroughly discussed in this chapter.

Algorithm

An algorithm is defined as a step-by-step procedure or method for solving a problem by a computer in a finite number of steps. Steps of an algorithm definition may include branching or repetition depending upon what problem the algorithm is being developed for. While defining an algorithm steps are written in human understandable language and independent of any programming language. We can implement it in any programming language of our choice.

Besides merely being a finite set of rules which gives a sequence of operations for solving a specific type of problem, a well defined algorithm has five important features:

- Finiteness: An algorithm must always terminate after a finite number of steps.

- Definiteness: Each step of an algorithm must be precisely defined; the actions to be carried out must be rigorously and unambiguously specified for each case.

- Input: An algorithm has zero or more inputs, i.e, quantities which are given to it initially before the algorithm begins.

- Output: An algorithm has one or more outputs i.e, quantities which have a specified relation to the inputs.

- Effectiveness: An algorithm is also generally expected to be effective. This means that all of the operations to be performed in the algorithm must be sufficiently basic that they can in principle be done exactly and in a finite length of time.

Let's say that you have a friend arriving at the airport, and your friend needs to get from the airport to your house.

Here are four different algorithms that you might give your friend for getting to your home:

1. The Taxi Algorithm:

    - Go to the taxi stand.

    - Get in a taxi.

    - Give the driver my address.

2. The Call-me Algorithm:

    - When your plane arrives, call my cell phone.

    - Meet me outside baggage claim.

3. The Rent-a-car Algorithm:

    - Take the shuttle to the rental car place.

    - Rent a car.

    - Follow the directions to get to my house.

4. The Bus Algorithm:

    - Outside baggage claim, catch bus number 70.

    - Transfer to bus 14 on Main Street.

    - Get off on Elm street.

    - Walk two blocks north to my house.

All four of these algorithms accomplish exactly the same goal, but each algorithm does it in completely different way. Each algorithm also has a different cost and a different travel time. Taking a taxi, for example, is probably the fastest way, but also the most expensive. Taking the bus is definitely less expensive, but a whole lot slower. You choose the algorithm based on the circumstances.

In computer programming, there are often many different ways -- algorithms -- to accomplish any given task. Each algorithm has advantages and disadvantages in different situations. Sorting is one place where a lot of research has been done, because computers spend a lot of time sorting lists. Here are five different algorithms that are used in sorting:

- Bin sort

- Merge sort

- Bubble sort

- Shell sort

- Quicksort

If you have a million integer values between 1 and 10 and you need to sort them, the bin sort is the right algorithm to use. If you have a million book titles, the quicksort might be the best algorithm. By knowing the strengths and weaknesses of the different algorithms, you pick the best one for the task at hand.

Applications of Algorithm

As mentioned before, algorithms can be used in many areas, and they are often represented in flowchart form for visual understanding. In other words, a flowchart is a diagram that represents an algorithm, showing the steps in various boxes and displays the process by connecting the boxes together. Here are some examples for algorithm application in flowchart forms:

1. Algorithm Application for Math

Determine and Output Whether Number N is Even or Odd.

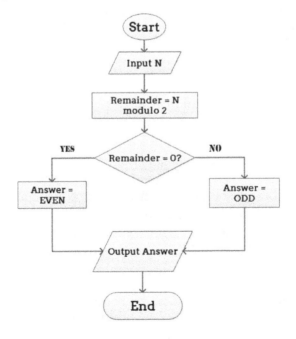

2. Algorithm Application for Computer Programming

Draw a flowchart for computing factorial N (N!).

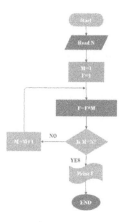

3. Algorithm Application for Daily Life

Determine Whether the Student Passed the Exam or Not.

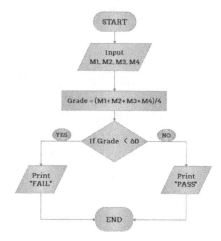

The examples above give a clear demonstration of the applicaitons of algorithms in math, computer programming and daily life. Creating a flowchart might be the best way to represent an algorithm.

Algorithm Design

An algorithm is a series of instructions, often referred to as a "process," which is to be followed when solving a particular problem. While technically not restricted by definition, the word is almost invariably associated with computers, since computer-processed algorithms can tackle much larger problems than a human, much more quickly. Since modern computing uses algorithms much more frequently than at any other point in human history, a field has grown up around their design, analysis, and refinement. The field of algorithm design requires a strong mathematical background, with computer science degrees being particularly sought-after qualifications. It offers a growing number of highly compensated career options, as the need for more (as well as more sophisticated) algorithms continues to increase.

Conceptual Design

At their simplest level, algorithms are fundamentally just a set of instructions required to complete a task. The development of algorithms, though they generally weren't called that, has been a popular habit and a professional pursuit for all of recorded history. Long before the dawn of the modern computer age, people established set routines for how they would go about their daily tasks, often writing down lists of steps to take to accomplish important goals, reducing the risk of forgetting something important. This, essentially, is what an algorithm is. Designers take a similar approach to the development of algorithms for computational purposes: first, they look at a problem. Then, they outline the steps that would be required to resolve it. Finally, they develop a series of mathematical operations to accomplish those steps.

From Small Tasks to Big Data

A simple task can be solved by an algorithm generated with a few minutes, or at most a morning's work. The level of complexity runs a long gauntlet, however, arriving at problems so complicated that they have stymied countless mathematicians for years — or even centuries. Modern computer confronts problems at this level in such areas as cyber-security, as well as big data handling — the efficient and thorough sorting of sets of data so large that even a standard computer would be unable to process them in a timely fashion. Examples of big data might include "every article on Wikipedia," "every indexed and archived webpage going back to 1998," or "the last six months of online purchases made in America."

Algorithm Design Techniques

The following is a list of several popular design approaches:

1. Divide and Conquer Approach: It is a top-down approach. The algorithms which follow the divide & conquer techniques involve three steps:

   - Divide the original problem into a set of subproblems.

   - Solve every subproblem individually, recursively.

   - Combine the solution of the subproblems (top level) into a solution of the whole original problem.

2. Greedy Technique: Greedy method is used to solve the optimization problem. An optimization problem is one in which we are given a set of input values, which are required either to be maximized or minimized (known as objective), i.e. some constraints or conditions.

- Greedy Algorithm always makes the choice (greedy criteria) looks best at the moment, to optimize a given objective.

- The greedy algorithm doesn't always guarantee the optimal solution however it generally produces a solution that is very close in value to the optimal.

3. Dynamic Programming: Dynamic Programming is a bottom-up approach we solve all possible small problems and then combine them to obtain solutions for bigger problems.

   This is particularly helpful when the number of copying subproblems is exponentially large. Dynamic Programming is frequently related to Optimization Problems.

4. Branch and Bound: In Branch & Bound algorithm a given subproblem, which cannot be bounded, has to be divided into at least two new restricted subproblems. Branch and Bound algorithm are methods for global optimization in non-convex problems. Branch and Bound algorithms can be slow, however in the worst case they require effort that grows exponentially with problem size, but in some cases we are lucky, and the method coverage with much less effort.

5. Randomized Algorithms: A randomized algorithm is defined as an algorithm that is allowed to access a source of independent, unbiased random bits, and it is then allowed to use these random bits to influence its computation.

6. Backtracking Algorithm: Backtracking Algorithm tries each possibility until they find the right one. It is a depth-first search of the set of possible solution. During the search, if an alternative doesn't work, then backtrack to the choice point, the place which presented different alternatives, and tries the next alternative.

7. Randomized Algorithm: A randomized algorithm uses a random number at least once during the computation make a decision.

Example: In Quick Sort, using a random number to choose a pivot.

Example: Trying to factor a large number by choosing a random number as possible divisors.

Algorithm Representation

As mentioned previously, algorithms are generally represented by either pseudocode or a flowchart. But what are these? It might be accurate to claim that each is merely a means of representing an algorithm, but that would hardly move the discussion along. Instead, let's focus on what features we need our means of algorithm representation to have in order for it to be a meaningful and useful representation.

- Show the logic of how the problem is solved - not how it is implemented.
- Readily reveal the flow of the algorithm.
- Be expandable and collapsible.
- Lend itself to implementation of the algorithm.

Essential Elements of a Good Representation

Show the Logic

One of the most difficult things for people just learning problem solving - especially when it involves computer programming - is to clearly distinguish between the concept of problem logic and implementation logic. The former is independent of the details of how the problem solution is implemented. If you are trying to find the radius of a sphere having a specific surface area, then you need to find out what that area is, you need some means of dividing that area by 4pi, and you need some means of taking the square root of the result. It doesn't matter whether you are solving the problem with a C program, a Java program, a calculator, a pencil and paper, or in your head - those elements are part of the logic of solving the problem. The logic involved in taking the square root of a number, on the other hand, is germane primarily to the logic of how you are implementing your solution. In other words, for most purposes I can communicate the logic behind how to determine the radius of a sphere with a specific surface area by going into no more detail than to note that, at some point, it is necessary to take the square root of a number.

Your algorithm representation should focus on the logic of the problem, and not the logic of the eventual implementation. More specifically, the upper levels of your representation should, to the degree possible, be devoid of implementation details - these should be relegated to the lower levels of the representation.

Reveal the Flow

Most problems, especially if they are intended to be solved with the aid of a computer program, involve flow control. In the "structured programming" paradigm, this flow control consists of sequences, selections, and repetitions. This may not be readily apparent at the topmost level where the algorithm can be represented by a list of tasks that are to be performed one after another in a specific sequence. But at some point, as each of those tasks is developed, decisions will have to be made and different steps taken depending on the outcome of those decisions. The representation method used should be compatible with this and clearly show the points at which decisions are made and what the various courses of action are that can result.

Be Expandable and Collapsible

Our algorithm representation should be flexible and allow us to readily collapse it so as to show less detail and focus on the more abstract elements of the algorithm or to expand it so as to get as detailed as necessary in order to actually implement the solution. Unstated in this is an acknowledgement that, as we expand our algorithm and become more detailed, at some point we have to get into the logic of the implementation issues.

For instance, if we expand the step that says to take the square root of a number, we have to start describing the specific method that will be used to do this and that method is highly dependent on the eventual implementation. At that point, our algorithm is becoming "locked" to that particular implementation. This is perfectly acceptable. The reason that we should be asking for more detail on how to take the square root is because we are now dealing with implementation issues and therefore expect that the steps will be specific to the implementation.

If we have structured our representation properly, then we can always back up. If our original implementation was with a C program and now we want to implement the algorithm in assembly on a PIC microcontroller, then we simply collapse our algorithm until the implementation dependent portions are gone and then re-expand the high level logic that was left in such a way that it can now be implemented on a PIC. If our high level logic is geared towards a particular implementation and our problem-oriented tasks are contained at lower levels, then this because very difficult to do.

Aid in Implementation

At the end of the day, the goal is usually to actually implement a solution to the problem being solved. If our method of representing our algorithm does not lend itself to an orderly implementation of that algorithm, then our method is seriously flawed. Conversely, if our method of representation lends itself to a systematic implementation of the algorithm, then our method is extremely useful.

By "systematic implementation" we mean that we should be able to take our represented algorithm and break it into easily identifiable fragments each of which can be readily translated into one of the structures, such as a while() loop or an if()/else block, available to us in our chosen implementation scheme be it a C program, an assembly language routine, an electronic circuit, or a physical mechanism.

This is one of the reasons why we seldom use flowcharts for algorithms that are slated for implementation using a physical circuit - flowcharts do not lend themselves to aiding such an implementation. But schematics do and properly developed schematics possess all of the properties described above. Likewise, schematics are seldom used to develop algorithms slated for implementation with a computer program for the same reason. However, when collapsed to their most abstract level - the topmost level or two - a well-structured flowchart and a well-structured schematic for a program and circuit, respectively, that solve the same problem may will look nearly identical. The reason is that, in each case, the topmost levels are representing only the logic of the problem and do not contain much, if any, information specific to the eventual means of implementation.

Implementation Independence

From this point forward, we will restrict the discussion to algorithms that are intended for eventual implementation using a computer program - but the concepts described can be readily generalized to any type of implementation and you should read them with the intent of grasping those generalized concepts.

Most texts maintain that the pseudocode or flowchart for a problem should represent the solution in a manner that is independent of how that solution will eventually be implemented and sufficiently complete such that the person developing the conceptual solution, who may have little if any programming background, can turn the material over to a programmer who could, in turn, decide what programming language to use and proceed to implement the solution without even understanding any of the conceptual goals behind the code being written. For instance, we should be able to give you a flowchart for a function that accepts one value and that then uses that value to produce and return another value. If we have done our job adequately, you should be able to write the function to accomplish this task in any language you are familiar and comfortable with without ever knowing or caring that the function is actually implementing a Bessel Function of Order Zero using truncated Chebyshev polynomials.

But such a philosophy is needlessly restrictive and fails to recognize some important realities. Some effort should be put into making the upper levels of the represented algorithm implementation independent. If it is practical to halt the expansion of the algorithm at the point where dealing with implementation specifics is feasible - great. This is likely to be the case if the the purpose of the given flowchart or pseudocode is to communicate the overall approach to a potential investor or an end-user. But generally it is necessary to carry the algorithm development at least a bit further - to step over the "implementation boundary" far enough that the people actually implementing and testing the code can be confident that the level of detail has truly made it into "their world" and that they are dealing only with implementation issues and not problem logic issues.

In point of fact, in the "real world" pseudocode and flowcharts are used in a variety of ways. On rare occasion reality and ideality actually come close to each other and they are used precisely. But, flowcharts also commonly serve as formal documentation for the high level structure of programs and, when used as such, generally offer very little detail but, instead, illustrate the overall flow of the program. In these cases, avoiding implementation details is usually pretty important. Other times they are used specifically to show the detailed steps necessary to carry out a specific implementation and, when used this way, are completely dependent on the language and, perhaps, even the processor being used. For instance, the algorithm could be for a new means of computing trigonometric functions using the latest processor instructions so as to increase speed and reduce memory usage. Such an algorithm is fundamentally tied to the implementation - but then so is the very problem that is being solved. The problem isn't how to compute the value of the sine of an angle, the problem is how to efficiently use the latest processor resources to compute the value of the sine of an angle - a subtle but critical distinction.

However, the vast majority of cases falls somewhere between these two extremes. From a code development point of view, pseudocode and flowcharts are generally very informal and incomplete - their purpose is to guide the programmer's thoughts just far enough to enable them to proceed with the coding directly. This is particularly the case when the person writing the pseudocode and the person writing the source code are one and the same but it is also quite common even when one person (or team) is preparing the flowcharts and another person (or team) is writing the code, especially if there is good communication back and forth. It is not uncommon to see a flow chart that is very chaotic in that one section has virtually no detail while other parts are documented in excruciating detail. The sparse sections probably represent portions where the programmer is comfortable with the tasks and needs very little guidance while the highly detailed sections are probably where the programmer is unfamiliar with the concepts or having a difficult time getting correct results.

Just like in the "real world", the guidelines in this course reflect the purposes of the pseudocode or flowchart being submitted - and there are two of them. In addition to guiding your own code development efforts, what is submitted must also serve to satisfy the grader that you have an adequate understanding of the problem being solved and have a viable approach to its solution. Keep in mind that the grader's sole insight into whether you know how to perform a particular task is what you have presented. The grader is not a mind reader and is not expected to make any effort to become one. A useful guideline for how detailed your pseudocode or flowchart should be is that it should be reasonable for you to hand it to another student in the course who is about average in their performance and who has been keeping up with the material to date (but no further) and expect them to be able to implement the code with little or no difficulty even if they have not seen the problem previously.

Imbedded in this guideline are a few subtleties. As we reach new material, your pseudocode and flowcharts should be more detailed with regards to that material than it needs to be when dealing with material from considerably earlier in the course. It will be understood that your programming skills are improving and that your pseudocode and flowcharts don't need to be as detailed about material that you should be familiar with. However, if your source code demonstrates that you are not yet adequately comfortable and proficient with a particular topic, don't be surprised to lose points for inadequately detailed pseudocode or flowcharts. In general you will not lose points for presenting your pseudocode/flowcharts in too detail.

Pseudocode is ideally language independent, however the reality is that all of the pseudocode you write in this course will be used to implement source code in a specific programming language, namely C. It is therefore permissible for you to use C statements and constructs in your pseudocode and flowcharts. By similar reasoning, it is NOT permissible to use statements and constructs from Matlab, Basic, Java, or any other language you might be familiar with. This is not to say that you can't use these in pseudocode or flowcharts that you are using strictly for yourself but only that the pseudocode you submit for grading must be free of them. Be aware that there is a danger to using language elements within your pseudocode - which is one of the reasons why the use is generally frowned upon. By using language elements it becomes very easy to lose focus on representing the logic of the problem solution and begin focusing on the logic of the implementation. Keep in mind that pseudocode and flowcharts are not simply another way of expressing your program - they are to represent the logic behind how the problem is solved.

Even if you don't use actual C statements within your pseudocode or flowchart, it is highly encouraged that the structure of your algorithm be laid to match the control structures available to you in C. Doing so will drastically decrease the amount of time you spend converting the algorithm to viable C code.

Pseudocode

To a much greater degree than programming style guidelines, there are very few commonly accepted standards for how pseudocode is written. This generally reflects the fact that it is used primarily as a rather short-term communication between members working on a specific project - the code itself and other documents are used for long-term archival purposes. Where those other documents use algorithm representations, flowcharts tend to be the preferred means because they convey structure much more effectively at that level. Therefore, pseudocode tends to be much more informal and a case of "whatever works". Some people choose to write their pseudocode very much as though it were a true programming language with very formal constructs. In fact, a common project in some software engineering courses is to devise a formal pseudocode and a translator that converts the pseudocode into actual code in some programming language. On the other end of the spectrum, some people write their pseudocode almost like a free-verse description of what the program needs to do.

The authors of your text tend to be more toward the latter end of the spectrum. You will probably notice that they seldom present highly detailed steps and generally prefer to describe what the input is, what the output should be, and then discuss how they go about producing that output. This is perfectly acceptable. You should probably also note that when they do represent an algorithm as a list of steps, they tend to use statements like "Repeat lines 15 through 17 while x < 4". This is also perfectly valid, but I think you will quickly discover a major disadvantage to writing your pseudocode this way. The frequent references to specific line numbers does not present a problem to someone reading the pseudocode, but when you're writing your pseudocode you will find two things to be very true - you will frequently be referring to lines that haven't been written yet meaning that you will have to go back and add the line numbers, once known, to earlier instructions. Worse, you will find that the line numbers keep changing as you add and delete lines. Just adding a single line at the top of your list means that every line number that appears in any instruction now has to be updated.

Fortunately, this last drawback can be avoided in a couple of ways. The first way is to provide labels for some of the instructions - namely the lines referred to in other instructions. The other way is to use indenting or some other means of showing that some instructions are controlled by other, higher level instructions.

Fortunately again, there is a pretty easy way around this as well, though your authors elect not to use it. It is called the "legal outline". In legal documents it is necessary to be able to refer to specific sections or even specific clauses of the document in an unambiguous fashion and a simple means of numbering sections and their component parts was adopted for that purpose. This, combined with a commitment to adhere to the use of structured programming constructs (sequence, selection, and repetition), allows the pseudocode to be written entirely without the need to refer to line numbers within any of the instructions.

But using the legal outline notation has drawbacks as well - most notably, it is cumbersome, especially if you are doing it on paper. You can avoid most of this by using the indenting alone to show the structure and adding in the outline numbers at the end. Or, you could completely forego the outline numbers altogether - but if you do that you must be certain that the indenting structure is very clear. This is reasonably easy to accomplish with a fixed-pitch font but can be difficult to accomplish with a proportional pitch font. Another way to circumvent this - and in fact to use it to your advantage - is to develop your pseudocode with a tool that is set up to work with legal outlines. Fortunately, most reasonably featured word processors, including Word, are capable of doing this. Although you cannot submit a Word document as your pseudocode, you can copy and paste the contents of the Word document to an ASCII text file (using Notepad, for instance) and the numbering will be carried over in the operation, which is very convenient.

A Recommended Pseudocode Format

To aid in communication - particularly between you and the grader (the value of which should be relatively obvious) it is recommended that the problem be decomposed into a set of hierarchical tasks. The lowest-level tasks should either be tasks that are very straightforward to implement directly in C (using your level of knowledge) or the specific instructions for performing the task should be provided. By beginning each line with one of the keywords discussed below, the chance for miscommunication between you and the grader is greatly diminished.

Documentation Keywords

Documentation keywords describe what needs to be done or provides information about why something is being done. You will quickly discover that, if you have done a decent job of writing your pseudocode, that these lines make very useful comment lines in your final code.

- TASK:

A TASK statement is something that the program must perform but that is described at a level more abstract than what can be coded directly. One way to think of it is that you break a problem down into a set of TASKs. Each TASK can, in turn, be broken down into more narrowly defined TASKs. At some point, the TASK can be described in terms of steps that can be directly implemented. From one perspective, anytime a TASK: keyword is used, it means that there should (or at least could) be a subordinate level of the hierarchy which is the pseudocode for that TASK. In practice, that pseudocode need not be present if the TASK is sufficiently narrow that the person implementing it can go directly from the TASK description to the actual code without the benefit of the detailed steps.

- REM:

A REM statement is merely a remark or comment. They are useful if the TASK statement proves to be insufficient to convey all the desired information or if the reason that something is done or why it works is not obvious..

Action Keywords

Action keywords are the lines that actually do the work. There are three basic actions that can be carried out: changing the value stored at some location in memory, getting input from some device, or generating output to some device. We will use the SET, GET, and PUT keywords for these actions respectively.

- SET:

This is an "action" keyword that denotes performing some operation that changes a value in memory. The most common example would be the evaluation of some equation.

- PUT:

This is an "action" keyword that denotes an output operation, generally to the screen. If the destination is anything other than the screen, such as a file or the serial port, then that should be explicitly stated.

- GET:

This is an "action" keyword that denotes in input operation, generally from the keyboard. It is generally understood that there is an implied SET action involved where the value brought in gets stored in some memory location. If the source is anything other than the keyboard, such as a file or the serial port, then that should be explicitly stated.

Flow Control Keywords

While the action keywords perform the actual work, they are insufficient in and of themselves to write all but the most trivial programs. Of the three structured programming constructs, the action keywords are only sufficient to implement the first of them, namely a sequence of instructions. A program's true power comes from the other two - selection and repetition - because they give it the ability to select whether a particular action will actually be carried out based on the information made available to it at the time that it is executed. This ability is the result of controlling the flow of the program which is the purpose of the flow control keywords.

Because flow control is a more complex task that merely executing a single statement, all but the simplest flow control keywords are used in groups and there are some options in how to use them depending on the specific situation.

Selection - Case 1

- SEL: (test condition)

    o TRUE:

- Statement(s) to be executed if test condition is TRUE

    o FALSE

- Statement(s) to be executed if test condition is FALSE

Selection - Case 2

- IF: (test condition)

    o Statement(s) to be executed if test condition is TRUE

- ELSE:

    o Statement(s) to be executed if test condition is FALSE

The advantage of Case 1 is that it clearly identifies the block as a selection construct, but it is a bit more involved than is usually necessary. The format of Case 2 is very close to the format of the actual C code that would result and is therefore a bit more straightforward to convert in the coding process, but not enough so as to be a significant factor.

In a legal outline, the ELSE: statement in Case 2 would be numbered one more than the IF: statement - in other words, if the IF: statement was numbered 3.4.2.6) then the ELSE: statement would be numbered 3.4.2.7). This can be useful or confusing depending upon how you thing of it. If you think of the test condition controlling a single selection construct, then it would be nice if the controlling expression was one level in the outline and everything it controls was at a lower level. So this could be a bit confusing. However, this format actually emphasizes the fact that, in C, an "else" statement truly is a separate statement and that it must immediately follow an "if" statement that is at the same level of control. Neither convention is significantly better than the other - and you should quickly get comfortable with whichever you choose to use.

Repetition - Case 1

- LOOP:

    o   WHILE: (test condition)

    o   Statement(s) to be executed if test condition is TRUE

Repetition - Case 2

- LOOP:

    o   Statement(s) to be executed if test condition is TRUE

    o   WHILE: (test condition)

These two cases map directly into the while() and do/while() looping constructs of the C language. In Case 1, the test condition is evaluated prior to making the first pass through the statements controlled by it and, as a result, the possibility exists that those statements won't be executed even once. The only difference in Case 2 is that the statements controlled by the test condition are executed one time and the test is evaluated after that first pass. If the test condition is TRUE then another pass is made - and the test condition evaluated at the end of that and each succeeding pass until the test finally fails.

While the two cases above are more than adequate to represent any looping logic - in fact, either one of them by itself is sufficient, just more cumbersome in some cases - the logic is sometime clearer to the reader if it is expressed in terms of repeating the loop until some some condition is met - meaning that the loop is terminated as soon as the test condition becomes TRUE.

Repetition - Case 3

- LOOP:

    o   UNTIL: (test condition)

    o   Statement(s) to be executed if test condition is FALSE

Repetition - Case 4

- LOOP:

    o Statement(s) to be executed if test condition is FALSE

    o UNTIL: (test condition)

Although C does not support a "loop until" construct (some languages do) converting Case 3 to an equivalent form of Case 1 is trivial - you simply invert the test condition. Similarly, Case 4 can be converted to Case 2 by the same mechanism.

Just as the selection construct can be streamlined, so too can a couple of the repetition constructs.

Repetition - Case 5 (streamlined version of Case 1)

- WHILE: (test condition)

    o Statement(s) to be executed if test condition is TRUE

Repetition - Case 6 (streamlined version of Case 3)

- UNTIL: (test condition)

    o Statement(s) to be executed if test condition is FALSE

Streamlining the other two is more difficult because, since the test comes at the end of the statement within the loop, it is very useful to mark the beginning of those statements in such a way that the fact that it is a loop is readily apparent to the reader. The LOOP: statement does that about as well as any other option would.

As you code loops, you will discover that it is frequently the case that there are steps that are logically associated with the loop but which must reside outside of the loop code. The most common by far is the need to initialize certain variables, especially counters, prior to entering the loop. Much less frequently, it is necessary to perform some cleanup tasks immediately after the loop is exited. A pseudocode construct that gathers all of these together so that their association is obvious is the following:

Repetition - Case 7

- REP:

    o PRE:

- Statement(s) to be executed prior to entering loop

    o WHILE: (test condition)

- Statement(s) to be executed if test condition is TRUE

- o LOOP:

- o POST:

- Statement(s) to be executed prior after the loop is finished

The above can be easily altered so as to cover all four of the first four cases. As shown, it implements Case 1. By switching the WHILE: and LOOP: statements it implements Case 2. Similarly, Case 3 is obtained simply by changing the WHILE: to UNTIL: and swapping the UNTIL: with the LOOP: then generated Case 4.

Flowcharts

Flowcharts are a graphical means of representing an algorithm, as should be expected, they have advantages and disadvantages compared to pseudocode. One of their primary advantages is that they permit the structure of a program to be easily visualized - even if all the text were to be removed. The human brain is very good at picking out these patterns and keeping them "in the back of the mind" as a reference frame for viewing the code as it develops.

Most programmers also find it easier to sketch flowcharts on a piece of paper and to modify them by crossing out connection arrows and drawing new ones that they would working with pseudocode by hand. By the same token, most programmers do not like to develop flowcharts in an electronic format because the overhead of creating and modifying it is generally more than they want to deal with while pseudocode lends itself to such electronic development.

Furthermore, if the pseudocode is already in an electronic format that has been structured to lend itself to translation to the final language then doing so can be a very simply matter of copying the pseudocode to a new file, overlaying the necessary syntax associated with the language, and compiling the result. This can be a powerful advantage of pseudocode over flowcharts where the entire source code still has to be typed by hand unless you are fortunate to have a tool that can take a flowchart - typically developed using that same tool - and translating it to directly to code. Such tools do exist - and they tend to be rather expensive.

Now that we have looked as some of the pros and cons of flowcharts relative to pseudocode, let's delve into flowcharting itself. The idea behind a flowchart is that it links together a series of blocks each of which perform some specific task. Each of these tasks is represented by a block and has exactly one arrow leading to it and, more importantly, one arrow exiting from it. This is key to the concept of a "structured program".

The shape of the block may convey additional information about what is happening. For instance, a rectangular block is frequently used to indicated that a computation is occurring while a slanted parallelogram is used to indicate some type of input or output operation. The diversity of shapes that can be used and what they mean is staggering - for instance a different shape can be used to indicated output to a tape drive versus to a hard disk or to indicate output in text format verses binary format. By using such highly specialized symbols, much of what is happening can be conveyed by the symbols themselves. But the power of using these distinctions is generally only useful to people that work with flowcharts continuously, professionally, and who are describing very large and complex systems. At our level, it is far better to restrict ourselves to a minimum number of shapes and explicitly indicate any information that otherwise might have been implied by using a different shape.

Basic Flowchart Shapes

The shapes we will use are the circle, the rectangle, the parallelogram, the diamond, and the arrows that interconnect them.

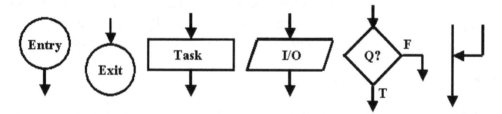

Circle - Entry/Exit Point

The circle indicates the entry and exit point for the program - or for the current segment of the program. The entry point has exactly one arrow leaving it and the exit point has exactly one arrow entering it. Execution of the program - or of that segment of the program - always starts at the entry point and finishes at the exit point.

Rectangle - Task

The rectangle represents a task that is to be performed. That task might be as simple as incrementing the value of a single variable or as complex as you can imagine. The key point is that it also has a single entry point and a single exit point.

Parallelogram - Input/Output

The parallelogram is used to indicate that some form in input/output operation is occurring. They must also obey the single entry single exit point rule which makes sense given that they are a task-block except with a slightly different shape for the symbol. We could easily eliminate this symbol and use the basic rectangle but the points at which I/O occur within our programs are extremely important and being able to easily and quickly identify them is valuable enough to warrant dealing with a special symbol.

Since a Task block can be arbitrarily complex, it can also contain I/O elements. Whether to use a rectangle or a parallelogram is therefore a judgment call. One way to handle this is to decide whether a task's primary purpose is to perform I/O. Again, that is a judgment call. Another option is to use a symbol that is rectangular on one side and slanted on the other indicating that it is performing both I/O and non-I/O tasks.

Diamond - Decision Point

The diamond represents a decision point within our program. A question is asked and depending on the resulting answer, different paths are taken. Therefore a diamond has a single entry point but more than one exit point. Usually, there are two exit points - one that is taken if the answer to the question is "true" and another that is taken if the answer to the question is "false". This is sufficient to represent any type of branching logic including both the typical selection statements and the typical repetition statements. However, most languages support some type of "switch" or "case" statement that allows the program to select one from among a potentially large set of possible paths. The basic two-exit-point diamond is fully capable of representing this construct, but it is generally cleaner and more useful to represent it using a as many exit points from the diamond as there are paths.

Arrow - Interblock Flow

The arrows simply show which symbol gets executed next. The rule is that once an arrow leaves a symbol, it must lead directly to exactly one other symbol - arrows can never fork and diverge. They can, however, converge and join arrows coming from other blocks.

Algorithm Implementation

In order to understand how to implement an Algorithm, we first need to conceptually understand what an Algorithm is. An Algorithm is a series of steps that you expect will arrive at a specific solution. Writing a program does not equal expressing code, that idea ignores and neglects the entire idea of writing code to solve a problem.

1. Establish the Rules of a Problem: Especially in a job interview, they'll ask you a problem that can be interpreted in many ways. They are looking for how you respond to those problems. Don't assume you know what the interviewer/your problem is meaning. It's almost inevitable that you'll go down the wrong path, but you need to get good at pivoting back on the right path. Figuring out that you have spent most of the morning wasting your time is what programming is about.

2. Explore the Problem Space: Don't put rigorous constraints on yourself. When people are thinking about the problem, often times they write steps, they then have a big list of steps that doesn't necessarily coincide with the steps of an Algorithm. It's OK to write down loose ideas of your plan, but acknowledge that

you're still just thinking about the problem. The list of ideas that you created aren't the new 10 commandments to solving your problem.

3. TDD: Write a Test that Would Verify a Solution: If you're doing TDD, which you should be, you're going to sort of invest in writing a test that does say what validates a correct solution. Skip this step if you're not doing TDD. In reality, you'll probably skip this step when you do a rough draft, then you should come back to it later.

4. Specify a Plan that Should Solve the Problem and Elaborate the Plan into Steps: Come up with a sequence of steps that you can explain to a very obedient pre-schooler. Don't use pronouns and be very specific. There should be no room for confusion for what these steps really mean.

   Optionally, verify each step in the process manually/mentally for some simple input. Be careful to not confuse what SHOULD happen with what is ACTUALLY happening. Pretend like you have no idea what the pseudocode is doing when you run through it.

5. Translate each step into a line of code: This step, believe it or not, is deterministic. The process of translating from one definitely clear solution in english can be easily translated to a correct programming language.

Algorithm Analysis

The most straightforward reason for analyzing an algorithm is to discover its characteristics in order to evaluate its suitability for various applications or compare it with other algorithms for the same application. Moreover, the analysis of an algorithm can help us understand it better, and can suggest informed improvements. Algorithms tend to become shorter, simpler, and more elegant during the analysis process.

Computational Complexity. The branch of theoretical computer science where the goal is to classify algorithms according to their efficiency and computational problems according to their inherent difficulty is known as computational complexity. Paradoxically, such classifications are typically not useful for predicting performance or for comparing algorithms in practical applications because they focus on order-of-growth worst-case performance.

Analysis of Algorithms. A complete analysis of the running time of an algorithm involves the following steps:

- Implement the algorithm completely.

- Determine the time required for each basic operation.

- Identify unknown quantities that can be used to describe the frequency of execution of the basic operations.

- Develop a realistic model for the input to the program.

- Analyze the unknown quantities, assuming the modelled input.

- Calculate the total running time by multiplying the time by the frequency for each operation, then adding all the products.

Classical algorithm analysis on early computers could result in exact predictions of running times. Modern systems and algorithms are much more complex, but modern analyses are informed by the idea that exact analysis of this sort could be performed in principle.

Analysis is done before coding. Profiling (a.k.a. benchmarking) is done after the code is written.

Measuring Time

The absolute running time of an algorithm cannot be predicted, since this depends on the programming language used to implement the algorithm, the computer the program runs on, other programs running at the same time, the quality of the operating system, and many other factors. We need a machine-independent notion of an algorithm's running time.

The current state-of-the-art in analysis is finding a measure of an algorithm's relative running time, as a function of how many items there are in the input, i.e., the number of symbols required to reasonably encode the input, which we call n. The n could be:

- The number of items in a container

- The length of a string or file

- The degree of a polynomial

- The number of digits (or bits) in an integer

The first three only make sense when each of the elements (items, characters, coefficients/

exponents) have a bounded-size. For example: if all items are 64-bit integers, then the number of items can be used for n, but if numeric values are unbounded, you have to count bits!

We count the number of abstract operations as a function of n.

Example: Printing each Element of an Array

```
for (int i = 0; i < a.length; i++) {

    System.out.println(a[i]);

}
```

Here $n = a.length$ (provided we know that all of the items in the array have a fixed size, which is often the case). We have

- 1 initialization of i
- n n comparisons of i against a.length
- n n increments of i
- n n array indexing operations (to compute a[i])
- n n invocations of System.out.println

so we write $T(n) = 4n + 1$

Or should we?

All operations are not created equal. The printing completely overwhelms the increments, compares and indexing operations. We might as well talk about having n compare-index-print-increment operations. Then $T(n) = n + 1$. While we're at it, we might as well realize that initialization doesn't mean much, so we're safe to write $T(n) = n$.

Example: Multiplying two Square Matrices

```
for (int i = 0; i < n; i++) {

    for (int j = 0; j < n; j++) {

        double sum = 0;

        for (int k = 0; k < n; k++) {

            sum += a[i][k] * b[k][j];

        }

        c[i][j] = sum;

    }

}
```

Working from the inside-out we see each iteration of the k -loop has 4 array indexing operations, one multiplication, one addition, and one assignment. Or, heck, one big $sum\ +=\ a[i][k]*b[k][j]$ operation. Inside the j -loop there are n of these, together with an initialization of sum and an assignment to $c[i][j]$.. Does this mean $n+2$? Hardly. Those other two operations don't count for much. By a similar argument we can ignore all the simple for-loop initializing, testing, and incrementing operations. They are fast. All we need to do is count the number of $sum\ +=\ a[i][k]*b[k][j]$ operations — that's really what counts.

So we have $T(n)=n^3$.

But is this a fair measure of the complexity? We counted operations relative to the width of the matrices. We can also count operations relative to the number of items in the two matrices, which is $2n^2$. Under this measure we'd say $T(n)=n^{1.5}$.

Example: An Interesting Nested Loop

```
for (int i = 1; i <= n; i *= 2) {

    for (int j = 0; j < n; j++) {

        count++;

    }

}
```

Here the outer loop is done $log\ n$ times and the inner loop is done n times, so $T(n)=n\log n$. (Yes, the default base for logarithms in Computer Science is 2.)

Example: Getting the Value of the Last Element from an Array

```
if (a.length > 0) {

    return a[a.length - 1];

} else {

    throw new NoSuchElementException();

}
```

Here $n = a.length$, and $T(n)=1$.

Example: Addition

```
x + y
```

If x and y are primitive int values that each fit in a word of memory, any computer can add them in one step: $T(n) = 1$, But if these are BigInteger values, then what matters is how many digits (or bits) there are in each value. Since we just have to add the digits in each place and propagate carries, we get $T(n) = n$.

Example: Finding the Index of a Given Value in an Array

```
for (int i = 0; i < a.length; i++) {

    if (a[i] == x) {

        return Optional.of(i);

    }

}

return Optional.empty();
```

Here we need to introduce the B (best-case) and W (worst-case) functions: $B(n) = 1$ and $W(n) = n$. (What about the average case? It's often difficult and sometimes impossible to compute an average case. You have to know something about the expected distributions of items.)

Time Complexity Classes

We can group complexity functions by their "growth rates" (something we'll formalize in a minute). For example:

Class	Example	Description
Constant	$\lambda n.1$	Fixed number of steps, regardless of input size
Logarithmic	$\lambda n.logn$	Number of steps proportional to log of input size
Polynomial	$\lambda n.n^k,\ k \geq 1$	Number of steps a polynomial of input size
Exponential	$\lambda n.c^n, c > 1$	Number of steps exponential of input size

Those are four useful families to be sure, but we can define lots more:

Class	Example $(\lambda n.)$	Description
Constant	1	Doing a single task at most a fixed number of times. Example: retrieving the first element in a list.
Inverse Ackermann	$\alpha(n)$	

Iterated Log	$log * n$	
Loglogarithmic	$loglogn$	
Logarithmic	$logn$	Breaking down a large problem by cutting its size by some fraction. Example: Binary Search.
Polylogarithmic	$(\log n)^c, c > 1$	
Fractional Power	$n, 0 < c < 1$	
Linear	n	"Touches" each element in the input. Example: printing a list.
N-log-star-n	$nlog * n$	
Linearithmic	$nlogn$	Breaking up a large problem into smaller problems, solving them independently, and combining the solutions. Example: Mergesort.
Quadratic	n^2	"Touches" all pairs of input items. Example: Insertion Sort.
Cubic	n^3	
Polynomial	$n^c, c \geq 1$	
Quasipolynomial	n^{logn}	
Subexponential	$2^{n^\varepsilon}, 0 < \varepsilon < 1$	
Exponential	$c^n, c > 1$	Often arises in brute-force search where you are looking for subsets of a collection of items that satisfy a condition.
Factorial	$n!$	Often arises in brute-force search where you are looking for permutations of a collection of items that satisfy a condition.
N-to-the-n	n^n	
Double Exponential	2^{2^n}	
Ackerman	$A(n)$	
Runs Forever	∞	

Comparison

To get a feel for the complexity classes consider a computer that performed one million abstract operations per second:

$T(n)T(n)$	10	20	50	100	1000	1000000
1	1 μs	1 μs	1 μs	1 μs	1 μs	1 μs
log n	3.32 μs	4.32 μs	5.64 μs	6.64 μs	9.97 μs	19.9 μs

n	10 μs	20 μs	50 μs	100 μs	1 msec	1 second
n log n	33.2 μs	86.4 μs	282 μs	664 μs	9.97 msec	19.9 seconds
n^2	100 μs	400 μs	2.5 msec	10 msec	1 second	11.57 days
1000 n^2	100 msec	400 msec	2.5 seconds	10 seconds	16.7 minutes	31.7 years
n^3	1 msec	8 msec	125 msec	1 second	16.7 minutes	317 centuries
$n^{\log n}$	2.1 ms	420 ms	1.08 hours	224 days	2.5×10^7 Ga	1.23×10^{97} Ga
1.01^n	1.10 μs	1.22 μs	1.64 μs	2.7 μs	20.9 ms	7.49×10^{4298} Ga
0.000001×2^n	1.02 ns	1.05 msec	18.8 minutes	40.2 Ga	3.40×10^{272} Ga	3.14×10^{301001} Ga
2^n	1.02 ms	1.05 seconds	35.7 years	4.02×10^7 Ga	3.40×10^{278} Ga	3.14×10^{301007} Ga
n!	3.63 seconds	771 centuries	9.64×10^{41} Ga	2.96×10^{135} Ga	1.28×10^{2545} Ga	—
n^n	2.78 hours	3323 Ga	2.81×10^{62} Ga	3.17×10^{177} Ga	3.17×10^{2977} Ga	—
2^{2n}	5.70×10^{285} Ga	2.14×10^{315630} Ga	—	—	—	—

By the way, Ga is a gigayear, or one billion years.

There is something. Compare the $2n$ row with the $0.000001 \cdot 2^n$ row. The latter represents something running one million times faster than the former, but still, even for an input of size 50, requires a run time in the thousands of centuries.

Asymptotic Analysis

Since we are really measuring growth rates, we usually ignore:

- all but the "largest" term, and

- any constant multipliers

so for example

$\lambda n.0.4n^5 + 3n^3 + 253$ behaves asymptotically like n^5

$\lambda n.6.22n \log n + \dfrac{n}{7}$ behaves asymptotically like $n \log n$

The justification for doing this is

The difference between $6n$ and $3n$ isn't meaningful when looking at algorithms abstractly, since getting a computer that is twice as fast makes the former look like the latter.

The difference between $2n$ and $2n + 8$ is insignificant as n gets larger and larger.

If you are comparing the growth rates of, say, $\lambda n.n3$ and $\lambda n.kn2$, the former will always eventually overtake the latter no matter how big you make k.

How can we formalize this? That is, how do we formalize things like "the set of all quadratic functions" or the "set of all cubic functions" or "the set of all logarithmic functions"?

Big-O: Asymptotic Upper Bounds

A function f is in $O(g)$ whenever there exist constants c and N such that for every $n > N, f(n)$ is bounded above by a constant times $g(n)$. Formally:

$$O(g) = def \{f \mid \exists cN. \forall n > N. \mid f(n) \mid \leq c \mid g(n) \mid\}$$

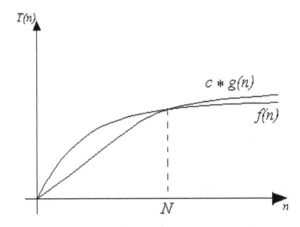

This means that $O(g)$ is the set of all functions for which g is an asymptotic upper bound of f.

Examples

- $\lambda n.0.4n^5 + 3n^3 + 253 \in O(\lambda n.n^5)$

- $\lambda n.6.22nlogn + n7 \in O(\lambda n.nlogn)$

Notation

By convention, people usually drop the lambdas when writing expressions involving Big-O, so you will see things like $O(n^2)$.

Well let's see why we should be able to, but only argue with one special case. (You can do the formal proof on your own.) Let's show that $7n^4 + 2n^2 + n + 20 \in O(n^4)$. We have to choose c and N. Let's choose $c = 30$ and $N = 1$. So since $n \geq 1$:

$$|7n^4 + 2n^2 + n + 20| \leq 7n^4 + 2n^2 + n + 20$$
$$\leq 7n^4 + 2n^4 + n^4 + 20n^4$$
$$\leq 30n^4$$

Big-O

Big-O notation is really only most useful for large n. The suppression of low-order terms and leading constants is misleading for small n. Be careful of functions such as

- ○ $n^2 + 1000n$

- ○ $0.0001n^5 + 10^6 n^2$

- ○ $10^{-4}2^n + 10^5 n^3$

- Large constants on the more significant terms signify overhead, for example when comparing

  - ○ $8n\log n$ and $0.01n^2$

note that the former is worse until n gets up to 10,710.

- Sedgewick writes "[Big-O analysis] must be considered the very first step in a progressive process of refining the analysis of an algorithm to reveal more details about its properties."

- Big-O is only an upperbound; it is not a tight upperbound. If an algorithm is in $O(n^2)$ it is also in $O(n^3)$, $O(n^{100})$, and $O(2^n)$. So it's not really right to say that all complexity functions in $O(2^n)$ are terrible, because that set properly includes the set $O(1)$.

Big-Ω: Asymptotic Lower Bounds

There is a Big-Ù notation for lower bounds.

A function f is in $\Omega(g)$ whenever there exist constants c and N such that for every $n > N, f(n)$ is bounded below by a constant times $g(n)$.

$$\Omega(g) = def\{f \mid \exists cN.\forall n > N.\mid f(n)\mid \geq c\mid g(n)\mid\}$$

Lower bounds are useful because they say that an algorithm requires at least so much time. For example, you can say that printing an array is $O(2^n)$ because $2n$ really is an upper bound, it's just not a very tight one! But saying printing an array is $Ù(n)$ means it requires at least linear time which is more accurate. Of course just about everything is $\Omega(1)$.

Big-Θ

When the lower and upper bounds are the same, we can use Big-Theta notation.

$$\Theta(g) = def\{f \mid \exists c_1 c_2 N.\forall n > N.c_1 \mid g(n)\mid \leq f(n)\mid \leq c_2 \mid g(n)\mid\}$$

Example: printing each element of an array is $\Theta(n)$. Now that's useful!

Most complexity functions that arise in practice are in Big-Theta of something. An example of a function that isn't in Big-Θ of anything is $\lambda n.n^2 cos n$.

Exercise: Why isn't that function in Big-Θ of anything?

Less-Common Complexity Functions

There are also little-oh and little-omega.

$$o(g) = def\{f \mid \lim_{x \to \infty} \frac{f(x)}{g(x)} = 0\}$$

$$\omega(g) = def\{f \mid \lim_{x \to \infty} \frac{f(x)}{g(x)} = 0\}$$

Exercise: Find functions f and g such that $f \in O(g)$ differs from $f \in o(g)$

There's also the Soft-O:

$$\tilde{O}(g) = def O(\lambda n.g(n)(\log g(n))^k)$$

Since a log of something to a power is bounded above by that something to a power, we have

$$\tilde{O}(g) \subseteq O(\lambda n.g(n)^{1+\varepsilon})$$

Determining Asymptotic Complexity

Normally you can just look at a code fragment and immediately "see" that it is $\Theta(1), \Theta(\log n), \Theta(n), \Theta(n \log n)$, or whatever. But when you can't tell by inspection, you can write code to count operations for given input sizes, obtaining $T(n)$. Then you "guess" different values of f for which $T \in \Theta(f)$. To do this, generate values of $\frac{T(n)}{f(n)}$ for lots of different f s and ns, looking for the f for which the ratio is nearly constant. Example:

```
package edu.lmu.cs.algorithms;


import java.util.Arrays;


/**

 * An application class that illustrates how to do an empirical

 * analysis for determining time complexity.

 */

public class PrimeTimer {
```

```
/**
 * A method that computes all the primes up to n, and returns the
 * number of "primitive operations" performed by the algorithm.
 */
public static long computePrimes(int n) {
    boolean[] sieve = new boolean[n];
    Arrays.fill(sieve, true);
    sieve[0] = sieve[1] = false;
    long ticks = 0;
    for (int i = 2; i * i < sieve.length; i++) {
        ticks++;
        if (sieve[i]) {
            ticks++;
            for (int j = i + i; j < sieve.length; j += i) {
                ticks++;
                sieve[j] = false;
            }
        }
    }
    return ticks;
}


/**
 * Runs the computePrimes() methods several times and displays the
 * ratio of the number of primitive operations to n, n*log2(log2(n)),
 * n*log2(n), and n*n, for each run.  The idea is that if the ratio is
 * nearly constant for any one of the expressions, that expression is
 * probably the asymptotic time complexity.
 */
```

```
public static void main(String[] args) {
    System.out.println("          n          T(n)/n  T(n)/nloglogn"
        + "      T(n)/nlogn          T(n)/n^2");
    for (int n = 100000000; true; n += 10000000) {
        double time = (double)computePrimes(n);
        double log2n = Math.log(n) / Math.log(2.0);
        double log2log2n = Math.log(log2n) / Math.log(2.0);
        System.out.printf("%9d%15.9f%15.9f%15.9f%18.12f\n",
            n, time / n, time / (n * log2log2n), time / (n * log2n),
            time / ((double)n * n));
    }
}
}
```

$ javac edu/lmu/cs/algorithms/PrimeTimer.java && java edu.lmu.cs.algorithms.PrimeTimer

n	T(n)/n	T(n)/nloglogn	T(n)/nlogn	T(n)/n^2
100000000	2.483153670	0.524755438	0.093437967	0.000000024832
110000000	2.488421536	0.525042572	0.093154203	0.000000022622
120000000	2.492800475	0.525216963	0.092881654	0.000000020773
130000000	2.496912269	0.525397614	0.092636275	0.000000019207
140000000	2.500607893	0.525543667	0.092406844	0.000000017861
150000000	2.504261540	0.525726296	0.092202718	0.000000016695
160000000	2.508113469	0.525989754	0.092029052	0.000000015676
170000000	2.511378312	0.526164370	0.091854066	0.000000014773
180000000	2.514174300	0.526271114	0.091679818	0.000000013968
190000000	2.517111653	0.526434419	0.091526593	0.000000013248
200000000	2.519476410	0.526502103	0.091366731	0.000000012597
210000000	2.521918771	0.526607744	0.091222446	0.000000012009
220000000	2.524643468	0.526791900	0.091099845	0.000000011476
230000000	2.526841665	0.526883963	0.090968655	0.000000010986
240000000	2.529254646	0.527037032	0.090854692	0.000000010539
250000000	2.531615772	0.527194102	0.090747527	0.000000010126

260000000	2.533554869	0.527276931	0.090633206	0.000000009744
270000000	2.535273511	0.527326521	0.090518378	0.000000009390
280000000	2.537081721	0.527406431	0.090413568	0.000000009061
290000000	2.538856217	0.527490156	0.090313866	0.000000008755
300000000	2.540369853	0.527529768	0.090210757	0.000000008468

.

.

.

580000000	2.573933419	0.529233035	0.088416447	0.000000004438
590000000	2.574801915	0.529278658	0.088371416	0.000000004364
600000000	2.575498323	0.529291236	0.088321815	0.000000004292
610000000	2.576229731	0.529313262	0.088274708	0.000000004223
620000000	2.576874421	0.529319651	0.088225880	0.000000004156
630000000	2.577634338	0.529351816	0.088182205	0.000000004091
640000000	2.578348789	0.529376678	0.088138140	0.000000004029
650000000	2.579215052	0.529434671	0.088100389	0.000000003968
660000000	2.579956808	0.529469006	0.088059472	0.000000003909
670000000	2.580654654	0.529496175	0.088018114	0.000000003852
680000000	2.581385994	0.529532005	0.087978922	0.000000003796
690000000	2.582226029	0.529591860	0.087944424	0.000000003742
700000000	2.582908279	0.529621034	0.087905512	0.000000003690
710000000	2.583473030	0.529627754	0.087863538	0.000000003639

.

.

.

What we're seeing here is that the ratio $\frac{T(n)}{n}$ is increasing, so the complexity is probably more than linear. The ratios $\frac{T(n)}{n \log n}$ and $\frac{T(n)}{n^2}$ are decreasing so those functions are probably upper bounds. But $\frac{T(n)}{n \log \log n}$ is also increasing, but the rate of increase seems to be slowing and who knows, might even converge. We could bet that the complexity $\in \Theta(n \log \log n)$, but we should really do a formal proof.

The Effects of Increasing Input Size

Suppressing leading constant factors hides implementation dependent details such as the speed of the computer which runs the algorithm. Still, you can some observations even without the constant factors.

For an algorithm of complexity	If the input size doubles, then the running time
1	stays the same
$logn$	increases by a constant
n	doubles
n^2	quadruples
n^3	increases eight fold
2^n	is left as an exercise for the reader

The Effects of a Faster Computer

Getting a faster computer allows to solve larger problem sets in a fixed amount of time, but for exponential time algorithms the improvement is pitifully small.

For an algorithm of complexity	If you can solve a problem of this size on your 100MHz PC	Then on a 500MHz PC you can solve a problem set of this size	And on a supercomputer one thousand times faster than your PC you can solve a problem set of this size
n	100	500	100000
n^2	100	223	3162
n^3	100	170	1000
2^n	100	102	109

More generally,

$T(n)T(n)$	On Present Computer	On a computer 100 times faster	On a computer 1000 times faster	On a computer one BIL-LION times faster
n	N	100N	1000N	1000000000N
n^2	N	10N	31.6N	31623N
n^3	N	4.64N	10N	1000N
n^5	N	2.5N	3.9N	63N
2^n	N	N + 6.64	N + 9.97	N + 30
3^n	N	N + 4.19	N + 6.3	N + 19

What if we had a computer so fast it could do One Trillion operations per second?

T(n)	20	40	50	60	70	80

n^5	3.2 µs	102 µs	313 µs	778 µs	1.68 msec	3.28 msec
2^n	1.05 msec	1.1 seconds	18.8 minutes	13.3 days	37.4 years	383 centuries
3^n	3.5 msec	4.7 months	227 centuries	1.3×10^7 centuries	7.93×10^{11} centuries	4.68×10^{16} centuries

As you can see, the gap between polynomial and exponential time is hugely significant. We can solve fairly large problem instances of high-order polynomial time algorithms on decent computers rather quickly, but for exponential time algorithms, we can network together thousands of the world's fastest supercomputers and still be unable to deal with problem set sizes of over a few dozen. So the following terms have been used to characterize problems:

Polynomial-time Algorithms	Exponential-time Algorithms
Good	Bad
Easy	Hard
Tractable	Intractable

Programming Language

A computer is a computational device which is used to process the data under the control of a computer program. Program is a sequence of instruction along with data. While executing the program, raw data is processed into a desired output format. These computer programs are written in a programming language which are high level languages. High level languages are nearly human languages which are more complex then the computer understandable language which are called machine language, or low level language.

Basic example of a computer program written in C programming language:

```
#include<stdio.h>

int main(void)

{

    printf("C is a programming language");

    return 0;

}
```

Between high-level language and machine language there are assembly language also called symbolic machine code. Assembly language are particularly computer architecture specific. Utility program (Assembler) is used to convert assembly code into executable machine code. High Level Programming Language are portable but require Interpretation or compiling toconvert it into a machine language which is computer understood.

Hierarchy of Computer Language –

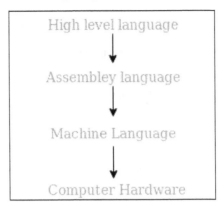

There have been many programming language some of them are listed below:

C	Python	C++
C#	R	Ruby
COBOL	ADA	Java
Fortran	BASIC	Altair BASIC
True BASIC	Visual BASIC	GW BASIC
QBASIC	PureBASIC	PASCAL
Turbo Pascal	GO	ALGOL
LISP	SCALA	Swift
Rust	Prolog	Reia
Racket	Scheme	Shimula
Perl	PHP	Java Script
CoffeeScript	VisualFoxPro	Babel
Logo	Lua	Smalltalk
Matlab	F	F#
Dart	Datalog	dbase
Haskell	dylan	Julia
ksh	metro	Mumps
Nim	OCaml	pick
TCL	D	CPL
Curry	ActionScript	Erlang
Clojure	DarkBASCIC	Assembly

Most Popular Programming Languages

- C
- Python
- C++
- Java
- SCALA
- C#
- R
- Ruby
- Go
- Swift
- JavaScript

Characteristics of a Programming Language

- A programming language must be simple, easy to learn and use, have good readability and human recognizable.
- Abstraction is a must-have Characteristics for a programming language in which ability to define the complex structure and then its degree of usability comes.
- A portable programming language is always preferred.
- Programming language's efficiency must be high so that it can be easily converted into a machine code and executed consumes little space in memory.
- A programming language should be well structured and documented so that it is suitable for application development.
- Necessary tools for development, debugging, testing, maintenance of a program must be provided by a programming language.
- A programming language should provide single environment known as Integrated Development Environment (IDE).
- A programming language must be consistent in terms of syntax and semantics.

Types of Programming Languages

Each of the different programming languages that we will mention can be broken into one or more of the following types (paradigms) of languages.

- High-level (most common) / low-level

- Declarative / imperative / procedural
- General-purpose / domain-specific
- Object-oriented / concurrent
- Command / Compiled / Script language
- Answer set

List of Computer Programming Languages

Today, there are hundreds of different programming languages. Here, we provide an index of the different programming and scripting languages.

A-C	D-K	L-Q	R-Z
ActionScript	D	LeLisp	R
ALGOL	DarkBASIC	Lisp	Racket
Ada	Dart	LiveScript	Reia
AIML *	Datalog	LOGO	RPG
Altair BASIC	dBASE	Lua	Ruby
Assembly	Dylan	MACLISP	Rust
AutoHotkey	EuLisp	Matlab	Scala
Babel	Elixir	Metro	Scheme
BASIC	F	MUMPS	Scratch
Batch file	F#	Nim	SGML *
BCPL	FORTRAN	Objective-C	Simula
BeanShell	FoxPro	OCaml	Smalltalk
Brooks	Franz Lisp	Pascal	SPL
C	Go	Perl	SQL *
C#	GW Basic	PHP	Stanford LISP
C++	Haskell	Pick	Swift
CL	HDML *	PureBasic	Tcl
Clojure	HTML *	Python	Turbo Pascal
COBOL	InterLisp	Prolog	True BASIC
CoffeeScript	ksh	QBasic	VHDL
Common Lisp	Java		Visual Basic
CPL	JavaScript		Visual FoxPro
CSS *	JCL		WML *
Curl	Julia		WHTML *
Curry	Kotlin		XLISP
			XML *
			YAML *
			ZetaLisp

Those new to computer programming may find the list above overwhelming. Figuring out where to start depends on the type of computer programming you want to do.

Applications and Program Development

Application and program development involves programs you work with on a daily basis. For example, the Internet browser you are using to view this web page is considered a program. If you are interested in developing a program, you should consider the following languages:

- C
- C#
- C++
- D
- Java
- Swift
- Tcl
- Visual Basic

Artificial intelligence development

Artificial intelligence or related fields involve creating the character interactions in computer games, portions of programs that make decisions, chatbots, and more. If you're interested in developing an AI, you should consider the following languages:

- AIML
- C
- C#
- C++
- Prolog
- Python

Database Development

Database developers create and maintain databases. If you're interested in creating or maintaining a database, you should consider any of the following languages:

- DBASE
- FoxPro

- MySQL
- SQL
- Visual FoxPro

Game Development

Game development involves creating computer games or other entertainment software. If you're interested in developing a game, you should consider the following languages:

- C
- C#
- C++
- DarkBASIC
- Java

Computer Drivers or other Hardware Development

Computer drivers and programming hardware interface support are a necessity for hardware functionality. If you're interested in developing drivers or software interfaces for hardware devices, you should consider the following languages:

- Assembly
- C

Internet and Web Page Development

Internet and web page development are the essence of the Internet. Without developers, the Internet would not exist. If you're interested in creating web pages, Internet applications, or other Internet-related tasks, you should consider the following languages:

- HDML
- HTML
- Java
- JavaScript
- Perl
- PHP
- Python
- XML

Script development

Although it is not likely to become a career, knowing how to create and develop scripts can increase productivity for you or your company, saving you countless hours. If you're interested in developing scripts, consider the following languages:

- AutoHotkey
- awk
- bash
- Batch file
- Perl
- Python
- Tcl

Programming Language Implementation

Levels of Languages

The task of a compiler may be more or less demanding. This depends on the distance of the languages it translates between. The situation is related to translation between human languages: it is easier to translate from English to French than from English to Japanese, because French is closer to English than Japanese is, both in the family tree of languages and because of cultural influences.

But the meaning of "closer" is clearer in the case of computer languages. Often it is directly related to the level of the language. The binary machine language is usually defined as the lowest level, whereas the highest level might be human language such as English. Usual programming languages are between these levels, as shown by the following very sketchy diagram:

```
--------------------------------------------- human

  human language

                        Haskell

                              Lisp          Prolog

Java

C

assembler

machine language ------------------------------------------------- machine
```

Because of the distance, high-level languages are more difficult to compile than low-level languages. Notice that "high" and "low" don't imply any value judgements here; the idea is simply that higher levels are closer to human thought, whereas lower levels are closer to the operation of machines. Both humans and machines are needed to make computers work in the way we are used to. Some people might claim that only the lowest level of binary code is necessary, because humans can be trained to write it. But to this one can object that programmers could never write very sophisticated programs by using machine code only—they could just not keep the millions of bytes needed in their heads. Therefore, it is usually much more productive to write high-level code and let a compiler produce the binary. The history of programming languages indeed shows a steady progress from lower to higher levels. Programmers can usually be more productive when writing in high-level languages, which means that high levels are desirable; at the same time, raising the level implies a challenge to compiler writers. Thus the evolution of programming languages goes hand in hand with developments in compiler technology. It has of course also helped that the machines have become more powerful. Compilation can be a heavy computation task, and the computers of the 1960's could not have run the compilers of the 2010's. Moreover, it is harder to write compilers that produce efficient code than ones that waste some resources.

Here is a very rough list of programming languages in the history, only mentioning ones that have implied something new in terms of programming language expressivity:

- 1940's: connecting wires to represent 0's and 1's
- 1950's: assemblers, macro assemblers, FORTRAN, COBOL, LISP
- 1960's: ALGOL, BCPL (-> B -> C), SIMULA
- 1970's: Prolog, ML
- 1980's: C++, Perl, Python
- 1990's: Haskell, Java

Compilation and Interpretation

In a way, a compiler reverts the history of programming languages. What we saw before goes from a "1960's" source language:

5 + 6 * 7

to a "1950's" assembly language

push 5 push 6 push 7 mul add

and further to a "1940's" machine language

0001 0000 0000 0101 0001 0000 0000 0110

0001 0000 0000 0111 0110 1000 0110 0000

The second step is very easy: you just look up the binary codes for each symbol in the assembly language and put them together in the same order. It is sometimes not regarded as a part of compilation proper, but as a separate level of assembly. The main reason for this is purely practical: modern compilers don't need to go all the way to the binary, but just to the assembly language, since there exist assembly programs that can do the rest.

A compiler is a program that translates code to some other code. It does not actually run the program. An interpreter does this. Thus a source language expression,

5 + 6 * 7

is by an interpreter turned to its value,

47

This computation can be performed without any translation of the source code into machine code. However, a common practice is in fact a combination of compilation and interpretation. For instance, Java programs are, as shown above, compiled into JVM code. This code is then in turn interpreted by a JVM interpreter.

The compilation of Java is different from for instance the way C is translated by GCC (GNU Compiler Collection). GCC compiles C into the native code of each machine, which is just executed, not interpreted. JVM code must be interpreted because it is not executable by any actual machine.

Sometimes a distinctin is made between "compiled languages" and "interpreted languages", C being compiled and Java being interpreted. This is really a misnomer, in two ways. First, any language could have both an interpreter and a compiler. Second, it's not Java that is interpreted by a "Java interpreter", but JVM, a completely different language to which Java is compiled.

Here are some examples of how some known languages are normally treated:

- C is usually compiled to machine code by GCC

- Java is usually compiled to JVM bytecode by Javac, and this bytecode is usually interpreted using JVM

- JavaScript is interpreted in web browsers

- Unix shell scripts are interpreted by the shell

- Haskell programs are either compiled using GHC, or interpreted (via bytecode) using Hugs or GHCI.

Compilation vs. interpretation is one of the important decisions to make when designing and implementing a new language. Here are some trade-offs:

Advantages of interpretation:

- Faster to get going,
- Easier to implement,
- Portable to different machines.

Advantages of compilation:

- If to machine code: the resulting code is faster to execute.
- If to machine-independent target code: the resulting code easier to interpret than the source code

The advent of virtual machines with actual machine language instruction sets, such as VMWare, is blurring the distinction. In general, the best tradeoffs are achieved by combinations of compiler and interpreter components, reusing as much as possible (as we saw is done in the reuse of the assembly phase). This leads us to the following topic: how compilers are divided into separate components.

Compilation Phases

A compiler even for a simple language easily becomes a complex program, which is best attacked by dividing it to smaller components. These components typically address different compilation phases. Each phase is a part of a pipeline, which transforms the code from one format to another. These formats are typically encoded in different data structures: each phase returns a data structure that is easy for the next phase to manipulate.

The following diagram shows the main compiler phases and how a piece of source code travels through them. The code is on the left, the down-going arrows are annotated by the names of the phases, and the data structure is on the right.

```
57+6*result              character string

| lexer

V

57 + 6 * result          token string

| parser

V

(+ 57 (* 6 result))      syntax tree

| type checker

V

([i+] 57 ([i*] 6 [i result]))    annotated syntax tree
```

```
| code generator

v

bipush 57                                    instruction list

bipush 6

iload 8

imul

iadd
```

With some more explaining words:

- The lexer reads a string of characters an chops it into tokens, i.e. to "meaningful words"; the figure represents the token string by putting spaces between tokens.

- The parser reads a string of tokens and groups it into a syntax tree, i.e. to a structure indicating which parts belong together and how; the figure represents the syntax tree by using parentheses.

- The type checker finds out the type of each part of the syntax tree that might have alternative types, and returns an annotated syntax tree; the figure represents the annotations by the letter i ("integer") in square brackets.

- The code generator converts the annotated syntax tree into a list of target code instructions. The figure uses normal JVM assembly code, where imul means integer multiplication, bipush pushing integer bytes, and iload pushing values of integer variables.

We want to point out the role of type checking in particular. In a Java-toJVM compiler it is an indispensable phase in order to perform instruction selection in the code generator. The JVM target language has different instructions for the addition of integers and floats, for instance (iadd vs. dadd), whereas the Java source language uses the same symbol + for both. The type checker analyses the code to find the types of the operands of + to decide whether integer or double addition is needed.

The difference between compilers and interpreters is just in the last phase: interpreters don't generate new code, but execute the old code. However, even then they will need to perform the earlier phases, which are independent of what the last step will be. This is with the exception of the type checker: compilers tend to require more type checking than interpreters, to enable instruction selection. It is no coincidence that untyped languages such as JavaScript and Python tend to be interpreted languages.

Compiler Errors

Each compiler phases has both a positive and a negative side, so to say. The positive side is that it converts the code to something that is more useful for the next phase, e.g. the syntax tree into a type-annotated tree. The negative side is that it may fail, in which case it might report an error to the user.

Each compiler phase has its characteristic errors. Here are some examples:

- Lexer errors, e.g. unclosed quote,

"hello

- Parse errors, e.g. mismatched parentheses,

- Type errors, e.g. the application of a function to an argument of wrong kind,

sort(45)

Errors on later phases are usually not supported. One reason is the principle (by Milner), that "well-typed programs cannot go wrong". This means that if a program passes the type checker it will also work on later phases. Another, more general reason is that the compiler phases can be divided into two groups:

- The front end, which performs analysis, i.e. inspects the program: lexer, parser, type checker.

- The back end, which performs synthesis: code generator.

It is natural that only the front end (analysis) phases look for errors.

A good compiler finds all errors at the earliest occasion. Thereby it saves work: it doesn't try to type check code that has parse errors. It is also more useful for the user, because it can then give error messages that go to the very root of the problem.

Of course, compilers cannot find all errors, for instance, bugs in the program. Errors such as array index out of bounds are another example of such errors. However, in general it is better to find errors at compile time than at run time, and this is one aspect in which compilers are constantly improving. One of the most important lessons of this book will be to understand what is possible to do at compile time and what must be postponed to run time.

A typical example is the binding analysis of variables: if a variable is used in an expression in Java or C, it must have been declared and given a value. For instance, the following function is incorrect in C:

```
int main () {

printf ("%d",x) ;

}
```

What is intuitively a problem, though, is that x has not been given a value. The corresponding function when compiled in Java would give this as an error.

Binding analysis cannot be performed in a parser, but must be done in the type checker. However, the situation is worse than this. Consider the function:

```
int main () {

int x ;

if (x!=0) x = 1 ;

 printf ("%d",x) ;

}
```

Here x gets a value under a condition. It may be that this condition is impossible to decide at compile time. Hence it is not decidable at compile time if x has a value—neither in the parser, nor in the type checker.

More Compiler Phases

The compiler phases discussed above are the main phases. There can be many more—here are a couple of examples:

1. Desugaring/normalization: remove syntactic sugar, i.e. language constructs that are there to make the language more convenient for programmers, without adding to the expressive power. Such constructs can be removed early in compilation, so that the later phases don't need to deal with them. An example is multiple declarations, which can be reduced to sequences of single declarations:

```
int i, j ; ---> int i ; int j ;
```

Desugaring is normally done at the syntax tree level, and it can be inserted as a phase between parsing and type checking. A disadvantage can be, however, that errors arising in type checking then refer to code that the programmer has never written herself, but that has been created by desugaring.

2. Optimizations: improve the code in some respect. This can be done on many different levels. For instance, source code optimization may precompute values known at compile time:

```
i = 2 + 2 ;                  ---> i = 4 ;
```

Target code optimization may replace instructions with cheaper ones:

```
bipush 31 ; bipush 31 ---> bipush 31 ; dup
```

Here the second bipush 31 is replaced by dup, which duplicates the top of the stack. The gain is that the dup instruction is just one byte, whereas bipush 31 is two bytes.

Modern compilers may have dozens of phases. For instance, GCC has several optimization phases performed on the level of intermediate code. This code is neither the source nor the target code, but something in between. The advantage is that the optimization phases can be combined with different source and target languages, to make these components reusable.

Theory and Practice

The complex task of compiler writing is greatly helped by the division into phases. Each phase is simple enough to be understood properly; and implementations of different phases can be recombined to new compilers. But there is yet another aspect: many of the phases have a clean mathematical theory, which applies to that phase. The following table summarizes those theories:

phase	theory
lexer	finite automata
parser	context-free grammars
type checker	type systems
interpreter	operational semantics
code generator	compilation schemes

The theories provide declarative notations for each of the phases, so that they can be specified in clean ways, independently of implementatiotion and usually much more concisely. They will also enable reasoning about the compiler components. For instance, the way parsers are written by means of context-free grammars can be used for guaranteeing that the language is unambiguous, that is, that each program can be compiled in a unique way.

Syntax-directed translation is a common name for the techniques used in type checkers, interpreters, and code generators alike. We will see that these techniques have so much in common that, once you learn how to implement a type checker, the other components are easy variants of this.

The Scope of the Techniques

The techniques of compiler construction are by no means restricted to the traditional task of translating programming language to machine language. The target of the translation can also be another programming language—for instance, the Google Web Toolkit is a compiler from Java into JavaScript, enabling the construction of web applications in a higher-level and typechecked language.

Actually, the modular way in which modern compilers are built implies that it is seldom necessary to go all the way to the machine code (or assembler), even if this is the target. A popular way of building native code compilers is via a translation to C. As soon as C code is reached, the compiler for the new language is complete.

The modularity of compilers also enables the use of compiler components to other tasks, such as debuggers, documentation systems, and code analysis of different kinds. But there is still a very good reason to learn the whole chain from source language to machine language: it will help you to decide which phases your task resembles the most, and thereby which techniques are the most useful ones to apply.

Important Programming Languages

Java

Java is a general-purpose computer programming language that is concurrent, class-based, object-oriented, and specifically designed to have as few implementation dependencies as possible. It is intended to let application developers "write once, run anywhere" (WORA), meaning that compiled Java code can run on all platforms that support Java without the need for recompilation.

For example, you can write and compile a Java program on UNIX and run it on Microsoft Windows, Macintosh, or UNIX machine without any modifications to the source code. WORA is achieved by compiling a Java program into an intermediate language called bytecode. The format of bytecode is platform-independent. A virtual machine, called the Java Virtual Machine (JVM), is used to run the bytecode on each platform.

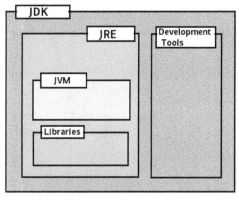

JDK vs JRE vs JVM

Java was originally developed by James Gosling at Sun Microsystems (which has since been acquired by Oracle Corporation) and released in 1995 as a core component of Sun Microsystems' Java platform. The language derives much of its syntax from C and C++, but it has fewer low-level facilities than either of them.

Oracle Corporation is the current owner of the official implementation of the Java SE platform, following their acquisition of Sun Microsystems on January 27, 2010. This implementation is based on the original implementation of Java by Sun. The Oracle implementation is available for Microsoft Windows, Mac OS X, Linux and Solaris.

The Oracle implementation is packaged into two different distributions:

- Java Runtime Environment (JRE) which contains the parts of the Java SE platform required to run Java programs and is intended for end users.

- Java Development Kit (JDK) which is intended for software developers and includes development tools such as the Java compiler, Javadoc, Jar, and a debugger.

Garbage Collection

Java uses an automatic garbage collector to manage memory in the object lifecycle. The programmer determines when objects are created, and the Java runtime is responsible for recovering the memory once objects are no longer in use. Once no references to an object remain, the unreachable memory becomes eligible to be freed automatically by the garbage collector.

Something similar to a memory leak may still occur if a programmer's code holds a reference to an object that is no longer needed, typically when objects that are no longer needed are stored in containers that are still in use. If methods for a nonexistent object are called, a "NullPointerException" is thrown.

Garbage collection may happen at any time. Ideally, it will occur when a program is idle. It is guaranteed to be triggered if there is insufficient free memory on the heap to allocate a new object; this can cause a program to stall momentarily. Explicit memory management is not possible in Java.

Java Hello World Program

The traditional "Hello, world!" program can be written in Java as:

HelloWorldApplication.java

```
public class HelloWorldApplication {

    public static void main(String[] args) {

        System.out.println("Hello World!");       // Prints Hello World! to the
console.

    }

}
```

Java Class File

- Java source files must be named after the public class they contain, appending the suffix .java, for example, HelloWorldApplication.java.

- It must first be compiled into bytecode, using a Java compiler, producing a file named HelloWorldApplication.class. Only then can it be executed, or 'launched'.

- The Java source file may only contain one public class, but it can contain multiple classes with other than public access and any number of public inner classes.

- When the source file contains multiple classes, make one class 'public' and name the source file with that public class name.

C

C is a general-purpose programming language that is extremely popular, simple and flexible. It is machine-independent, structured programming language which is used extensively in various applications.

C was the basics language to write everything from operating systems (Windows and many others) to complex programs like the Oracle database, Git, Python interpreter and more.

Language Rank	Types	Spectrum Ranking
1. Python	⊕ 🖥 ▮	100.0
2. C++	▯ 🖥 ▮	99.7
3. Java	⊕ ▯ 🖥	97.5
4. C	▯ 🖥 ▮	96.7
5. C#	⊕ ▯ 🖥	89.4
6. PHP	⊕	84.9
7. R	🖥	82.9
8. JavaScript	⊕ ▯	82.6
9. Go	⊕ 🖥	76.4
10. Assembly	▮	74.1

IEEE-the best 10 top programming language in 2018

It is said that 'C' is a god's programming language. One can say, C is a base for the programming. If you know 'C,' you can easily grasp the knowledge of the other programming languages that uses the concept of 'C'.

It is essential to have a background in computer memory mechanisms because it is an important aspect when dealing with the C programming language.

The base or father of programming languages is 'ALGOL.' It was first introduced in 1960. 'ALGOL' was used on a large basis in European countries. 'ALGOL' introduced the concept of structured programming to the developer community. In 1967, a new computer programming language was announced called as 'BCPL' which stands for Basic Combined Programming Language. BCPL was designed and developed by Martin Richards, especially for writing system software. This was the era of programming languages. Just after three years, in 1970 a new programming language called 'B' was introduced by Ken Thompson that contained multiple features of 'BCPL.' This programming language was created using UNIX operating system at AT&T and Bell Laboratories. Both the 'BCPL' and 'B' were system programming languages.

In 1972, a great computer scientist Dennis Ritchie created a new programming language called 'C' at the Bell Laboratories. It was created from 'ALGOL', 'BCPL' and 'B' programming languages. 'C' programming language contains all the features of these languages and many more additional concepts that make it unique from other languages.

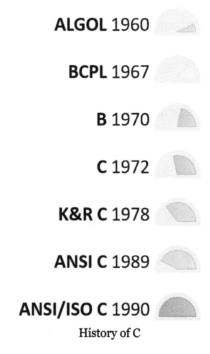

ALGOL 1960

BCPL 1967

B 1970

C 1972

K&R C 1978

ANSI C 1989

ANSI/ISO C 1990

History of C

'C' is a powerful programming language which is strongly associated with the UNIX operating system. Even most of the UNIX operating system is coded in 'C'. Initially 'C' programming was limited to the UNIX operating system, but as it started spreading around the world, it became commercial, and many compilers were released for cross-platform systems. Today 'C' runs under a variety of operating systems and hardware platforms. As it started evolving many different versions of the language were released. At times it became difficult for the developers to keep up with the latest version as the systems were running under the older versions. To assure that 'C' language will remain standard, American National Standards Institute (ANSI) defined a commercial standard for 'C' language in 1989. Later, it was approved by the International Standards Organization (ISO) in 1990. 'C' programming language is also called as 'ANSI C'.

Languages such as C++/Java are developed from 'C'. These languages are widely used in various technologies. Thus, 'C' forms a base for many other languages that are currently in use.

Key Applications

- 'C' language is widely used in embedded systems.

- It is used for developing system applications.

- It is widely used for developing desktop applications.

- Most of the applications by Adobe are developed using 'C' programming language.

- It is used for developing browsers and their extensions. Google's Chromium is built using 'C' programming language.

- It is used to develop databases. MySQL is the most popular database software which is built using 'C'.

- It is used in developing an operating system. Operating systems such as Apple's OS X, Microsoft's Windows, and Symbian are developed using 'C' language. It is used for developing desktop as well as mobile phone's operating system.

- It is used for compiler production.

- It is widely used in IOT applications.

Reason behind 'C' Learning

As we studied earlier, 'C' is a base language for many programming languages. So, learning 'C' as the main language will play an important role while studying other programming languages. It shares the same concepts such as data types, operators, control statements and many more. 'C' can be used widely in various applications. It is a simple language and provides faster execution. There are many jobs available for a 'C' developer in the current market.

'C' is a structured programming language in which program is divided into various modules. Each module can be written separately and together it forms a single 'C' program. This structure makes it easy for testing, maintaining and debugging processes.

'C' contains 32 keywords, various data types and a set of powerful built-in functions that make programming very efficient.

Another feature of 'C' programming is that it can extend itself. A 'C' program contains various functions which are part of a library. We can add our features and functions to the library. We can access and use these functions anytime we want in our program. This feature makes it simple while working with complex programming.

Various compilers are available in the market that can be used for executing programs written in this language.

It is a highly portable language which means programs written in 'C' language can run on other machines. This feature is essential if we wish to use or execute the code on another computer.

Working of 'C'

C is a compiled language. A compiler is a special tool that compiles the program and converts it into the object file which is machine readable. After the compilation process, the linker will combine different object files and creates a single executable file to run the program. The following diagram shows the execution of a 'C' program

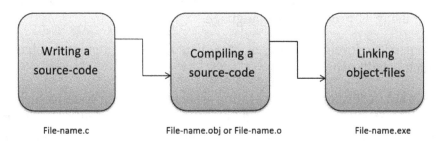

Nowadays, various compilers are available online, and you can use any of those compilers. The functionality will never differ and most of the compilers will provide the features required to execute both 'C' and 'C++' programs.

Following is the list of popular compilers available online:

- Clang compiler
- MinGW compiler (Minimalist GNU for Windows)
- Portable 'C' compiler
- Turbo C

C++

C++ is a high-level object-oriented programming language that helps programmers write fast, portable programs. C++ provides rich library support in the form of Standard Template Library (STL).

C++ Language Features

Some of the interesting features of C++ are:

- Object-oriented: C++ is an object-oriented programming language. This means that the focus is on "objects" and manipulations around these objects. Information about how these manipulations work is abstracted out from the consumer of the object.

- Rich library support: Through C++ Standard Template Library (STL) many functions are available that help in quickly writing code. For instance, there are standard libraries for various containers like sets, maps, hash tables, etc.

- Speed: C++ is the preferred choice when latency is a critical metric. The compilation, as well as the execution time of a C++ program, is much faster than most other general purpose programming languages.

- Compiled: A C++ code has to be first compiled into low-level code and then executed, unlike interpreted programming languages where no compilation is needed.

- Pointer Support: C++ also supports pointers which are widely used in programming and are often not available in several programming languages.

It is one of the most important programming languages because almost all the programs/systems that you use have some or the other part of the codebase that is written in C/C++. Be it Windows, be it the photo editing software, be it your favorite game, be it your web browser, C++ plays an integral role in almost all applications that we use.

Uses/Applications of C++ Language

After exploring C++ features, let's have look at some interesting areas where C++ is popularly used.

Operating Systems

Be it Microsoft Windows or Mac OSX or Linux – all of them are programmed in C++. C/C++ is the backbone of all the well-known operating systems owing to the fact that it is a strongly typed and a fast programming language which makes it an ideal choice for developing an operating system. Moreover, C is quite close to the assembly language which further helps in writing low-level operating system modules.

Browsers

The rendering engines of various web browsers are programmed in C++ simply because if the speed that it offers. The rendering engines require faster execution to make sure that users don't have to wait for the content to come up on the screen. As a result, such low-latency systems employ C++ as the programming language.

Libraries

Many high-level libraries use C++ as the core programming language. For instance, several Machine Learning libraries use C++ in the backend because of its speed. Tensorflow, one of the most widely used Machine Learning libraries uses C++ as the backend programming language. Such libraries required high-performance computations because they involve multiplications of huge matrices for the purpose of training Machine Learning models. As a result, performance becomes critical. C++ comes to the rescue in such libraries.

Graphics

All graphics applications require fast rendering and just like the case of web browsers, here also C++ helps in reducing the latency. Software that employ computer vision, digital image processing, high-end graphical processing – they all use C++ as the backend programming language. Even the popular games that are heavy on graphics use C++ as the primary programming language. The speed that C++ offers in such situations helps the developers in expanding the target audience because an optimized application can run even on low-end devices that do not have high computation power available.

Banking Applications

One of the most popularly used core-banking system – Infosys Finacle uses C++ as one of the backend programming languages. Banking applications process millions of transactions on a daily basis and require high concurrency and low latency support. C++ automatically becomes the preferred choice in such applications owing to its speed and multithreading support that is made available through various Standard Template Libraries that come as a part of the C++ programming kit.

Cloud/Distributed Systems

Large organizations that develop cloud storage systems and other distributed systems also use C++ because it connects very well with the hardware and is compatible with a lot of machines. Cloud storage systems use scalable file-systems that work close to the hardware. C++ becomes a preferred choice in such situations because it is close to the hardware and also the multithreading libraries in C++ provide high concurrency and load tolerance which is very much needed in such scenarios.

Databases

Postgres and MySQL – two of the most widely used databases are written in C++ and C, the precursor to C++. These databases are used in almost all of the well-known applications that we all use in our day to day life – Quora, YouTube, etc.

Embedded Systems

Various embedded systems like medical machines, smartwatches, etc. use C++ as the primary programming language because of the fact that C++ is closer to the hardware level as compared to other high-level programming languages.

Telephone Switches

Because of the fact that it is one of the fastest programming languages, C++ is widely used in programming telephone switches, routers, and space probes.

Compilers

The compilers of various programming languages use C and C++ as the backend programming language. This is because of the fact that both C and C++ are relatively lower level languages and are closer to the hardware and therefore are the ideal choice for such compilation systems.

These are a few uses and applications of C++ programming language. Now, let's know more about C++ advantages over other programming languages.

Advantages of C++ Language

C++ has the following 2 features that make it a preferred choice in most of the applications:

- Speed: C++ is faster than most other programming languages and it provides an excellent concurrency support. This makes it useful in those areas where performance is quite critical and the latency required is very low. Such requirements occur all the time in high-load servers such as web servers, application servers, database servers, etc. C++ plays a key role in such servers.

- Closer to hardware: C++ is closer to hardware than most other programming languages like Python, etc. This makes it useful in those areas where the software is closely coupled with hardware and a low-level support is required at the software level.

Python

In technical terms, Python is an object-oriented, high-level programming language with integrated dynamic semantics primarily for web and app development. It is extremely attractive in the field of Rapid Application Development because it offers dynamic typing and dynamic binding options.

Python is relatively simple, so it's easy to learn since it requires a unique syntax that focuses on readability. Developers can read and translate Python code much easier than other languages. In turn, this reduces the cost of program maintenance and development because it allows teams to work collaboratively without significant language and experience barriers.

Additionally, Python supports the use of modules and packages, which means that programs can be designed in a modular style and code can be reused across a variety of projects. Once you've developed a module or package you need, it can be scaled for use in other projects, and it's easy to import or export these modules.

One of the most promising benefits of Python is that both the standard library and the interpreter are available free of charge, in both binary and source form. There is no exclusivity either, as Python and all the necessary tools are available on all major platforms. Therefore, it is an enticing option for developers who don't want to worry about paying high development costs.

Python is a programming language used to develop software on the web and in app form, including mobile. It's relatively easy to learn, and the necessary tools are available to all free of charge.

That makes Python accessible to almost anyone. If you have the time to learn, you can create some amazing things with the language.

Use of Python

Python is a general-purpose programming language, which is another way to say that it can be used for nearly everything. Most importantly, it is an interpreted language, which means that the written code is not actually translated to a computer-readable format at runtime. Whereas, most programming languages do this conversion before the program is even run. This type of language is also referred to as a "scripting language" because it was initially meant to be used for trivial projects.

The concept of a "scripting language" has changed considerably since its inception, because Python is now used to write large, commercial style applications, instead of just banal ones. This reliance on Python has grown even more so as the internet gained popularity. A large majority of web applications and platforms rely on Python, including Google's search engine, YouTube, and the web-oriented transaction system of the New York Stock Exchange (NYSE). You know the language must be pretty serious when it's powering a stock exchange system.

In fact, NASA actually uses Python when they are programming their equipment and space machinery. Pretty neat, right?

Python can also be used to process text, display numbers or images, solve scientific equations, and save data. In short, it is used behind the scenes to process a lot of elements you might need or encounter on your device(s) - mobile included.

Ruby

Ruby is a pure Object-Oriented language developed by Yukihiro Matsumoto (also known as Matz in the Ruby community) in the mid 1990's in Japan. Everything in Ruby is an object except the blocks but there are replacements too for it i.e procs and lambda. The objective of Ruby's development was to make it act as a sensible buffer between human programmers and the underlying computing machinery. Ruby has similar syntax to that of many programming languages like C and Java, so it is easy for Java and C programmers to learn. It supports mostly all the platforms like Windows, Mac, Linux.

Ruby is based on many other languages like Perl, Lisp, Smalltalk, Eiffel and Ada. It is an interpreted scripting language which means most of its implementations execute instructions directly and freely, without previously compiling a program into machine-language instructions. Ruby programmers also have access to the powerful RubyGems (RubyGems provides a standard format for Ruby programs and libraries).

Beginning with Ruby Programming

1. Finding a Compiler

Before starting programming in Ruby, a compiler is needed to compile and run our programs. There are many online compilers that can be used to start Ruby without installing a compiler:

There are many compilers available freely for compilation of Ruby programs.

2. Programming in Ruby

To program in Ruby is easy to learn because of its similar syntax to already widely used languages.

Writing Program in Ruby

Programs can be written in Ruby in any of the widely used text editors like Notepad++, gedit etc. After writing the programs save the file with the extension .rb

Let's see some basic points of programming:

Comments: To add single line comments in Ruby Program, # (hash) is used.

Syntax:

```
# Comment
```

To add multi-line comments in Ruby, a block of =begin and =end (reserved key words of Ruby) are used.

Syntax:

```
=begin
```

```
Statement 1

Statement 2

...

Statement n

=end
```

Example:

A simple program to print "Hello Geeks!! Welcome to GeeksforGeeks".

Output

In the output screen, it can be seen how a program is made to run on prompt.

First line consist of single line comment with "#" as prefix. Second line consist of the message to printed and puts is used to print the message on the screen.

As everything has some advantages and disadvantages, Ruby also has some advantages along with some disadvantages.

Advantages of Ruby

- The code written in Ruby is small, elegant and powerful as it has fewer number of lines of code.

- Ruby allows simple and fast creation of Web application which results in less hard work.

- As Ruby is free of charge that is Ruby is free to copy, use, modify, it allow programmers to make necessary changes as and when required.

- Ruby is a dynamic programming language due to which there is no tough rules on how to built in features and it is very close to spoken languages.

Disadvantages of Ruby

- Ruby is fairly new and has its own unique coding language which makes it difficult for the programmers to code in it right away but after some practice its easy to use. Many programmers prefer to stick to what they already know and can develop.

- The code written in Ruby is harder to debug, since most of the time it generates at runtime, so it becomes difficult to read while debugging.

- Ruby does not have a plenty of informational resources as compared to other programming languages.

- Ruby is an interpreted scripting language, the scripting languages are usually slower than compiled languages therefore, Ruby is slower than many other languages.

Applications

- Ruby is used to create web applications of different sorts. It is one of the hot technology at present to create web applications.

- Ruby offers a great feature called Ruby on Rails (RoR). It is a web framework that is used by programmers to speed up the development process and save time.

Swift

Swift is a compiled programming language for iOS, macOS, watchOS, tvOS, and Linux applications. Here's what you need to know about Swift.

Created by Apple in 2014. Backed up by one of the most influential tech companies in the world, Swift is set to become the dominant language for iOS development and beyond.

- Open source: Swift creators acknowledged the fact that in order to build a defining programming language, the technology needs to be open for all. So, within its three years of existence, Swift acquired a large supportive community and an abundance of third-party tools.

- Safe: Its syntax encourages you to write clean and consistent code which may even feel strict at times. Swift provides safeguards to prevent errors and improve readability.

- Fast: Swift was built with performance in mind. Not only does its simple syntax and hand-holding help you develop faster, it also lives up to its name: as stated on apple.com, Swift is 2.6x faster than Objective-C and 8.4x faster than Python.

- In demand: As of March 2018, it's 12th most popular language, surpassing Objective-C, Go, Scala, and R. With more than 40K stars on GitHub and 187K StackOverflow questions, this young language is rightfully becoming one of the dominant technologies in the industry.

First introduced at Apple's 2014 Worldwide Developers Conference (WWDC), Swift programming language has generated considerable debate ever since. Chris Lattner, Apple's Senior Director, Developer Tools Department, started designing the basic concepts of the new language back in 2010.

"Initially, it was really just me messing around and nobody knew about it because it wasn't anything to know about. But eventually, it got a little bit more serious. So I started talking to my management and some of the engineers that were working on Clang, and they seemed excited about it. We got a couple people working on it part-time and I convinced my manager that it was interesting enough that we could have a couple of people work on it."

It wasn't until 2013 that the team was able to solve a strategic question about how the new language would fit in with the existing Objective-C ecosystem. Forcing all iOS developers to move to a new language could have had a major disruptive effect on the community. So, the company decided to continue investing in Objective-C while also committing to the development of a new "safe programming language."

One year later, the registered Apple developers were able to lay their hands on the beta version of the new language. In the first month post its release as a part of Xcode tools, it was downloaded over 11 million times, according to Tim Cook.

The initial reactions to Swift were mixed at best. Some developers were delighted with its features, flexibility, and simplicity, while others criticized it. Yet, most of them agreed that it was too early for Swift to be used in production. The language was evolving fast: major changes were introduced with every new release.

This, however, didn't prevent Swift from becoming the "most loved" technology, according to the 2015 StackOverflow Developer Survey.

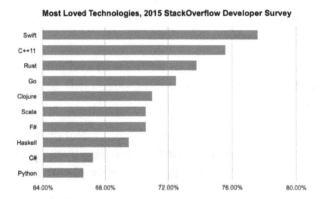

Most loved technologies, 2015 StackOverflow Developer Surve

At the same time, the language was listed among top 10 "most wanted" technologies.

2015 – turning Open Source

Since Apple decided to make Swift an open sourced language in 2015, its growth has been tremendous. Over 60,000 people took a clone of the Swift project in the first week after the announcement. Now, 2 years later, Swift is officially the fastest growing language in history, according to TIOBE Index: The language reached the top 10 in March, 2017.

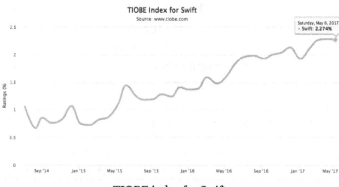

TIOBE index for Swift

Being free and open to all, the language is growing rapidly with rapidly with its last version, Swift 4.0, released September 2017. The language is actively deployed in iOS development, when building desktop apps for OSX, or even as a server-side technology, thanks to IBM.

One of the reasons that Swift has become so popular over such a short period is probably the fact that it was made by Apple. When a company with such global name recognition and a multimillion army of loyal followers does something, the chances are it is doomed for success (or at least good press coverage).

Now, let's take a closer look at the critical benefits and drawbacks that accompany Swift. What should you know about this language? Is it ready to be used in production? What are the risks involved in building a Swift app? We start with advantages that make it the darling of developers.

Pros of Using Swift for iOS Native Development

Often referred to as "Objective-C, without the C," Swift language is in many aspects superior to its predecessor. According to the official press release, "Swift combines the performance and efficiency of compiled languages with the simplicity and interactivity of popular scripting languages." Leaving technology details and marketing aside, let's see what it really means from a business perspective.

Rapid Development Process

A clean and expressive language with a simplified syntax and grammar, Swift is easier to read and write. It is very concise, which means less code is required to perform the same task, as compared to Objective-C. Automatic Reference Counting (ARC) does all the work tracking and managing the app's memory usage, so developers don't need to spend time and effort doing that manually. Accordingly, it usually takes less time to build iOS apps with Swift.

A shining example of this advantage is the new Lyft app: The company completely rewrote its iOS app using Swift. While the old codebase consisted of about 75,000 lines of code, the Swift version recreated the same functionality with less than a third of that. Moreover, the app now featured a new onboarding process: While the old one took more than a month and multiple engineers to implement, the new onboarding with Swift was completed within a week with only one engineer.

Easier to Scale the Product and the Team

In addition to faster development time, you get a product that is future-proof and can be extended with new features as needed. Thus, Swift projects are typically easier to scale. The fact that Apple is more likely to support Swift than Objective-C should also get serious consideration for long-term investment.

Moreover, Swift allows you to add more developers to your team if needed: The onboarding is relatively fast due to the simplicity and conciseness of the codebase.

Improved Safety and Performance

As suggested by its name, Swift is made to be well, swift. With a focus on performance and speed, the language was initially designed to outperform its predecessor. Namely, the initial release claimed a 40 percent increase in performance, as compared to Objective-C. Over the years, multiple benchmarks and tests conducted by individual developers have proved that. Moreover, there are many ways to optimize Swift code for even better performance.

Apple WWDC 2014 Presentation

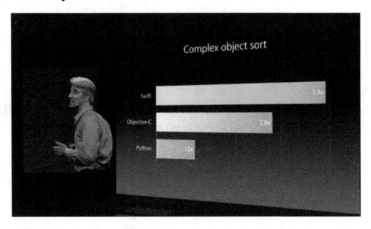

Another of Swift's strengths is its safety. Its strong typing system and error handling prevents code crashes and errors in production. Thus, Swift has a shorter feedback loop, allowing you to see the errors in the code instantly and fix them on the fly, greatly reducing the time and effort needed for bug fixing and eliminating the risks of deploying low quality code.

Decreased Memory Footprint

When you build an app, you use a lot of third-party code – reusable and often open source frameworks or libraries compiled into your app's code. These libraries can be static and dynamic (or shared). Swift first introduced dynamic libraries to iOS when it launched. You can probably guess that static libraries are locked into code at the time you compiled them, become the part of your executable file, thus increasing its size and load time. They also can't be automatically updated since they're stuck in the version you compiled at. Dynamic libraries, on the other hand, exist outside of your code and are uploaded only when needed. Static libraries need to have copies in all files of your program while dynamic ones only need one.

Though it takes more time to reach for the dynamic code from the outside than call to it when it's already included, you have a choice to keep using static libraries when you want to isolate apps that are not supposed to be shared.

Interoperability with Objective-C

As Jordan Morgan, iOS developer at Buffer, swift is the new toy and marked as the future. Objective-C is showing its age and will, eventually, be much less prevalent. But in the here and the now, the two must learn to coexist peacefully." Accordingly, there are two possible scenarios for using both in the same project: You either add new features in Swift to the existing Objective-C codebase, or use Objective-C elements in your new Swift project.

Either way, Swift language is perfectly compatible with Objective-C and can be used interchangeably within the same project. This is especially useful for large projects that are being extended or updated: You can still add more features with Swift, taking advantage of the existing Objective-C codebase. Thus, the porting process becomes easier and more risk-free.

Automatic Memory Management

Swift uses Automatic Memory Counting (ARC) – a technology aimed to add a garbage collector function that wasn't introduced to iOS before. Languages like Java, C#, and Go use garbage collectors to delete class instances that are no longer used. They are useful to decrease your memory footprint but can add up to 20 percent to CPU. Before ARC, iOS developers had to manage memory manually and constantly manage retain counts of every class. Swift's ARC determines which instances are no longer in use and gets rid of them on your behalf. It allows you to increase your app's performance without lagging your memory or CPU.

Full Stack Potential and Cross-device Support

Actively pushed forward by IBM, the initiative to put the language in the cloud has been pretty successful so far. Server-side Swift integrates with most of the popular backend technologies. Just like in full stack Javascript development, using Swift on both back-end and frontend of your app allows for extensive code sharing and reuse, speeding up the development process and reducing development efforts.

Moreover, Swift provides out-of-the-box support not only for iPhones and iPads, but for all Apple devices, including Apple TV, Apple Watch, and Mac. Aside from that, there is already support for Linux, and an intention to officially port it to the Windows platform. There were even some rumors that Google will drop Java in favor of Swift as a first-class language for Android development. However, the recent announcement from Google I/O shows that Kotlin is the future of Android.

Vibrant Open Source Community and Learnability

The next version of the language, Swift 5.0, will launch in late 2018, and many of the expecting features will solve most current issues such as callback-heavy code and problematic Cocoa SDK integration – Apple's API originally created for Objective-C. The company's persistent work towards making Swift not only the main language for all Apple devices, but also for building web servers, Linux, and Android applications, proves that it will become one of the most popular technologies on the market.

As Apple's Senior VP of Software Engineering, Craig Federighi, mentioned "We saw open sourcing as a critical element to make Swift reach its potential to be the language, the major language for the next 20 years of programming in our industry."

Indeed, with the strong corporate support from Apple and IBM, Swift has quickly gained one of the most active and vibrant open source communities. The adoption trends, mentioned earlier are the case in point. Besides, Swift is currently the most starred language on GitHub, followed by Google's Go.

For such a young language, Swift sure has an abundance of resources to help developers accelerate adoption. Apart from official e-books, there are tons of community guidelines, podcasts, online and even real-life courses, third-party apps, and of course Swift Playgrounds – a gamified learning experiences from Apple.

The Cons of Swift Programming Language

While there seem to be so many reasons to love Swift, the language is still far from perfect. Many developers and business owners are overly cautious when it comes to switching to the new language. There are several reasons for that.

The Language is still Quite Young

Swift might be the fastest and most powerful language in the world, but still too young. It has many issues that need to be addressed and "growing pains" to experience. After all, three years is too little time for any language to mature, even if it is Swift.

Moreover, Swift still has a very limited number of "native" libraries and tools: Many of the available resources and tools dedicated to earlier Swift versions are useless with the newer releases.

Swift is Considered a "Moving Target"

That said, it follows that Swift is often considered to be unstable due to the major changes that are introduced with every new release. One of the key problems articulated by many developers is the lack of backward compatibility with the older language versions. Consequently, developers are forced to completely rewrite their projects if they want to switch to the latest Swift version.

While Xcode provides a tool to help developers update their Swift code to newer versions, it doesn't fix all the issues. Thus, porting your project to a newer Swift version can be time consuming and costly. The latest update of Xcode IDE along with Swift 4.0 have partially solved this problem by supporting all versions starting from Swift 3.2. You can also compile each target separately in case some third-party libraries haven't updated yet. Though you'll still have to do some manual updating to your code – Apple's SDK has gone through some changes too. If you have a very large project or a project that you don't plan to update too often, Swift might be not the best option for you, at least for now.

Limited Talent Pool

While the Swift community is growing fast, it is still significantly smaller as compared to any other open source language. According to the latest StackOverflow Developer Survey, only 8.1 percent of the 78,000 respondents use Swift. At the same time, Upwork.com, a global freelance marketplace, finds that the demand for Swift programmers is growing, which might result in a talent gap.

While there are not many Swift developers out there, even fewer of them have decent hands-on experience with the language. There is probably only one person who has such experience with Swift, but Tesla already snagged that player for their roster.

Poor Interoperability with Third-party Tools and IDEs

Largely due to frequent updates and lacking backward compatibility, as mentioned above, it is often hard to find the right tools to help with the certain tasks. Moreover, the official Apple IDE, XCode, lags in terms of tooling and support for Swift. Developers often report issues with syntax highlighting, autocomplete, refactoring tools, and compilers.

Lack of Support for Earlier iOS Versions

You can only use Swift in the apps that target iOS7 and later. That said, Swift can't be used for legacy projects running on older versions of the operating system.

However, per recent research, less than 5% of Apple devices currently run on iOS6 or earlier.

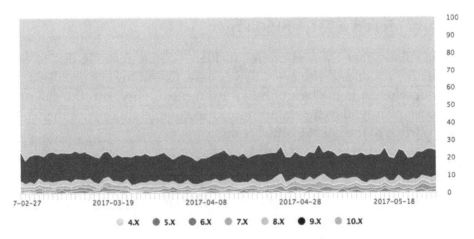

IDEs to be used with Swift

IDE (Integrated Development Environment) is the main point of the interaction with the language.

- Xcode: As mentioned above, working with Swift using the native Apple IDE Xcode isn't always the best choice. In most cases, Xcode will be enough for Swift engineering. It has a convenient interface, autocompletion support, and many other feature that make Swift engineering smooth. However, if you also need to use HTML, CSS, and JavaScript, Xcode will turn into a simple text editor lacking instruments available with Objective-C and Swift.

- Atom: Atom text editor and IDE was created by GitHub. It shines if you combine plain iOS development with other platforms and languages. While Atom itself is basic, it has a great number of open source packages built by the GitHub community which will allow you to customize the IDE for cross-platform and versatile development with autocompletion, advanced navigation, and other useful features.

- AppCode: This IDE for iOS and macOS developers was designed by JetBrains. The product is aimed at improving development performance by providing some refactoring tools similar to those available in Android Studio. And this perhaps is one of the main reasons why you might consider AppCode over Xcode. Unfortunately, AppCode still has limited functionality with Swift compared to Xcode, lacking storyboards, app validation, and submission. On top of that, AppCode comes with a subscription fee.

While you can also consider Visual Studio and some other IDEs for Swift these three are on the list to check first as each one of them provides unique benefits of working with this language.

Comparing Objective-C and Swift

A big part of making a choice between programming languages is your team's experience and programming preferences. If you have developers skilled at Objective-C, having them all migrate to Swift may not be an option. Let's unpack in which cases you might want to stick with Objective-C over Swift.

Old OS Versions Support

Being a new language, Swift supports only iOS 7 and macOS 10.9 or higher. If you have a reason to build apps that should run on older versions, you don't have other choice rather than using Objective-C.

Tight Deadlines

Learning a language, even a simple one like Swift, takes time and effort that many projects lack. If you don't have a luxury of postponing your app release until members of your team get comfortable with Swift, you should consider sticking to ObjC. In case the time allows, learning Swift would definitely be beneficial in the long run, considering that Apple doesn't plan to stop its development.

Big Project Size

Swift is young, which is why smaller apps can get around updates much easier. We mentioned that rewriting your program with each version release may be a struggle, so until this issue is fully fixed, you wouldn't want to risk long lists of changes.

Using C or C++ Third-party Frameworks

Being a superset of C, Objective-C allows you to comfortably and smoothly use C and C++ libraries. While the need to exclusively import C++ files is a rare case, you should be aware that Swift doesn't have that supported.

Object Oriented Programming

Object Oriented programming is a programming style which is associated with the concepts like class, object, Inheritance, Encapsulation, Abstraction, Polymorphism. Most popular programming languages like Java, C++, C#, Ruby, etc. follow an object-oriented programming paradigm. As Java being the most sought-after skill, we will talk about object-oriented programming concepts in Java. An object-based application in Java is based on declaring classes, creating objects from them and interacting between these objects.

Object Oriented Programming: Inheritance

In OOP, computer programs are designed in such a way where everything is an object that interact with one another. Inheritance is one such concept where the properties of one class can be inherited by the other. It helps to reuse the code and establish a relationship between different classes.

Inheritance - object oriented programming - Edureka

As we can see in the image, a child inherits the properties from his father. Similarly, in Java, there are two classes:

1. Parent class (Super or Base class)

2. Child class (Subclass or Derived class)

A class which inherits the properties is known as Child Class whereas a class whose properties are inherited is known as Parent class.

Inheritance is further classified into 4 types:

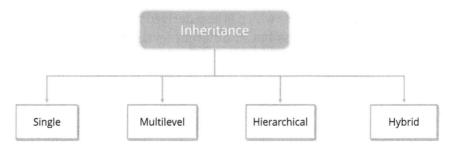

So let's begin with the first type of inheritance i.e. Single Inheritance:

Single Inheritance

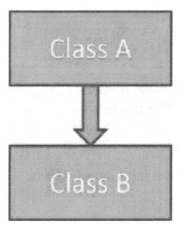

In single inheritance, one class inherits the properties of another. It enables a derived class to inherit the properties and behavior from a single parent class. This will in turn enable code reusability as well as add new features to the existing code.

Here, Class A is your parent class and Class B is your child class which inherits the properties and behavior of the parent class.

Let's see the syntax for single inheritance:

```
1              Class A
2                 {
3                 ---
4                 }
5          Class B extends A {
6                 ---
7                 }
```

Multilevel Inheritance

When a class is derived from a class which is also derived from another class, i.e. a class having more than one parent class but at different levels, such type of inheritance is called Multilevel Inheritance.

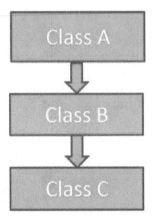

If we talk about the flowchart, class B inherits the properties and behavior of class A and class C inherits the properties of class B. Here A is the parent class for B and class B is the parent class for C. So in this case class C implicitly inherits the properties and methods of class A along with Class B. That's what is multilevel inheritance.

Let's see the syntax for multilevel inheritance in Java:

```
1           Class A{
2              ---
3                 }
4     Class B extends A{
5              ---
6                 }
7     Class C extends B{
8              ---
9                 }
```

Hierarchical Inheritance

When a class has more than one child classes (sub classes) or in other words, more than one child classes have the same parent class, then such kind of inheritance is known as hierarchical.

If we talk about the flowchart, Class B and C are the child classes which are inheriting from the parent class i.e Class A.

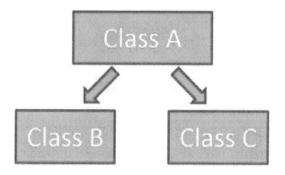

Let's see the syntax for hierarchical inheritance in Java:

```
1          Class A{
2             ---
3              }
4      Class B extends A{
5             ---
6              }
7      Class C extends A{
8             ---
9              }
```

Hybrid Inheritance

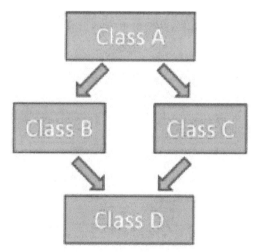

Hybrid inheritance is a combination of multiple inheritance and multilevel inheritance. Since multiple inheritance is not supported in Java as it leads to ambiguity, so this type of inheritance can only be achieved through the use of the interfaces.

If we talk about the flowchart, class A is a parent class for class B and C, whereas Class B and C are the parent class of D which is the only child class of B and C.

Now we have learned about inheritance and their different types. Let's switch to another object oriented programming concept i.e Encapsulation.

Object Oriented Programming : Encapsulation

Encapsulation is a mechanism where you bind your data and code together as a single unit. It also means to hide your data in order to make it safe from any modification. What does this mean? The best way to understand encapsulation is to look at the example of a medical capsule, where the drug is always safe inside the capsule. Similarly, through encapsulation the methods and variables of a class are well hidden and safe.

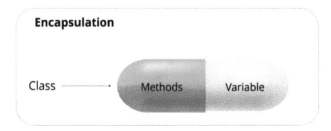

We can achieve encapsulation in Java by:

- Declaring the variables of a class as private.

- Providing public setter and getter methods to modify and view the variables values.

Let us look at the code below to get a better understanding of encapsulation:

```
1        public class Employee {
2            private String name;
3        public String getName() {
4                return name;
5                    }
6        public void setName(String name) {
7                this.name = name;
8                    }
9        public static void main(String[]
                    args) {
10                    }
11                }
```

Let us try to understand the above code. I have created a class Employee which has a private variable name. We have then created a getter and setter methods through which we can get and set the name of an employee. Through these methods, any class which wishes to access the name variable has to do it using these getter and setter methods.

Let's move forward to our third Object-oriented programming concept i.e. Abstraction.

Object Oriented Programming : Abstraction

Abstraction refers to the quality of dealing with ideas rather than events. It basically deals with hiding the details and showing the essential things to the user. If you look at the image here, whenever we get a call, we get an option to either pick it up or just reject it. But in reality, there is a lot of code that runs in the background. So you don't know the internal processing of how a call is generated, that's the beauty of abstraction. Therefore, abstraction helps to reduce complexity. You can achieve abstraction in two ways:

a) Abstract Class

b) Interface

Let's understand these concepts in more detail.

1. Abstract class: Abstract class in Java contains the 'abstract' keyword. Now what does the abstract keyword mean? If a class is declared abstract, it cannot be instantiated, which means you cannot create an object of an abstract class. Also, an abstract class can contain abstract as well as concrete methods.

To use an abstract class, you have to inherit it from another class where you have to provide implementations for the abstract methods there itself, else it will also become an abstract class.

Let's look at the syntax of an abstract class:

```
1      Abstract class Mobile {    // abstract class mobile
2          Abstract void run();      // abstract method
```

2. Interface: Interface in Java is a blueprint of a class or you can say it is a collection of abstract methods and static constants. In an interface, each method is public and abstract but it does not contain any constructor. Along with abstraction, interface also helps to achieve multiple inheritance in Java.

So an interface basically is a group of related methods with empty bodies. Let us understand interfaces better by taking an example of a 'ParentCar' interface with its related methods.

```
1            public interface ParentCar {
2        public void changeGear ( int newValue);
3         public void speedUp(int increment);
4        public void applyBrakes(int decrement);
5                         }
```

These methods need be present for every car, right? But their working is going to be different.

Let's say you are working with manual car, there you have to increment the gear one by one, but if you are working with an automatic car, that time your system decides how to change gear with respect to speed. Therefore, not all my subclasses have the same logic written for change gear. The same case is for speedup, now let's say when you press an accelerator, it speeds up at the rate of 10kms or 15kms. But suppose, someone else is driving a super car, where it increment by 30kms or 50kms. Again the logic varies. Similarly for applybrakes, where one person may have powerful brakes, other may not.

Since all the functionalities are common with all our subclasses, we have created an interface 'ParentCar' where all the functions are present. After that, we will create a child class which implements this interface, where the definition to all these method varies.

Next, let's look into the functionality as to how you can implement this interface.

So to implement this interface, the name of your class would change to any particular brand of a Car, let's say We'll take an "Audi". To implement the class interface, we will use the 'implement' keyword as seen below:

```
1            public class Audi implements ParentCar {
2                      int speed=0;
3                      int gear=1;
4            public void changeGear ( int value){
5                      gear=value;
6                         }
7            public void speedUp ( int increment)
8                         {
9                 speed=speed+increment;
10                        }
11           public void applyBrakes(int decrement)
12                        {
13                speed=speed-decrement;
```

```
14
                    void printStates(){
15
      System.out.println("speed:"+speed+"gear:"+gear);
16
                            }
17
        public static void main(String[] args) {
18
            // TODO Auto-generated method stub
19
                Audi A6= new Audi();
20
                    A6.speedUp(50);
21
                    A6.printStates();
22
                    A6.changeGear(4);
23
                    A6.SpeedUp(100);
24
                    A6.printStates();
25
                        }
26
                        }
27
```

Here as you can see, we have provided functionalities to the different methods we have declared in my interface class. Implementing an interface allows a class to become more formal about the behavior it promises to provide. You can create another class as well, say for example BMW class which can inherit the same interface 'car' with different functionalities.

Finally, the last Object oriented programming concept is Polymorphism.

Object Oriented Programming : Polymorphism

Polymorphism means taking many forms, where 'poly' means many and 'morph' means forms. It is the ability of a variable, function or object to take on multiple forms. In other words, polymorphism allows you define one interface or method and have multiple implementations.

Let's understand this by taking a real-life example and how this concept fits into Object oriented programming.

Let's consider this real world scenario in cricket, we know that there are different types of bowlers i.e. Fast bowlers, Medium pace bowlers and spinners. As you can see in the above figure, there is a parent class- BowlerClass and it has three child classes: FastPacer, MediumPacer and Spinner. Bowler class has bowlingMethod() where all the child classes are inheriting this method. As we all know that a fast bowler will going to bowl differently as compared to medium pacer and spinner in terms of bowling speed, long run up and way of bowling, etc. Similarly a medium pacer's implementation of bowlingMethod() is also going to be different as compared to other bowlers. And same happens with spinner class.

The point of above discussion is simply that a same name tends to multiple forms. All the three classes above inherited the bowlingMethod() but their implementation is totally different from one another.

Polymorphism in Java is of two types:

- Run time polymorphism

- Compile time polymorphism

Run time polymorphism: In Java, runtime polymorphism refers to a process in which a call to an overridden method is resolved at runtime rather than at compile-time. In this, a reference variable is used to call an overridden method of a superclass at run time. Method overriding is an example of run time polymorphism. Let us look the following code to understand how the method overriding works:

```
1              public Class BowlerClass{
2                  void bowlingMethod()
3                        {
4          System.out.println(" bowler ");
5                        }
6                  public Class FastPacer{
7                  void bowlingMethod()
8                        {
9          System.out.println(" fast bowler ");
10                       }
11      Public static void main(String[] args)
12                       {
```

```
13              FastPacer obj= new FastPacer();
14                  obj.bowlingMethod();
15                          }
16                          }
```

Compile time polymorphism: In Java, compile time polymorphism refers to a process in which a call to an overloaded method is resolved at compile time rather than at run time. Method overloading is an example of compile time polymorphism. Method Overloading is a feature that allows a class to have two or more methods having the same name but the arguments passed to the methods are different. Unlike method overriding, arguments can differ in:

- Number of parameters passed to a method

- Datatype of parameters

- Sequence of datatypes when passed to a method.

Let us look at the following code to understand how the method overloading works:

```
1                   class Adder {
2           Static int add(int a,  int b)
3                           {
4                       return a+b;
5                           }
6       static double add( double a,  double b)
7                           {
8                       return a+b;
9                           }
10
11      public static void main(String args[])
12                           {
13      System.out.println(Adder.add(11,11));
14      System.out.println(Adder.add(12.3,12.6));
15                           }
16                           }
```

References

- What-is-an-algorithm, dsa, tech-interview: cs-fundamentals.com, Retrieved 15 May, 2019

- What-is-a-computer-algorithm: howstuffworks.com, Retrieved 13 January, 2019

- Algorithm-definition: edrawsoft.com, Retrieved 2 June, 2019

- What-is-algorithm-design: computersciencedegreehub.com, Retrieved 9 August, 2019

- Daa-algorithm-design-techniques: javatpoint.com, Retrieved 10 February, 2019

- Algorithm Representation, Static: dragonwins.com, Retrieved 8 July, 2019

- Steps-to-implementing-an-algorithm: tylermcginnis.com, Retrieved 27 January, 2019

- Alganalysis: lmu.edu, Retrieved 22 May, 2019

- Introduction-to-programming-languages: geeksforgeeks.org, Retrieved 26 March, 2019

- Programming-language, jargon: computerhope.com, Retrieved 19 July, 2019

- What-is-java-programming-language, basics, java: howtodoinjava.com, Retrieved 24 April, 2019

- C-programming-language: guru99.com, Retrieved 12 June, 2019

- Features-uses-applications-of-c-plus-plus-language: hackr.io, Retrieved 5 February, 2019

- What-is-python, learn-python: pythonforbeginners.com, Retrieved 29 August, 2019

- Ruby-programming-language: geeksforgeeks.org, Retrieved 9 May, 2019

- The-good-and-the-bad-of-swift-programming-language, engineering: altexsoft.com, Retrieved 31 July, 2019

- Object-oriented-programming: edureka.co, Retrieved 18 March, 2019

6

Data Structures and Databases

A data organization, management and storage format that facilitates efficient access and modification is known as a data structure. It provides a means to manage large amounts of data such as large databases and internet indexing services for various uses. An organized collection of data that is generally stored and accessed electronically from a computer system is termed as database. The topics elaborated in this chapter will help in gaining a better perspective about computer databases and data structures.

Data Structures

At the backbone of every program or piece of software are two entities: data and algorithms. Algorithms transform data into something a program can effectively use. Therefore, it is important to understand how to structure data so algorithms can maintain, utilize, and iterate through data quickly.

Data structures are the way we are able to store and retrieve data. You may already be familiar with Python lists and dictionaries, or JavaScript arrays and objects. If so, you know that lists and arrays are sequential with data accessed by index while dictionaries and objects use a named key to store and retrieve information.

The data structures that exist in programming languages are pretty similar to real-world systems that we use outside of the digital sphere. Imagine that you go to the grocery store. At this particular grocery store, the frozen pizza is stored next to the bell peppers and the toothbrushes are next to the milk. The store does not have signs that indicate where different items are located. In this disorganized grocery store, you would have a pretty difficult time trying to find what you were looking for.

Fortunately, most grocery stores have a clear order to the way the store is stocked and laid out. Similarly, data structures provide us with a way to organize information (including other data structures!) in a digital space.

Use of Data Structures

Data structures handle four main functions for us:

- Inputting information
- Processing information

- Maintaining information

- Retrieving information

Inputting is largely concerned with how the data is received. What kind of information can be included? Will the new data be added to the beginning, end, or somewhere in the middle of the existing data? Does an existing point of data need to be updated or destroyed?

Processing gets at the way that data is manipulated in the data structure. This can occur concurrently or as a result of other processes that data structures handle. How does existing data that has been stored need to change to accommodate new, updated, or removed data?

Maintaining is focused on how the data is organized within the structure. Which relationships need to be maintained between pieces of data? How much memory must the system reserve (allocate) to accommodate the data?

Retrieving is devoted to finding and returning the data that is stored in the structure. How can we access that information again? What steps does the data structure need to take to get the information back to us?

Different types and use cases for data will be better suited to different manners of inputting, processing, storing, and retrieving. This is why we have several data structures to choose from and the ability to create our own.

Choosing the Best Data Structure

Your plumber probably would not be the best professional to diagnose an illness and your doctor probably wouldn't be the best person to do your taxes — they are each better suited for other tasks! Similarly, different data structures are better suited for different tasks. Choosing the wrong data structure can result in slow or unresponsive code (and mess up your program!), so it's important to consider a few factors as you make your decision:

1. What is the intended purpose for the data? Do any data structures have built-in functionality that is ideally suited for this purpose? Do you want to search, sort, or iterate data in a way in which certain data structures would be better suited than others?

2. Do you want or need control over how memory is set aside to store your data?

Data structures that use *static memory allocation* (e.g., stacks or arrays) will manage memory for you and assume a fixed amount of memory upon instantiation with a cap on how much data may be added.

Data structures that utilize *dynamic memory allocation* (e.g., heaps or linked lists) allow you to allocate and reallocate memory within the life of the program.

While memory allocation is not something that you'll need to consider in languages like Python or Javascript (these languages will manage memory for you, regardless of which data structure you use), it is something to bear in mind when working in other languages like C.

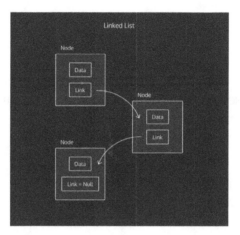

3. How long will it take different data structures to accomplish various tasks relative to other data structures?

Technically, two data structures may both be able to accomplish the same task for you, but one may be quite a bit faster. This consideration, known as runtime will be covered further in depth when you explore all the nifty tricks of asymptotic notation.

As you've seen, data structures are the essential building blocks that we use to organize all of our digital information. Choosing the right data structure allows us to use the algorithms we want and keeps our code running smoothly. Understanding data structures and how to use them well can play a vital role in many situations including:

- Technical interviews in which you may be asked to evaluate and determine runtime for data structures given specific algorithms.

- Day-to-day work for many software engineers who manipulate data stored in structures.

- Data science work where data is stored and accessed through data structures

- A whole lot more.

Types of Data Structures

Anything that can store data can be called as a data structure, hence Integer, Float, Boolean, Char etc, all are data structures. They are known as Primitive Data Structures.

Then we also have some complex Data Structures, which are used to store large and connected data. Some example of Abstract Data Structure(ADT) are :

- Stack

- Queue

- Linked List

- Tree

- Graph

All these data structures allow us to perform different operations on data. We select these data structures based on which type of operation is required.

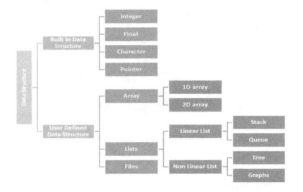

Descriptions:

Linear:

In Linear data structures,the data items are arranged in a linear sequence.

Example: Array

Non-Linear:

In Non-Linear data structures,the data items are not in sequence.

Example: Tree, Graph

Homogeneous:

In homogeneous data structures,all the elements are of same type.

Example: Array

Non-Homogeneous:

In Non-Homogeneous data structure, the elements may or may not be of the same type.

Example: Structures

Static:

Static data structures are those whose sizes and structures associated memory locations are fixed, at compile time.

Example: Array

Dynamic:

Dynamic structures are those which expands or shrinks depending upon the program need and its execution. Also, their associated memory locations changes.

Example: Linked List created using pointers

Array

Arrays are a very simple data structure and may be thought of as a list of a fixed length. Arrays are nice because of their simplicity, and are well suited for situations where the number of data items is known (or can be programmatically determined). Suppose you need a piece of code to calculate the average of several numbers. An array is a perfect data structure to hold the individual values, since they have no specific order, and the required computations do not require any special handling other than to iterate through all of the values. The other big strength of arrays is that they can be accessed randomly, by index. For instance, if you have an array containing a list of names of students seated in a classroom, where each seat is numbered 1 through n, then studentName[i] is a trivial way to read or store the name of the student in seat i.

An array might also be thought of as a pre-bound pad of paper. It has a fixed number of pages, each page holds information, and is in a predefined location that never changes.

Linked Lists

A linked list is a data structure that can hold an arbitrary number of data items and can easily change size to add or remove items. A linked list, at its simplest, is a pointer to a data node. Each data node is then composed of data (possibly a record with several data values), and a pointer to the next node. At the end of the list, the pointer is set to null.

Queues

A queue is a data structure that is best described as "first in, first out". A real-world example of a queue is people waiting in line at the bank. As each person enters the bank, he or she is "enqueued" at the back of the line. When a teller becomes available, they are "dequeued" at the front of the line.

Priority Queues

In a typical breadth-first search (BFS) algorithm, a simple queue works great for keeping track of what states have been visited. Since each new state is one more operational step than the current state, adding new locations to the end of the queue is sufficient to ensure that the quickest path is found first. However, the assumption here is that each operation from one state to the next is a single step.

Stacks

Stacks are, in a sense, the opposite of queues, in that they are described as "last in, first out". The classic example is the pile of plates at the local buffet. The workers can continue to add clean plates to the stack indefinitely, but every time, a visitor will remove from the stack the top plate, which is the last one that was added.

Trees

Trees are a data structure consisting of one or more data nodes. The first node is called the "root", and each node has zero or more "child nodes". The maximum number of children of a single node, and the maximum depth of children are limited in some cases by the exact type of data represented by the tree.

Binary Trees

A special type of tree is a binary tree. A binary tree also happens to be one of the most efficient ways to store and read a set of records that can be indexed by a key value in some way. The idea behind a binary tree is that each node has, at most, two children.

Hash Tables

Hash tables are a unique data structure and are typically used to implement a "dictionary" interface, whereby a set of keys each has an associated value. The key is used as an index to locate the associated values. This is not unlike a classical dictionary, where someone can find a definition (value) of a given word (key).

Database

Database, also called as electronic database, is any collection of data, or information, that is specially organized for rapid search and retrieval by a computer. Databases are structured to facilitate the storage, retrieval, modification, and deletion of data in conjunction with various data-processing operations. A database management system (DBMS) extracts information from the database in response to queries.

A database is stored as a file or a set of files on magnetic disk or tape, optical disk, or some other secondary storage device. The information in these files may be broken down into records, each of which consists of one or more fields. Fields are the basic units of data storage, and each field typically contains information pertaining to one aspect or attribute of the entity described by the database. Records are also organized into tables that include information about relationships between its various fields. Although database is applied loosely to any collection of information in computer files, a database in the strict sense provides cross-referencing capabilities. Using keywords and various sorting commands, users can rapidly search, rearrange, group, and select the fields in many records to retrieve or create reports on particular aggregates of data.

Database records and files must be organized to allow retrieval of the information. Queries are the main way users retrieve database information. The power of a DBMS comes from its ability to define new relationships from the basic ones given by the tables and to use them to get responses to queries. Typically, the user provides a string of characters, and the computer searches the database for a corresponding sequence and provides the source materials in which those characters appear; a user can request, for example, all records in which the contents of the field for a person's last name is the word Smith.

The many users of a large database must be able to manipulate the information within it quickly at any given time. Moreover, large business and other organizations tend to build up many independent files containing related and even overlapping data, and their data-processing activities often require the linking of data from several files. Several different types of DBMS have been developed to support these requirements: flat, hierarchical, network, relational, and object-oriented.

Early systems were arranged sequentially (i.e., alphabetically, numerically, or chronologically); the development of direct-access storage devices made possible random access to data via indexes. In flat databases, records are organized according to a simple list of entities; many simple databases for personal computers are flat in structure. The records in hierarchical databases are organized in a treelike structure, with each level of records branching off into a set of smaller categories. Unlike hierarchical databases, which provide single links between sets of records at different levels, network databases create multiple linkages between sets by placing links, or pointers, to one set of records in another; the speed and versatility of network databases have led to their wide use within businesses and in e-commerce. Relational databases are used where associations between files or records cannot be expressed by links; a simple flat list becomes one row of a table, or "relation," and multiple relations can be mathematically associated to yield desired information. Various iterations of SQL (Structured Query Language) are widely employed in DBMS for relational databases. Object-oriented databases store and manipulate more complex data structures, called "objects," which are organized into hierarchical classes that may inherit properties from classes higher in the chain; this database structure is the most flexible and adaptable.

The information in many databases consists of natural-language texts of documents; number-oriented databases primarily contain information such as statistics, tables, financial data, and raw scientific and technical data. Small databases can be maintained on personal-computer systems and may be used by individuals at home. These and larger databases have become increasingly important in business life, in part because they are now commonly designed to be integrated with other office software, including spreadsheet programs.

Typical commercial database applications include airline reservations, production management functions, medical records in hospitals, and legal records of insurance companies. The largest databases are usually maintained by governmental agencies, business organizations, and universities. These databases may contain texts of such materials as abstracts, reports, legal statutes, wire services, newspapers and journals, encyclopaedias, and catalogs of various kinds. Reference databases contain bibliographies or indexes that serve as guides to the location of information in books, periodicals, and other published literature. Thousands of these publicly accessible databases now exist, covering topics ranging from law, medicine, and engineering to news and current events, games, classified advertisements, and instructional courses.

Increasingly, formerly separate databases are being combined electronically into larger collections known as data warehouses. Businesses and government agencies then employ "data mining" software to analyze multiple aspects of the data for various patterns. For example, a government agency might flag for human investigation a company or individual that purchased a suspicious quantity of certain equipment or materials, even though the purchases were spread around the country or through various subsidiaries.

Types of Database

- Centralised Database

This database can be accessed by users from different locations at the central database. The central database saves data and programs to central computing facility for processing.

- Operational Database

This is a basic form of data that contain information regarding the operations of an enterprise. These databases are organised for marketing, production and others.

- End-user Database

This is a database shared among users and intended for use by the end users, for example, managers of different departments. This database presents the summary of the information.

- Commercial Database

This is a database that holds information that external users need. But, it's not cost efficient for the end users to maintain such database by themselves. Commercial database is a paid service for the user as the databases are subject specific. The access is given through commercial links.

Some commercial databases are offered on CD-ROMs where cost of communication is reduced.

- Personal Database

The personal databases are maintained on personal computers. They contain information meant for use of a limited number of users.

- Distributed Database

These databases have inputs from common databases. The data remains shared at different sites in the organisation. As the sites are connected to each other, the entire collection of data makes up the database of the organisation.

Nowadays, data warehouses exist where separate databases are combined electronically. These data warehouses are analysed using data mining software. These are widely used in business and government agencies.

Database Management System

A DBMS is defined as system software that enables to store, modify, manipulate and extract data from a database.

For example, from a small startup firm to the multinational companies and industries managing a huge amount of data becomes a mess. So, the software like the DBMS brought a revolution in many fields regarding efficient information management.

Users of DBMS: There are different types of users and can retrieve data on demand using the applications and interfaces provided by DBMS. They are:

- Native user

- Online user

- Application programmers

- Sophisticated users

- Database administrators

Uses of DBMS: It is used in wide range in many sectors like banking, airlines, universities, human resources, manufacturing and selling and many more. This is used because of the following useful parameters of it:

- Not only efficient but also effective in data management.

- Easy to understand.

- Strictly secured.

- Ability to query processing.

- Sharing of information.

- Facility of better decision making.

- Best access to accurate data in searching.

Components of DBMS: The DBMS has five important components in it which plays a major role in it and they are as follows:

- Hardware

- Software

- Data

- Users

- Procedures

The hardware is nothing but the actual computer system which is used for keeping and accessing database and DBMS hardware has the secondary storage devices like the hard disks, database machines. These secondary storage devices are designed specifically to support the database.

Software is the actual DBMS and between the actual stored data and the users of the system there is a presence of a layer of software called DBMS. It can control the access and can maintain the consistency of the information.

The most vital component of the DBMS environment is none other than the data from the user point of view. It acts as a machine between the machine components and the user components, database should contain all the data needed by the organization i.e. user.

Well, user can access the data on demand by using the applications and interfaces provided by the database management system. The types of users are as follows:

- Native user

- Online user

- Application programmers

- Sophisticated users

- Database administrator

Procedures refer to the instructions and rules that govern the design of database along with that we require the following procedure to run the system:

- Log onto DBMS,

- Use a particular DBMS facility,

- Start and stop the DBMS,

- Make backup copies of database, and

- Handle hardware or software failures.

Types of DBMS

There are many types of DBMS available in the market today and they are as below:

- IMS

- DB2

- MYSQL

- Dbase

- FoxPro

- SQLservers

- NOSQL (Not only SQL)

- RDBMS which stands for relational database management system and examples of it are oracle, Sybase, ingress, Informix, Microsoft access.

- Network DBMS and in this pascal, cobol and FORTAN are used to implement records and set structures.

- Object oriented database

- Hierarchical DBMS.

Advantages of Database Management System: Database management system has many advantages and they are like:

- In DBMS the redundancy problem can be solved,

- Has a very high security level,

- Presence of referential integrity,

- Support multiple users,

- Independency of data,

- Avoidance of inconsistency,

- Shared data,

- Enforcement of standards,

- Prefer to solve enterprise requirement than individual requirement,

- Any unauthorized access is restricted,

- Provide backup of data,

- Recovery of data,

- Affordable cost of manufacturing and developing,

- Control on concurrency, and

- Can develop data models.

So, because of such advantages and parameters to overcome the disadvantages this has become a worldwide phenomenon in all the organizations by solving their issues and being a part in making profit.

Disadvantages of Database Management System: Along with the advantages we have some disadvantages to everything and likewise it is to this and the disadvantages are as follows:

- Complexity is a parameter of it because when the internal structure is observed it is very complex.

- Size becomes an issue because in some databases have large size.

- Performance may not run as fast as desired.

- Impact of failure is higher i.e. it makes damage to many parts of the system.

- Some DBMS have unaffordable prices.

- The requirement of the additional hardware increases cost.

- Also have the cost of conversion.

Relational Data Model

The relational model represents the database as a collection of relations. A relation is nothing but a table of values. Every row in the table represents a collection of related data values. These rows in the table denote a real-world entity or relationship.

The table name and column names are helpful to interpret the meaning of values in each row. The data are represented as a set of relations. In the relational model, data are stored as tables. However, the physical storage of the data is independent of the way the data are logically organized.

Some popular Relational Database management systems are:

- DB2 and Informix Dynamic Server - IBM

- Oracle and RDB – Oracle

- SQL Server and Access – Microsoft

Relational Model Concepts

1. Attribute: Each column in a Table. Attributes are the properties which define a relation. e.g., Student_Rollno, NAME,etc.

2. Tables – In the Relational model the, relations are saved in the table format. It is stored along with its entities. A table has two properties rows and columns. Rows represent records and columns represent attributes.

3. Tuple – It is nothing but a single row of a table, which contains a single record.

4. Relation Schema: A relation schema represents the name of the relation with its attributes.

5. Degree: The total number of attributes which in the relation is called the degree of the relation.

6. Cardinality: Total number of rows present in the Table.

7. Column: The column represents the set of values for a specific attribute.

8. Relation instance – Relation instance is a finite set of tuples in the RDBMS system. Relation instances never have duplicate tuples.

9. Relation key - Every row has one, two or multiple attributes, which is called relation key.

10. Attribute domain – Every attribute has some pre-defined value and scope which is known as attribute domain.

Table also called Relation

Primary Key   Domain
     Ex: NOT NULL

© guru99.com

CustomerID	CustomerName	Status
1	Google	Active
2	Amazon	Active
3	Apple	Inactive

Tuple OR **Row**
Total # of rows is **Cardinality**

Column OR **Attributes**
Total # of column is **Degree**

Relational Integrity Constraints

Relational Integrity constraints is referred to conditions which must be present for a valid relation. These integrity constraints are derived from the rules in the mini-world that the database represents.

There are many types of integrity constraints. Constraints on the Relational database management system is mostly divided into three main categories are:

1. Domain constraints

2. Key constraints

3. Referential integrity constraints

Domain Constraints

Domain constraints can be violated if an attribute value is not appearing in the corresponding domain or it is not of the appropriate data type.

Domain constraints specify that within each tuple, and the value of each attribute must be unique. This is specified as data types which include standard data types integers, real numbers, characters, Booleans, variable length strings, etc.

Example:

Create DOMAIN CustomerName

CHECK (value not NULL)

The example shown demonstrates creating a domain constraint such that Customer-Name is not NULL.

Key Constraints

An attribute that can uniquely identify a tuple in a relation is called the key of the table. The value of the attribute for different tuples in the relation has to be unique.

Example:

In the given table, CustomerID is a key attribute of Customer Table. It is most likely to have a single key for one customer, CustomerID =1 is only for the CustomerName =" Google".

CustomerID	CustomerName	Status
1	Google	Active
2	Amazon	Active
3	Apple	Inactive

Referential Integrity Constraints

Referential integrity constraints is base on the concept of Foreign Keys. A foreign key is an important attribute of a relation which should be referred to in other relationships. Referential integrity constraint state happens where relation refers to a key attribute of a different or same relation. However, that key element must exist in the table.

Example:

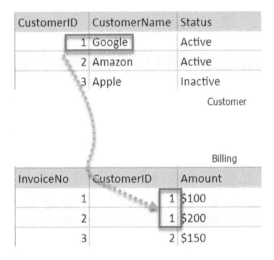

In the above example, we have 2 relations, Customer and Billing.

Tuple for CustomerID =1 is referenced twice in the relation Billing. So we know CustomerName=Google has billing amount $300.

Operations in Relational Model

Four basic update operations performed on relational database model are:

Insert, update, delete and select.

- Insert is used to insert data into the relation.

- Delete is used to delete tuples from the table.

- Modify allows you to change the values of some attributes in existing tuples.

- Select allows you to choose a specific range of data.

Whenever one of these operations are applied, integrity constraints specified on the relational database schema must never be violated.

Inset Operation

The insert operation gives values of the attribute for a new tuple which should be inserted into a relation.

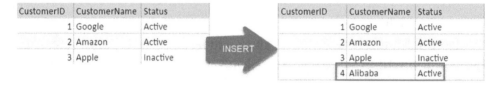

Update Operation

You can see that in the below-given relation table CustomerName= 'Apple' is updated from Inactive to Active.

Delete Operation

To specify deletion, a condition on the attributes of the relation selects the tuple to be deleted.

In the above-given example, CustomerName= "Apple" is deleted from the table.

The Delete operation could violate referential integrity if the tuple which is deleted is referenced by foreign keys from other tuples in the same database.

Select Operation

CustomerID	CustomerName	Status
1	Google	Active
2	Amazon	Active
4	Alibaba	Active

SELECT →

CustomerID	CustomerName	Status
2	Amazon	Active

In the above-given example, CustomerName="Amazon" is selected

Best Practices for creating a Relational Model

- Data need to be represented as a collection of relations.
- Each relation should be depicted clearly in the table.
- Rows should contain data about instances of an entity.
- Columns must contain data about attributes of the entity.
- Cells of the table should hold a single value.
- Each column should be given a unique name.
- No two rows can be identical.
- The values of an attribute should be from the same domain.

Advantages of using Relational Model

- Simplicity: A relational data model is simpler than the hierarchical and network model.
- Structural Independence: The relational database is only concerned with data and not with a structure. This can improve the performance of the model.
- Easy to use: The relational model is easy as tables consisting of rows and columns is quite natural and simple to understand.
- Query capability: It makes possible for a high-level query language like SQL to avoid complex database navigation.
- Data independence: The structure of a database can be changed without having to change any application.
- Scalable: Regarding a number of records, or rows, and the number of fields, a database should be enlarged to enhance its usability.

Disadvantages of using Relational Model

- Few relational databases have limits on field lengths which can't be exceeded.

- Relational databases can sometimes become complex as the amount of data grows, and the relations between pieces of data become more complicated.

- Complex relational database systems may lead to isolated databases where the information cannot be shared from one system to another.

Object Oriented Database

When the database techniques are combined with object oriented concepts, the result is an object oriented management system (ODBMS). Today's trend in programming languages is to utilize objects, thereby making OODBMS is ideal for Object Oriented programmers because they can develop the product, store them as objects, and can replicate or modify existing objects to make new objects within the OODBMS. Object databases based on persistent programming acquired a niche in application areas such as engineering and spatial databases, telecommunications, and scientific areas such as high energy physics and molecular biology.

List of Object Oriented Database Standards

Some of the Object oriented DBMS standards are:

- Object data management group

- Object database standard ODM 6.2.0

- Object query language

- Object query language support of SQL 92

Object Oriented Data Model (OODM)

Object oriented data models are a logical data models that capture the semantics of objects supported on object oriented programming. OODMs implement conceptual models directly and can represent complexities that are beyond the capabilities of relational systems. OODBs have adopted many of the concepts that were developed originally for object oriented programming language. An object oriented database is a collection of objects defined by an object oriented data model. An object oriented database can extend the existence of objects so that they are stored permanently. Therefore, the objects persist beyond program termination and can be retrieved later and shared by other programs.

Characteristics of Object Oriented Database

The characteristics of object oriented database are listed below:

- It keeps up a direct relation between real world and database objects as if objects do not loose their integrity and identity.

- OODBs provide system generated object identifier for each object so that an object can easily be identified and operated upon.

- OODBs are extensible, which identifies new data types and the operations to be performed on them.

- Provides encapsulation, feature which, the data representation and the methods implementation are hidden from external entities.

- Also provides inheritance properties in which an object inherits the properties of other objects.

Object, Attributes and Identity

- Attributes : The attributes are the characteristics used to describe objects. Attributes are also known as instance variables. When attributes are assigned values at a given time, it is assumed that the object is in a given state at that time.

- Object : An object is an abstract representation of the real world entity which has a unique identity, embedded properties, and the ability to interact with other objects and itself.

- Identity : The identity is an external identifier- the object ID- maintained for each object. The Object ID is assigned by the system when the object is created, and cannot be changed. It is unlike the relational database, for example, where a data value stored within the object is used to identify the object.

Object Oriented Methodologies

There are certain object oriented methodologies are use in OODB. These are:

- Class: A class is assumed as a group of objects with the same or similar attributes and behavior.

- Encapsulation: It is the property that the attributes and methods of an object are hidden from outside world. A published interface is used to access an object's methods.

- Inheritance: It is the property which, when classes are arranged in a hierarchy, each class assumes the attributes and methods of its ancestors. For example, class students are the ancestor of undergraduate students and post graduate students.

- Polymorphism : It allows several objects to represent to the same message in different ways. In the object oriented database model, complex objects are modeled more naturally and easily.

Benefit of Object Orientation in Programming Language

The benefits of object orientation in programming language are:

- Minimizes number of lines of code.
- Reduces development time.
- Increases the reusability of codes.
- Makes code maintenance easier.
- Increased productivity of programmers.

Merits of Object Oriented Database

OODBs provide the following merits:

- OODBs allow for the storage of complex data structures that cannot be easily stored using conventional database terminology.
- OODBs support all the persistence required for object oriented applications.
- OODBs contain active object servers which support both distribution of data and distribution of work.

Advantages of Object Oriented Data Model over Relational Model

When compared with the relational model, the object oriented data model has the following advantages:

- Reusability: generic objects can be defined and then reused in numerous application.
- Complex data types: Can manage complex data such as document, graphics, images, voice messages, etc.
- Distributed databases: Due to mode of communication between objects, OODBMS can support distribution of data across networks more easily.

Object Oriented Model vs Entity Relationship Model

An entity is simply a collection of variables or data items.

When an application is running, the ER Model will tells how the application's data will be persisted but the Object Oriented Model will decide that how that data will be stored in the memory.

Advantages of OODB Over RDBMS

Object oriented database advantages over RDBMS:

- Objects do not require assembly and dis-assembly saving coding time and execution time to assemble or disassemble objects,

- Reduced paging,

- Easier navigation,

- Better concurrency control,

- Data model is based on the real world,

- Works well for distributed architectures, and

- Less code required when applications are object oriented.

References

- Why-data-structures: codecademy.com, Retrieved 3 April, 2019

- Various-data-structures: atnyla.com, Retrieved 17 February, 2019

- Database, technology: britannica.com, Retrieved 14 May, 2019

- What-is-a-database: teachcomputerscience.com, Retrieved 24 January, 2019

- Relational-data-model-dbms: guru99.com, Retrieved 29 June, 2019

- Object-oriented-database: oureducation.in, Retrieved 7 March, 2019

Permissions

We would like to thank the editorial team for lending their expertise to make the book truly unique. They have played a crucial role in the development of this book. Without their invaluable contributions this book wouldn't have been possible. They have made vital efforts to compile up to date information on the varied aspects of this subject to make this book a valuable addition to the collection of many professionals and students.

This book was conceptualized with the vision of imparting up-to-date and integrated information in this field. To ensure the same, a matchless editorial board was set up. Every individual on the board went through rigorous rounds of assessment to prove their worth. After which they invested a large part of their time researching and compiling the most relevant data for our readers.

The editorial board has been involved in producing this book since its inception. They have spent rigorous hours researching and exploring the diverse topics which have resulted in the successful publishing of this book. They have passed on their knowledge of decades through this book. To expedite this challenging task, the publisher supported the team at every step. A small team of assistant editors was also appointed to further simplify the editing procedure and attain best results for the readers.

Apart from the editorial board, the designing team has also invested a significant amount of their time in understanding the subject and creating the most relevant covers. They scrutinized every image to scout for the most suitable representation of the subject and create an appropriate cover for the book.

The publishing team has been an ardent support to the editorial, designing and production team. Their endless efforts to recruit the best for this project, has resulted in the accomplishment of this book. They are a veteran in the field of academics and their pool of knowledge is as vast as their experience in printing. Their expertise and guidance has proved useful at every step. Their uncompromising quality standards have made this book an exceptional effort. Their encouragement from time to time has been an inspiration for everyone.

The publisher and the editorial board hope that this book will prove to be a valuable piece of knowledge for students, practitioners and scholars across the globe.

Index

www.ingramcontent.com/pod-product-compliance
Lightning Source LLC
Jackson TN
JSHW052200130125
77033JS00004B/195